the

SECRET
POWER
of
YOU

Decode Your Hidden Destiny
with Astrology, Tarot, Palmistry, Numerology, and the Enneagram

MEERA LESTER, AUTHOR OF *THE EVERYTHING® LAW OF ATTRACTION BOOK*

Aadamsmedia
Avon, Massachusetts

Published by
Adams Media, a division of F+W Media, Inc.
57 Littlefield Street, Avon, MA 02322. U.S.A.
www.adamsmedia.com

ISBN 10: 1-4405-4013-6
ISBN 13: 978-1-4405-4013-4
eISBN 10: 1-4405-4181-7
eISBN 13: 978-1-4405-4181-0

Printed in the United States of America.

10   9   8   7   6   5   4   3   2   1

Acknowledgments

Thanks to Victoria Sandbrook, Peter Archer, and Katie Corcoran Lytle, three masterful editors of consummate skill. What a pleasure to work with you all.
—Meera Lester

Contents

INTRODUCTION / 7

Part One   ASTROLOGY / 9

Part Two   THE TAROT / 67

Part Three   PALMISTRY / 143

Part Four   NUMEROLOGY / 189

Part Five   THE ENNEAGRAM / 241

Part Six   CONCLUSION: PUTTING IT ALL TOGETHER / 289

Appendix A   THE ENNEAGRAM SELF-TEST / 293

Appendix B   GLOSSARY / 339

INDEX / 348

INTRODUCTION

Welcome, Reader. Get ready to launch your life on a new and mind-bending journey. The power to transform your world is greater than you might ever imagine. Until now, it has remained hidden inside you, but that circumstance is about to change. You are going to see what that hidden power can do.

This book will help you unlock that power, using nontraditional methods that have been around for centuries. These methods have stood the test of time and are practiced today by people around the globe. With them, you'll reach deep into yourself and find the central kernel that is the essence of you—your authentic Self. You'll see how knowing this Self can also help you better know others, and finally, you'll learn how it can help you remake your world in terms of money, friendship, relationships, your job, and sex.

So hold tight! Ready . . . liftoff!

Part One

ASTROLOGY

A child is born on that day and at that hour when the celestial rays are in mathematical harmony with his individual karma.

—Sri Yukteswar (1855–1936), monastic name of Priyanath Karar, educator, astronomer, **yogi**, and expert on Vedic astrology

Your soul selected the circumstances into which you were born—and that included choosing the exact moment that best depicted your personality, strengths, and desires. From that moment on, the stars and planets in the sky would act as a beacon to help you develop spiritually, giving you a way to forever interpret who you are and what destiny will most fulfill your soul. The ancient art of astrology shows you where you'll find your greatest passion in various areas of your life; what life lessons, obstacles, and opportunities you might encounter; and how to achieve the greatness that is meant just for you as you unmask your real Self.

What Is Astrology?

Astrology is an ancient system based on the belief that the position of the Sun, Moon, and planets at the time of people's birth impacts their lives through energy shifts that mold their personalities, influence their romantic relationships, and forecast their potential destinies.

You might wonder how astrology differs from astronomy since both involve the study of celestial objects. Astronomy, considered a natural science, focuses on celestial objects beyond Earth's atmosphere, including their positions and motion, compositions, chemistry, energy, and evolution.

Astrology, an arcane art that has survived thousands of years, does not discount scientific discoveries of astronomy; however, it aligns more closely with ancient metaphysical beliefs about the symbolic relationships of celestial bodies and their effects on human affairs.

THE BASICS

Look through a telescope on a clear night and see for yourself how distant images conjure the mythical stories of the Greco-Roman gods and goddesses. Look at the rings of Saturn, the red dust of Mars, and the stark landscape of the Moon—do you have an intuitive insight about why the ancient astrologers called Mars the god of war, Mercury the messenger, and Neptune ruler of the seas? Or how they differentiated between the polarities of planetary energies?

NEGATIVE AND POSITIVE ENERGIES

Planetary energy, as viewed through the lens of astrology, is neither positive nor negative; however, tradition assigns each planet's energy as such. Jupiter towers as the great benefic, the planet that blesses. Venus commands a close second. The Sun, Moon, and Mercury line up behind Venus, exerting positive energy and influence.

Saturn is the bad guy of the group whose life lessons tend to be harsh. The energy of Mars, Uranus, Neptune, and Pluto is viewed somewhat negatively as well.

THE TWELVE HOUSES

Think of the sky as a circle. Now divide it into twelve parts. Each part is a house. As the Sun travels over the course of a year, it makes a circle, passing from one house to the next. Your "Sun sign" is where the Sun was on the day you were born, in relation to where you were born, i.e., which part of the world. Your ascendant is determined by what hour and minute of the day you were born in relation to this.

YOUR SIGN

Think of your Sun sign as the pattern of your overall personality. It represents your ego. The sign in which your Sun falls influences your aspirations and how you accomplish your goals. By learning the basics of astrology such as your Sun sign and your rising sign (or ascendant) and whether or not you were born on the cusp of a sign, you can pinpoint not only your powerful traits but also your weaknesses, as these can help or hinder your efforts at realizing your loftiest goals and dreams.

SIGNS ON THE CUSP

If you were born on the cusp (or, between two houses and their respective signs), read the interpretations for the sign closest to yours. For instance, if you were born on August 19, the cutoff date for Leo, also read the interpretation for Virgo for attributes that you might have.

INTUITION AND OBSERVATION

As your "ruling" planet moves through its orbit and touches on a particular point or house in the heavens, it creates an energetic ripple in your life. To become fully aware of this, you must cultivate keen powers of observation, strengthen your intuition, and heighten your sensitivity to subtle energy shifts if you are to apply the power of astrology to your life.

FREE WILL

The concept of astrology and free will working together seems deceptively easy to grasp at first. But as you work with both, peeling back the layers, you realize that everything that happens to you—from the grand to the mundane—is the result of a belief that you hold. And if it's simply your belief, you can change it. When you change a core belief, your experience also changes. This ability to change is what empowers you.

SIGNS AND SYMBOLS

See the signs and symbols used in astrology as a type of shorthand. Once you learn about them, working with astrology and understanding astrological charts will be much easier. When working with astrology and other arcane arts on your journey to self-discovery and empowerment, your grasp of astrological shorthand will prove extremely beneficial. The next three tables show the various symbols you'll soon recognize and use.

Signs and Symbols

There are twelve signs and each has a symbol:

Sign	Symbol	Sign	Symbol
Aries	♈	Libra	♎
Taurus	♉	Scorpio	♏
Gemini	♊	Sagittarius	♐
Cancer	♋	Capricorn	♑
Leo	♌	Aquarius	♒
Virgo	♍	Pisces	♓

Planets and Symbols

Besides the Sun and the Moon, we'll be using eight planets,
two nodes, and the Part of Fortune in birth charts:

Planet/Node	Symbol	Planet/Node	Symbol
Sun	☉	Saturn	♄
Moon	☽	Uranus	♅
Mercury	☿	Neptune	♆
Venus	♀	Pluto	♇
Mars	♂	North Node	☊
Jupiter	♃	South Node	☋

Aspects and Symbols

Due to the placement of planets in the houses, geometric angles are created between the planets and also between the planets and the angles of the houses. These angles are called aspects. Each aspect has a particular symbol and meaning. In this chapter, the following aspects are used:

Aspect	Symbol	Meaning
Conjunction	☌	A separation of 0 degrees between two or more planets
Sextile	✶	A separation of 60 degrees between two or more planets
Square	□	A separation of 90 degrees between two or more planets
Trine	△	A separation of 120 degrees between two or more planets
Opposition	☍	A separation of 180 degrees between two or more planets

Other symbols used in a birth chart are:

- **Ascendant or Rising Sign (AS):** The sign and degree of the zodiac rising at the time of birth.
- **Descendant (DS):** Opposite the ascendant, cusp of the seventh house.
- **Midheaven or Medium Coeli (MC):** The highest point of the zodiac at the time of birth.
- **Imum Coeli or Nadir (IC):** The zodiac point opposite the midheaven.

Other symbols you'll see in the charts, but which won't be discussed in this book because they are much more complicated, are:

- **Equatorial Ascendant (Eq):** The ascendant of the chart if you were born at the equator. Symbolizes who you think you are.
- **Vertex (Vtx):** A point of fate or destiny.

Birth Charts

Think of an astrological birth chart (also known as a natal chart) as an organic whole, a living pattern that depicts who the individual is and what he or she could become—in short, a blueprint of the soul's intent. Certain aspects (or geometrical angles formed between planets) in a person's birth chart coincide with certain tensions and stresses in that individual's life; additionally, some aspects also match up to areas of ease and pleasure.

NATAL CHART SPECIFICS

A birth chart is circular, with 360 degrees. The ascendant, represented by a horizontal line through the middle of the chart (Figure 1), forms the horizon. The space above it is south of the horizon; the space below it is north. The ascendant (AS) is intersected by the meridian, the axis that connects the midheaven (MC) and the nadir or Imum Coeli (IC), the lowest heaven. The space to the left of the meridian is east; the space to the right is west.

FIGURE 1.

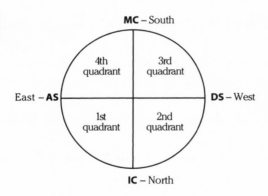

These directions are the opposite of what they usually are because we live in the northern hemisphere, on the "top" of the planet. This means the Sun is due south when it reaches the peak of its daily arc at noon.

The birth chart (Figure 2) shows an ascendant in Pisces, a Sun in Virgo, and a Moon in Virgo. The numbers inside each of the pieces of the circular pie represent the houses. In the lower left-hand corner is a graph that depicts the various aspects of the chart.

This is a chart for a 1989 birth year. The chart is quite straightforward and shows clearly defined areas of the soul's intent.

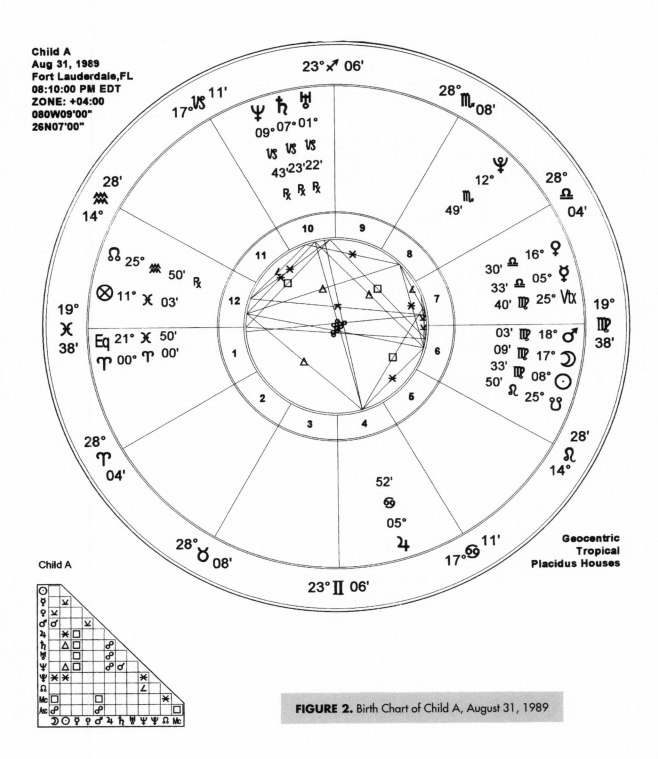

FIGURE 2. Birth Chart of Child A, August 31, 1989

HOUSES AND HOUSE CUSPS

Think of the sky as a circle. Now divide that space into twelve parts. Each part is a house. With the Earth's rotation during the span of a year, the Sun transits from one house to the next. Your Sun sign is determined by the Sun's position on that circle at the moment of your birth relative to where you were born. The division between one house and another is called the cusp. For example, if you have Taurus rising—on the cusp of the first house—then Gemini sits on the cusp of your second house, Cancer on the cusp of the third, and so on around the horoscope circle.

On the Cusp

Because there are no "lines" in the sky dividing up the universe into precise parts, we have to consider some discrepancies when determining a person's Sun sign. Those who were born at the edge of a house—during the days when the Sun transits from one house to another—are considered to have been born "on the cusp" and may show traits from the two signs they border. For instance, if you were born on April 19, the cutoff date for Aries, also read the interpretation for Taurus, because some of those attributes probably apply to you.

In the natural order of the zodiac, the signs begin with Aries and progress through the months to Pisces. Part of the reason for the order is the nature of the signs themselves. In astrology, Aries is often depicted as the pioneer who goes out into the world first. Pisces swims through the waters of the imagination, and his dreams eventually root in the physical world and become the reality of Aries.

THE INTERCEPTED SIGN

The exception to this structure is an "intercepted sign," which means a sign that doesn't appear on the cusp of a house but is completely contained within the house. The chart in Figure 3 shows an interception in the sixth house and in the opposite twelfth house as well. In the first instance, the cusps leap from Virgo on the cusp of the sixth to Scorpio on the cusp of the seventh. Libra has been swallowed. Directly opposite, the cusp of the eleventh house leaps from Taurus on the ascendant to Pisces. Aries has been subsumed.

In the birth chart in Figure 3, ruling planets affected by the interception are Neptune, which rules Pisces, and Mars, which rules Aries.

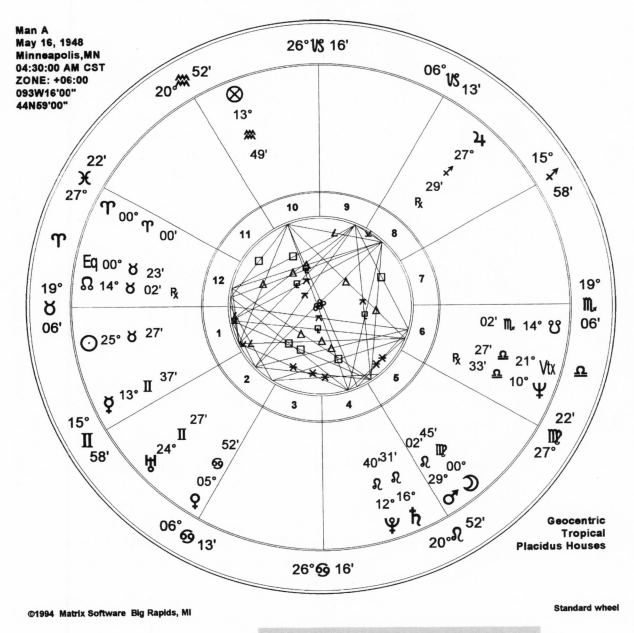

FIGURE 3. Birth Chart for Man A, May 16, 1948

RULERSHIP OF THE CUSP

Each house cusp is ruled by the planet that governs the sign on the cusp. In Figure 3, Taurus is on the ascendant, so Venus rules the first house. Since the Sun is so close to the ascendant in this chart, the Sun could be said to co-rule. Gemini is on the cusp of the second house, so Mercury is the ruler of that house.

NATURAL RULERS

However, the natural order of the horoscope begins with Aries, then Taurus, then Gemini, and so on around the zodiac. This means that regardless of what sign is on the cusp, Mars is the natural ruler of the first house because Mars governs Aries. You must take into account the attributes of the natural rulers when interpreting a chart.

UNDERSTANDING THE PLANETS

You can see from the following list the way each planet influences your life:

- Sun and Moon—your ego and **emotions**
- Mercury—your intellect
- Venus—your love life
- Mars—your energy
- Jupiter—your luck, your higher mind
- Saturn—your responsibilities, karma
- Uranus—your individuality
- Neptune—your visionary Self, your illusions
- Pluto—your transformation and regeneration (or recreation) of your life

NODES OF THE MOON

The lunar nodes are the degrees where the planet or the Moon's orbit intersects or crosses the ecliptic (Earth's orbit around the Sun). In Western astrology, the North Node is considered Jupiter's equivalent, with the South Node as Saturn's. Another theory ties the nodes in your chart to ideas of reincarnation—the South Node represents your **karma**, deeply embedded patterns of behavior and thought acquired in previous lives that must be overcome through the North Node's influence (the area of your most profound growth) in this life.

Know Your Nodes

Another way to think about nodes and polarity is to consider the South Node as an unconscious bias—either from previous incarnations or that which builds up during our lives. It's what we need to release in order to grow. The North Node sign and house placement indicate the area of our lives we need to expand so we can evolve toward our fulfillment as spiritual beings.

PLANETS IN THE SIGNS

The sign a planet occupies describes how that particular energy permeates your personality and influences your life. Here are the influences of the planets in their signs:

- The Moon: Instinct
- Mercury: Communication
- Venus: Love
- Mars: Stamina and Sex Drive
- Jupiter: Moral and Spiritual Beliefs
- Saturn: The Karmic Planet
- Uranus: Individuality
- Neptune: Intuition
- Pluto: Transformation

A sign seldom occupies only one house but rather partially occupies two houses as it transits around the circle. A sign that occupies only one house completely is called an intercepted sign. When a planet hovers between the lower meridian and eastern horizon, it is said to be ascending (due to the Earth's rotation). When it has reached the last degree of the nighttime semi-arc, it arrives at the ascendant.

Generalities in your chart—using just Sun signs without Moon, ascendant, etc.—aren't wrong, but they're hardly the full story. They don't take into account the vast diversity inherent in every human being. However, they are a convenient way to immediately get a handle on someone you've just met.

SUN SIGNS

The twelve Sun signs are divided roughly by months, but because those divisions don't follow the months exactly, you may have been born on the cusp between two signs. If you were, then read the interpretations for both signs. Each sign is associated with both a planet and with one of the four natural elements: air, earth, fire, and water. These elements provide further clues to the personality traits associated with the signs.

- **Aries**—April 18–May13—Mars (fire) is bold, courageous, and resourceful. Arian individuals always seem to know what they believe, what they want from life, and where they're going. They're dynamic and aggressive (sometimes to a fault) in pursuing their goals. These individuals sometimes lose interest if they don't see rapid results. But this tendency is compensated for by their ambition and drive to succeed. They can be argumentative, lack tact, and have bad tempers. But they are also the hardworking trailblazers, symbolized by the sure-footed ram.

- **Taurus**—May 13–June 21—Venus (earth) symbolized by the bull, is patient, determined, and singular in his pursuit of goals. Lacking versatility because of the fixed nature of the sign, they compensate by enduring whatever they have to in order to get what they want. As a result, they often succeed where others fail. Most Taureans like the fine arts and enjoy music (often with a talent for it themselves). They also like working with their hands—gardening, woodworking, and sculpting. It takes a lot to anger a Taurus person, but once you do, clear out. The "bull's rush" can be fierce. Venus rules this sign; therefore, Taurus people are usually sensual and romantic.

- **Gemini**—June 21–July 20—Mercury (air) is the sign of individuals who use their rational intellect to explore and understand their world. Their inquisitiveness compels them to visit foreign countries, particularly if the Sun is in the ninth house, where their need to explore other cultures and traditions ranks high. The Gemini's mind demands one thing, and his heart clamors for the opposite, accounting for his frequent moodiness. These individuals are fascinated by relationships and connections among people, places, and objects. Their need to analyze everything can be annoying. When this quality leads a Gemini into an exploration of psychic and spiritual realms, it grounds him. The heart of a Gemini is won by seduction of the mind.

- **Cancer**—July 20–August 10—Moon (water) people need roots, a place, or even a state of mind they can call their own. They need a safe harbor, a refuge in which to retreat. Imagination, sensitivity, and the nurturing instinct characterize this sign. Cancerians are generally kind people but when hurt can become vindictive and sharp spoken. They forgive easily, but rarely forget. Affectionate, passionate, and even possessive, Cancerians may be overprotective as parents and smothering as parents and lovers. Cancerians act and react emotionally in the same way the crab moves—sideways. They avoid confrontations, are reluctant to reveal their real selves, and may hide behind their protective urges, preferring to tend to the needs of others. Cancers are often intuitive and psychic, as experience flows through them emotionally.

- **Leo**—August 10–September 16—Sun (fire) loves being the center of attention. These individuals often surround themselves with admirers. Leo offers generosity, warmth, and compassion to those in her orbit who are loyal. As a fixed sign, Leos stand firm in their belief systems. They are optimistic, honorable, loyal, and ambitious. Leos have an innate dramatic sense, and life is their stage. Their flamboyance and personal magnetism extend to every facet of their lives. They seek to succeed and make an impact in every situation. It is no surprise that the theater and allied arts fall under the rule of Leo.

- **Virgo**—September 16–October 30—Mercury (earth) is mentally quick and agile. The popular image of a Virgo as a picky, critical, and compulsively tidy person is misleading. Virgos tend to be detail oriented and delve deeply into subjects they study. They are career-oriented people and seem to be interested in doing their jobs efficiently and well. They're happiest when engaged in something that benefits society at large. Virgos tend to be attracted to people who are intellectually stimulating or eccentric in some way. Their standards are high when it comes to romantic relationships, and unless the mental connection exists, the relationship won't last long. Young adult Virgos (those in their twenties) may fall for those who aren't quite good enough for them—people who are too critical or not appreciative—an unhealthy match for the Virgos and their partners.

- **Libra**—October 30–November 23—Venus (air) seeks balance and may find it through **meditation**. Librans come in three distinct types: those who are decisive, those who aren't, and those who seek harmony for its own sake. Librans have an inherent need to act democratically, diplomatically, and fairly. Even though Librans are courteous, amiable people, they are not pushovers. They use diplomacy and intelligence to get what they want.

- **Scorpio**—November 23–December 17—Mars and Pluto (water) includes people who are intense, passionate, and strong-willed. They often impose their will on others. For less evolved Scorpios, this willfulness can manifest negatively as cruelty, sadism, and enmity; in Scorpios who are more highly evolved, their will transforms lives for the better. Like Aries, Scorpios aren't afraid of anything. Their endurance allows them to plow ahead and overcome opposition. Individuals of this sign don't know the meaning of indifference. You're either a friend or an enemy—no in-betweens for this sign. A Scorpio is loyal unless you hurt him or someone he loves. Then Scorpio can become vindictive (biting sarcasm is associated with this sign). The more highly evolved people in this sign are often very psychic, with rich inner lives and passionate involvement in metaphysics. Scorpios are excellent workers: industrious and relentless, excelling at types of work associated with the eighth house—trusts and inheritances, mortuaries, psychological counselors, and the occult.

- **Sagittarius**—December 17–January 20—Jupiter (fire) seeks the truth, expresses it as he sees it—and doesn't care if anyone else agrees with him. Sagittarians see the large picture of any issue and can't be bothered with the mundane details. They are always outspoken and can't understand why other people aren't as candid. After all, what is there to hide? Logic reigns supreme in this sign. But the mentality differs from Gemini, the polar opposite of Sagittarius, in several important ways. A Gemini is concerned with the here and now: he needs to know how and why things and relationships work in his life. A Sagittarian focuses on the future and on the larger family of humanity. Despite the Sagittarian's propensity for logic, he is often quite prescient, with an uncanny ability to glimpse the future. Sagittarians love their freedom and chafe at restrictions. Their versatility and natural optimism win them many friends, but only a few ever really know the heart of the Sagittarian.

- **Capricorn**—January 20–February 16—Saturn (earth) is serious-minded, aloof, and in tight control of his emotions. Even as youngsters, Capricorns exhibit a mature air as if they were born with a profound core. Capricorns's slow, steady rise through the world resonates with the image of the goat—their sign's symbol. Easily impressed by trappings of success, they are more interested in the power that wealth represents than money itself. They feel the need to rule whatever kingdom they occupy whether this is their home, work place, or business. Although Capricorns prize power and mastery over others, they tend to be subtle about it. Capricorns are industrious, efficient, and disciplined workers. Their innate common sense gives them the ability to plan ahead and to work out practical ways of approaching goals, and they often succeed in their endeavors. Capricorns possess a quiet dignity but have a tendency to worry.

- **Aquarius**—February 16–March 11—Uranus (air) is an original thinker, often eccentric, who prizes individuality and freedom above all else. The tribal mentality goes against the grain of Aquarians. They chafe at the restrictions placed upon them by society and seek to follow their own paths. Aquarius is the sign of true genius; these people generally have the ability to think in unique ways. Once they make up their minds about something, nothing can convince them to think otherwise. This stubbornness is a double-edged sword; it can sustain them or destroy them. Even though compassion is a hallmark of this Sun sign, Aquarians usually don't become emotionally involved with the causes they promote. Their compassion, while genuine, rises from the intellect rather than the heart.

- **Pisces**—March 11–April 18—Neptune (water) needs to explore the world through the emotions. They can easily become a kind of psychic sponge, absorbing the emotions of people around them. People born under this sign usually have wonderful imaginations and great creative resources. They gravitate toward the arts, specifically to theater and film. Because they are so attuned to the thoughts of people around them, they excel as managers and administrators. However, Pisceans can be ambivalent and indecisive because they're so impressionable. In highly evolved types, mystical tendencies are well developed, and the individuals possess deep spiritual connections. Pisces people need time alone to center themselves. Their moods range from joyful giddy heights to the depths of despair. Love and romance fulfill Pisces emotionally, and they generally flourish within stable relationships.

Use Astrology to Unearth the Power of You

Now that you know the basics of astrology, your intuition can bring clarity to any astrological chart configuration and interpretation. Intuition is the essential connection that links the various astrological pieces into a coherent whole—a living story. Without intuition, you're just reading symbols. Choosing to align specific areas of your life in harmony with the energies of the planets gives you the power to make wiser choices that facilitate dramatic and empowering change.

Relationships

Comparing your Sun sign with that of another person will give you a basic idea of whether or not you'll get along but such a simple observation lacks the depth and breadth that a comparison of natal horoscopes would provide. Fire signs form relationships quickly but they can also become easily bored. They are bold and bright, often the aggressors and like being in the spotlight, not good for partners who might easily become jealous. Water signs are emotionally intense, often spiritually inclined, and have a mysterious air about them, but they can be moody. Air sign individuals are quick and mentally agile, and they like to stir things up. They're all havoc seekers on some level. Libra does it quietly; Gemini is a drama queen and a gossip; and Aquarius is hard to pin down. They give any relationship that uncertainty factor. In romantic relationships, earth signs can fall hard. They will struggle and protest along the way. They're ten times more sensitive than people think they are—only because they don't necessarily wear their hearts on their sleeves. When they love, they love truly and deeply.

ARIES IN LOVE

Aries man has a penchant for doing things his way. He's as sharp as a tack, and those with whom he forms a relationship respect him, even though they think he's bossy and domineering. He'll decide how he wants things done, and he's a perfectionist about it. If you get into a fight with him, watch out! There is no better debater than Aries. He must win every argument—even when he's wrong.

Jealousy's a Losing Game

Never get too jealous with Aries man or Aries woman. They both hate it. They need to know that they can do whatever it is they want to do. If you're too jealous, they'll run out and start a fling, just to prove that they're in charge.

Aries woman, on the other hand, handles people with more charm and finesse. She's a lot less aggressive than Aries man—on the outside—though her thought process is very similar. Where he drives forward, she'll pull back and wait for her lover to come to her—and they always do. When it comes to love, she's just as fickle and stubborn as Aries man.

Stay Skeptical

With Aries, take everything with a grain of salt, and you'll be ahead of the game. Remember that they're the children of the zodiac, too, and that they'll always want more of what they cannot truly have. With Aries, you have to change the rules frequently, or they'll get bored.

Aries, unfortunately, can woo you into bed with well-placed words. Once there, his skill depends on each Aries. He's confident—too confident in bed. And he's sensitive, too. He might tell you about his own downfalls, but he'll absolutely freak out if you start listing them.

Aries can be a bit selfish in bed, too. Sure, he's creative, exciting, and extremely inventive. He thinks he's sensitive but he's not necessarily—unless his Venus is in Taurus, Cancer, or Pisces. If his Venus is in Aquarius or Aries, beware! He can woo you to the ends of the earth, but he can also be detached. You'll believe you know him, and then he'll change right before your eyes.

TIPS

Aries can be incredibly loving and sweet, and she almost always gets what she wants in love. Her only regret is that someone she loves may not be good enough for her, as she perceives it. Most times, once she falls out of love, it's gone forever.

Go slow with Aries and make her work for everything. Never put her on a pedestal—treat her as an equal. Praise her only when she deserves it. Make her listen to you but understand that she'll only see her side of it. Accept this. Don't ever try to control her, or she'll run the other way. Give her freedom but also set boundaries.

MATCHES WITH ARIES

If you want an Aries who lives for love, find an Aries with his Venus in Cancer or Pisces. Aries, because it's a fire sign, is often attracted to other fire signs—Sagittarius or Leo. But generally, unless aspects in the chart indicate otherwise, romance with another fire sign can be explosive. Aries gets along well with air signs—Gemini, Libra, Aquarius—or a sign that's sextile (60 degrees) or trine (120 degrees) from Aries. Sometimes, an earth sign helps ground all that Aries energy. In chart comparisons, a Venus or Moon in Aries in the other person's chart would indicate compatibility.

Give Him His Space

If Aries pulls away, let him. Don't go chasing after him, or he'll run away even faster. When he's ready, he'll come back. Aries likes to test. He wants to make sure you're independent enough for him. Be strong and don't be too needy.

TAURUS IN LOVE

In romance with a Taurus, a lot goes on beneath the surface. Taureans are subtle and quiet about what they feel. Once they fall, though, they fall hard. In fact, their inherently fixed natures simply won't allow them to give up. Perhaps this tendency sounds like it could be good for you and bad for them. But Taurus people get in way over their heads and then find that there's no turning back.

However, a Taurus will never really fall in love unless he thinks he can trust you. Trust goes a long way with Taurus. Deep down, Taurus knows that he's sensitive and that he takes himself a little too seriously. His sense of responsibility weighs heavily on his shoulders, and he'll always fulfill any task he believes he must.

But, remember: he'll also feel like it's up to him to judge the world. If he's critical, take it as a warning. He has an idea in his head of how things should be, and he'll try to mold you into how he sees you or how he'd like to see you. Pay close attention to his naggings because, though it may seem otherwise, he means every word he says.

Go with Your Gut

Sometimes, it's not clear if a Taurus is in love with you or in love with the *idea* of you. Ego comes into play with a Taurus and sometimes his "win, win" attitude will outweigh his real need for you. If you're not sure, trust your gut. Deep down, you'll know the difference.

As a Venus-ruled sign, Taureans are true sensualists and romantic lovers. Their romantic attachments ground and stabilize them. Love is like air to them: they need it to breathe. Again, they'll want to trust and rely on you. This is essential. In fact, it's very easy to see if Taurus trusts you, at least to some degree. Taurus can't touch and make love unless he feels he can. Taurus and Virgo may be the only men in the zodiac who are like this. They might entertain a fling or two in their lifetime, but that's not what they're about.

Light My Fire

Taurus women (and sometimes men) have a habit of falling for fire signs. In the beginning, the fire sign will conquer her. But once she starts getting comfortable, he begins flirting with others and testing her. If she lightens up, she just may be able to keep him.

Taurus individuals are looking for meaning and true love—someone who'll put up with their obstinate nature and even revel in it. Most of the Taurus men are quite macho. Like the bull, they're quite direct and will usually take a problem on—head on (quite the opposite of the way Cancer would handle it). Give them a good love challenge and they won't shy away. Taurus is built for competition. The problem is, he may never really stop to consider if you two are actually good for one another.

Mind Before Body

Unlike most other signs, don't deal with a Taurean on a physical level when the two of you fight. You'll probably need to talk things out before you make love again. Remember, Taurus is sensitive and puts his heart into lovemaking. Don't try to make up with him with kisses.

Grapple with issues as they come up. Don't go to bed angry. Work out your problems. Taurus is good at dealing with the issues at hand. However, if he pushes them deeper and deeper, you will never get them out of him again. When you bring it up, he'll look at you like he has no idea what you're talking about—even if he's steaming inside. Instead, he'll talk about it years from now when you least expect it.

In fact, Taurus is capable of holding a grudge for decades. It's very difficult for him to let go of the past. He remembers everything and never forgets anything. Try to be direct and honest with Taurus all the time. And don't let him get on a self-pity track; it's his armor. If a partner from his past has wronged him, he'll look for every conceivable indication that you'll do the same to him.

TIPS

Find out where he's sensitive and make sure you stay far away from that route. If an ex cheated on him, go out of your way to show him that you're more than trustworthy. If an ex was using him for money (or, more likely, he was simply convinced that she was), make sure he knows that you're just the opposite.

When he's relaxed, you can give him a massage or touch him in any way—he'll get the hint. He's sensitive with touch as well. Just don't rush things. Make sure he's in love before you go to bed with him. If you don't, he'll lose respect for you and think that you do the same with everyone.

The Food of Love
Taurus loves all sensual things—including food! And he loves domestic prowess. Cook a wonderful dinner for Taurus man or Taurus woman and you'll get extra potential husband or wife brownie points.

Also, a woman Taurus wants to know that she's truly loved before she'll hit the sack with a man. She can have flings but, as she gets older and gets to know herself better, she'll realize that this is not the best of all possible worlds. She'll want to wait and be romanced. And there's no one else who knows how to seduce and romance like Taurus.

MATCHES WITH TAURUS

Air signs mesh well with earth signs, too, because they're both thinking signs, whereas water and fire signs are more spontaneous and apt to follow their hearts more. Gemini will entertain Taurus, but Taurus won't necessarily trust her. Libra may be a good bet for Taurus, as both have an incredible affinity for an elegant, sumptuous, and refined life. Libra and Taurus manage to acquire it together by spurring each other on. Aquarius's lifestyle will drive conservative Taurus crazy, despite his attraction to her.

GEMINI IN LOVE

The problem with Gemini is that he doesn't really know what he wants. He thinks he knows, but then it changes. Gemini needs to work for love—then he'll give his all. Also, he needs a partner who makes him laugh—but not about himself. Geminis can be touchy and sensitive when the humor comes at their expense.

Geminis love first with their minds. Even a relationship that begins primarily because of a sexual attraction won't last if there's no mental connection. Quite often, Geminis seek friendship first with the opposite sex and, once a mental rapport is established, the friendship deepens into love. But this happens when they're really ready for something serious. True, they can be quite fickle in their affections, sometimes carrying on simultaneous relationships. But once their hearts are won, they love deeply.

When It's Done, It's Done

Once Gemini is over you, it's really over. Don't ever take a "break" with Gemini—the relationship won't ever come back around to the way it was. Gemini has this power to cut it off clean and never look back once he's decided it's through.

Geminis have a "need to try everything once" attitude. They're like children who need to stick their hands in the cookie jar. True, there are some Geminis who won't sleep with a person if they're not in love, but chances are, they'll try it all with the one they're with at the moment.

Geminis can also be drama queens (and kings). They like to entertain people, make others laugh, and give good, grown-up advice (that they only wish they could follow themselves). No one can tell a story like a Gemini. She'll use her eyes and her body to create a moment. And she'll get as emotionally worked up the seventh time she tells a tale as she did the first time. Don't ever take the stories at face value, though. Gemini has a habit of exaggerating, even when she doesn't mean to.

Let Me Entertain You!

Gemini, in love, always likes to leave a few options open. Before you get comfy and cozy with a Gemini, make sure he's smitten! Boredom, to a Gemini, is death. He needs the challenge of tempting and wooing you. Let him court you fully before you succumb!

Although Geminis give great advice, they're not good at taking advice from others. And they change their minds frequently, so it's sometimes difficult for them to get to the heart of the matter. Geminis do love wholeheartedly. Capable of diplomacy, they use it when they feel the need but not when it involves love, romance, and you.

If you have a head for business or simply a good job, this will impress Gemini to the umpteenth degree. He wants to respect his partner and know that his partner has big ambitions. Gemini is not a wallflower. He wants to brag about what a great person he's got at his side.

You're a Prize, Not a Trophy

Gemini needs to feel like he's got the prize that other people covet. In other words, it's not just okay that he thinks you're great; he needs to know that his friends think you're amazing, too. So, don't hang on him at parties. Show that you're independent but that you're on his side.

Gemini has a bit of a paranoid, insecure thing. You may not see it right away, but it's there. Never go against Gemini in front of his friends. He'll be instantly offended and look elsewhere for romantic company (who will be "faithful," in his eyes). You don't have to show him your love and devotion immediately; just make sure you agree with him in front of people he deems important.

TIPS

Gemini really does need a little drama to know that you're interested, but he doesn't like being alone for long. He can get caught up with his work for a while, but work will never be the most important thing in his life—not deep down. Love is the real focus. In fact, he'll stay with someone he thinks is the best thing he can find. And if you stay on top, for him, he'll be with you—always.

▲▲▲▲▲▲▲▲▲▲▲▲▲▲▲▲▲▲▲▲▲▲▲▲▲▲▲

The Line Between Jealous and Crazy

There's a fine line between making Gemini jealous and making him insane. If you make him jealous in an innocent way—but he still trusts you—it's fine. If you truly make him jealous, there's no one more vindictive and crazy than he will be. You won't like this side of him at all. It's not pretty.

▼▼▼▼▼▼▼▼▼▼▼▼▼▼▼▼▼▼▼▼▼▼▼▼▼▼▼

Geminis also know that sarcasm and humor with an edge is the best remedy for everything. Make a Gemini laugh—at himself and at others, in general—and he'll instantly think you're smart. With Gemini, it's not always about book-smarts; it's about street-smarts and ironic, sarcastic comebacks that are funny, not biting or nasty. Geminis can be sensitive, in general, but they love to gossip and to make fun of others.

MATCHES WITH GEMINI

Geminis are social enough to get along with and be attracted to just about anyone on a superficial basis. They feel most at home with other air signs, particularly Aquarians, whose minds are as quick as theirs. They also get along with Sagittarius, their polar opposites in the zodiac, who share some of the same attributes. Again, though, these are broad generalizations. It's important to compare the individual charts.

When Gemini is ready to settle down, an earth sign may be a good option for a partner. A Virgo will be a bit too critical for the thin-skinned Gemini, but a Taurus, with his feisty sensual side, may just be what the doctor ordered. Capricorn can go either way, but most Capricorns won't put up with Gemini's otherwise flighty antics or superficial skimming of political ideas that hold great truths for Capricorns.

Again, an air sign like Libra may be ideal for Gemini if they can find a balance of minds. If anyone can find that rare balance, it's Libra. The only problem is that Libra despises confrontation and Gemini tends to go that way.

Water signs are probably too sidestepping for feisty Gemini—unless they have a lot of earth or air in their charts. Scorpio and Gemini match up well in bed, but Scorpio sometimes can drag down a Gemini when he wants to go out and play. Leo can be a fun dating partner for Gemini—with a lot of laughter—but Leo may get annoyed when Gemini doesn't praise the ground she walks on. If Gemini does, it's a match made in heaven.

CANCER IN LOVE

Cancers can be evasive when it comes to romance. They flirt coyly, yet all the while they're feeling their way through the maze of their own emotions. Cancers feel deeply; but Cancers are also very good at putting their feelings "on hold." In other words, if they're not already in love with you, they can pull back and see the relationship for what it is at a distance.

On the one hand, if they're in love, it's not so easy for Cancer to let go. On the other hand, Cancers might just cheat on you rather than confess that they are unhappy in your relationship. Cancers excel at dodging questions and confronting important issues. They find it difficult to open up and talk about their true, personal feelings. If they do, with you, you've got an edge over all the others. The whole sidestepping part of Cancer is true. True to their crab sign, they mimic the crustacean with surprising accuracy.

Right to the Point

Some Cancers dislike the courtship of romance altogether and prefer to get right down to the important questions: Are we compatible? Do we love each other? The problem is, they tend to go through this by themselves or with a very close friend—not with you. In this case, you must be direct and ask what's going on.

Cancers are homebodies and enjoy entertaining at home where they feel most relaxed and secure. They feel comfortable around water, too. From the fluidity and calmness of water spring their vivid, fantastical imaginations. Cancers are "idea" people—and can truly explain any strange, unusual, or outrageous concept to you.

Just remember: to live with and love a Cancer, you have to accept the intensity of their emotions. It's a war they have within themselves, and they'll want to embroil you in it.

Be Playful

Cancers like to poke and prod. They like to make fun—and will do it just to get your goat. Play along. If you act too touchy, they'll think you're rigid and that could trigger one of their many unfathomable moods.

TIPS

Perhaps the worst thing you can do with a Cancer is to take everything too literally. If you don't understand the idea of "concept" and the subtleties of grand schemes, forget Cancer. They're good at seeing the big picture. They stall at the idea of future and forever after, but they'll know, deep down, when they get there. One thing is for sure: Cancers don't have to be faithful at all, but once they make a strong commitment, they're bound by it.

MATCHES WITH CANCER

On the surface, Pisces, as the other dreamy water sign, would seem to be the most compatible with a Cancer. But Pisces's all-over-the-map style, combined with Cancer's sidestepping, could be frustrating for both. Plus, the duality of Pisces would, most likely, drive a Cancer person crazy. One of the best combinations here is water sign Scorpio. Cancer manages Scorpio with bravado and knows how to get the ever-changing Scorpio hooked. A little mystery goes a long way with Scorpio, and, in the case of this match, Cancer cannot help but induce a little intrigue with her onslaught of bottled-up emotions that just lie beneath the surface. Scorpio might just bring those emotions out of Cancer.

Earth signs—Taurus, Virgo, and Capricorn—are particularly good for Cancers because they are sextile to Cancer. Fire signs with Cancer, on the other hand, tend to bring out the worst in Cancer. In rare cases, Leos do well with Cancers (especially if the Leo is the man).

LEO IN LOVE

Leos are passionate. They can also be impulsive and irrational, but it's all part of the charm. They're fickle, and they like to test their partners before they put their hearts into anything. They're difficult, too, particularly when their egos need to be stroked. If you treat a Leo with anything but the ultimate respect, he may not say anything, but he'll remember it—and count it against you in the game of love.

▲▲▲▲▲▲▲▲▲▲▲▲▲▲▲▲▲▲▲▲▲▲▲▲▲▲▲▲▲

Special on the Inside

Though Leo gives the appearance of being confident and secure, this is often an act. Leo's innermost desire is to be accepted for who he is, and his biggest worry is that he'll soon discover he's just normal or boring. It's very important for a Leo to feel special.

▼▼▼▼▼▼▼▼▼▼▼▼▼▼▼▼▼▼▼▼▼▼▼▼▼▼▼▼▼

Leo fights fiercely, so be sure to stick up for yourself with him. On the other hand, arguing for the sake of arguing will make a Leo insane. Leos are intense and will argue, but their sunny, calm natures are truly made for being content and feeling safe and comfortable with a partner.

TIPS

Make a Leo feel secure and he'll be more likely to fall in love with you. But making him secure doesn't mean making yourself a doormat. Let Leo know he can be himself with you—that you won't judge him—and he'll relax in your presence and velvet his claws. For the most part, Leos need to feel needed and want to know they are loved before they commit entirely. Once they're committed, everything is bigger than life and brighter than the Sun. They're known to be loyal, but this is only true after they've found themselves. If they haven't, and they're not yet emotionally evolved or secure, they can be as two-faced as Gemini can be.

Leo needs to believe that a relationship is his idea. If you push too hard, you'll scare him off. He likes to win—always likes a prize. *You* need to be the prize he wins. Leo won't mind putting up a fight for you. There needs to be a fine line, though. If you make Leo work too hard, he'll just walk away. This, for example, isn't true of Aries, another fire sign.

Get Him to Lay It All Out

If you're involved with a Leo, make sure you know his intentions with you. Ask him. He'll tell you. Leo is not a very good liar. If you ask him in person, chances are that you'll get the truth from him. (Or you'll at least read it in his facial expressions—pay attention.)

MATCHES WITH LEO

Another fire sign is good for a Leo because the energy levels are similar. Any sign that is sextile—that is, an angle of separation of 60 degrees or more between two planets—(Gemini, for instance) or trine—an angle of separation of 120 degrees between two planets—(Aries) would be fine, too—though Leo has little patience for Aries who aren't spiritually evolved. True, he may win her for a while, but then what? He can be too headstrong. Aries is a lot like Sagittarius with Leo—lots of fire, but not the same temperament. Sagittarius can be a bit too wise and quiet (or even too superficial or stubborn) for Leo; Aries can be too demanding and controlling.

The polarity between Leo and Aquarius, its polar opposite sign, may elevate a Leo's consciousness to where it succeeds best—to the wider world beyond himself—if the Leo has some air signs in his chart. Capricorn can be an interesting match and Scorpio seems like a go until Leo realizes that she may not like the way he may raise their children. But they're surely a good match in bed.

VIRGO IN LOVE

Virgos are inscrutable in the affairs of the heart. They seem remote and quiet one minute, then open and talkative the next. This is due only to Virgo's battle within himself. He's sensitive but doesn't like to show it. Sometimes he'll need to show you how he feels; other times, he'll keep his feelings a secret. Unfortunately, he doesn't always let you see this true side of himself. He's too busy weighing all the options and trying to act the way he thinks he should, not how he truly feels.

Virgos always need to perfect everything: every moment, every deed, and every word. They're idealists, but in a practical way. They believe that everything should fall into place on its own (even if it shows no sign of happening) and tend to stay in relationships much longer than they should because they don't want to give up and walk away. To them, you are the investment of their precious time. They also hold on to the past like Cancers and, unfortunately, apply past experiences to present ones. In a perfect world, this would make sense (to them). Unfortunately, each situation is different, and Virgos must face this fact.

The Boneyard in the Closet

The world is a complicated place, and most of us have skeletons in our closets. But for Virgo, there are too many skeletons. He wants perfection (mostly from himself). He'll generally keep his imperfections in the dark, though he'll be the first to point out some of his more superficial flaws. Pay attention to what Virgo tells you, as it's usually all true.

It is said that Virgos generally don't entertain romantic illusions. There is truth to this, but it's not the whole story. Virgos are incredibly romantic when they feel it. They have a wonderful appreciation of love—and know how to woo the right way. They *seem* more practical than idealistic but deep down, Virgos suffer for love and feel their emotions intensely.

Virgos try to make everything fit into their idea of a perfect world. For example, they're very serious about the words they and others use. If you tell a Virgo something, he expects you to follow through on your promise. He's put his heart and soul into finding a solution for you. If you don't at least try it his way, he'll seriously discredit you.

Critical Mass

Virgos are critical, and they can't help it. Don't take it personally, though. A Virgo is never harder on the people he loves than he is on himself. Virgo needs to analyze, sort through, and mentally take stock once in a while in order to feel grounded and stable.

Here's the bottom line: If you ask Virgo for advice, you'd better take it or at least make him think you're doing something practical about your situation. Like Sagittarius, Virgo will always tell you what to do and expect you to do it. If you get advice from Virgo and ignore it, he'll be less likely to help you in the future.

▲▲▲▲▲▲▲▲▲▲▲▲▲▲▲▲▲▲▲▲▲▲▲▲▲▲▲

Do the Work

You have to do some grunt work to get on a Virgo's good side. If you show a Virgo that you're easy to get along with and can take his criticism with a healthy show of acceptance, he'll feel more comfortable with you and will eventually let his guard down completely.

▼▼▼▼▼▼▼▼▼▼▼▼▼▼▼▼▼▼▼▼▼▼▼▼▼▼▼

Virgos are conflicted within and, therefore, will come across as being nit-picky or too precise. The truth is, they've got thin skins.

TIPS

The best way to handle a Virgo's lecturing and criticizing you is to tell her she's right about whatever she's picking at, at the moment. Then bring it up later to dispute, if you like. Although Virgos must have a sense that they're right, they're also self-aware. In fact, they'll be the first to admit that they're difficult and hardheaded.

MATCHES WITH VIRGO

Virgos are mentally attracted to Geminis, but they find the twins a bit hard to take for the long run. The light, airy nature of Geminis, too, contrasts with Virgo's obstinate nature. Gemini likes interesting discussions (as does Virgo) and entertains Virgo well, but Virgo sometimes fights more than Gemini would like.

Instead, the "grounding" present in other earth signs may seem appealing on the surface, but leave it to a Virgo to find fault with his fellow earth signs. Scorpios and Cancers may be the best bets, with mystical Pisces a close second. Libra sometimes goes well with Gemini but it may seem like Virgo is always just 'round the bend with Libra—never quite getting all the love and devotion he wants. Libra makes it tough.

Fire signs can be great friends with Virgo, but the two might never truly understand the other's intentions. It depends on the rest of their charts. Virgo can patronize without knowing it, and sensitive fire signs take offense. In the end, anyone with a good heart and a sensitive but practical nature will get along well with Virgo.

LIBRA IN LOVE

Libras are drawn to beauty, whatever its form. The only thing they enjoy as much as beauty is harmony. Even when a relationship has gone sour, a Libra hesitates to be the one who ends it. Libras can't stand hurting anyone's feelings; emotional rawness is one of those ugly realities that they don't like to see. As a result, they may remain in a relationship longer than they should because disharmony is so distasteful. Libras seek harmony because, in their hearts, they know that enlightenment lies at the calm center of the storm.

In fact, Libra is just that—the eye of the storm. He'll start something and then walk away to watch things unfold at a distance, where it's safe. Libra is the ultimate watcher of human behavior. He studies it—studies you—and determines what he knows and what he believes from that. He'll have his friends study you and see if you're faithful and worthy. Ultimately, he'll make up his own mind. But if a Libra doesn't trust you, you're history. He'll never put the time in to get to know you.

The Ideal Partner
Libra has a very fixed idea in his head of what he's looking for. If you don't fit that perfect mold, he's not going to waste his time on you. Find out what Libra wants. If you don't, you may seduce him for one night, but he won't get serious with you.

It seems as if Libra has many friends. True, he has a wonderful social circle and many people who believe in him. But watch closely. Libra keeps his true self hidden from the world. There's usually only one person he truly trusts—often a family member. If he opens up to you completely on a consistent basis, you've got a real mate for life.

In fact, Librans can be very stubborn when deciding what the roads of life all lead to. It's sometimes difficult for them to make a tough decision, but when they do, no one can talk them out of it. Librans believe in signs, red flags, and even superstitions. They'll consider omens and apply them to their own lives.

Also, Librans want to be calm and comfortable in a relationship. Many Libra men choose younger women just to have this feeling of ultimate control. Sometimes they also pick women a lot older than they are so the woman does all of the deciding. You'll also find that Librans are mostly faithful when they find the one with whom they want to spend time. True, they may set up strange arrangements, but when they love, they love deeply.

Librans have a tough time figuring out what they really want. On one hand, they want a partner who's carefree and easy to deal with. On the other hand, they want someone who's a true confidant and partner for life. Let them battle it out on their own. If they haven't yet determined what they want, stay away.

TIPS

Remember, too, that Libra likes to feel in control. In this way, you may have to be demure in the beginning. Let Libra chase you. Don't let his friends know that you're interested. Libra will get the hint just by looking you in the eyes. His eyes are the key to his soul. In fact, that's how you'll know that a Libra is interested.

Libras are very sensitive, so try not to make the first move. Because of the internal battle all Libras must face, they like to have dominance in the situation, and they tend to judge a mate unfairly if she's too aggressive. Once again, let Libra man steer the conversation and the relationship. Pull back, at first, and let him court you. He'll do it in a grand way, and you'll be glad you did.

MATCHES WITH LIBRA

Librans can get along with just about anyone. They are most compatible with other air signs, Aquarius and Gemini. Though seriously outgoing, Geminis can sometimes scare them—they understand the way Librans think. Scorpios get to the heart of the matter with Libra; they have the intensity and emotional depth that Librans crave. In fact, Librans might even get attached to Scorpios in a volatile and unhealthy way if they're not careful. Though Scorpios can be a good match for Libras, they should watch out for signs of control. If Librans feel they're being manipulated in any way, they'll be out the door in a flash.

Librans also gravitate toward people who reflect their refined tastes and aesthetic leanings, like Leo. Also, an earth sign may provide a certain grounding that a Libran needs. Taurus is a wonderful, sensual match with Libra. A water sign, like Cancer, may offer a fluidity of emotion that a Libran may lack, but this combination may be an uphill battle. Cancers can be too moody, sometimes, and too self-involved for harmony-seeking Librans.

Since opposites attract, Aries can sometimes be a good fit for Librans—though Aries needs to have spiritually found herself before this match can work. On another note, a Libra with a Libra can be a good match—but watch out! Two of the same signs together can be wonderful or a big mess.

▲▲▲▲▲▲▲▲▲▲▲▲▲▲▲▲▲▲▲▲▲▲▲▲▲▲▲▲

Finding Yourself in Your Partner

When you pick someone of the same Sun sign as you, it will magnify all of your good traits—and your bad ones, too. It's like looking in the mirror. Do you like what you see? Or does the similarity bring up issues for you? Always choose a partner who brings out your best side.

▼▼▼▼▼▼▼▼▼▼▼▼▼▼▼▼▼▼▼▼▼▼▼▼▼▼▼▼

SCORPIO IN LOVE

You don't know the meaning of the word "intensity" unless you've been involved with a Scorpio. No other sign brings such raw power to life. The rawness probably isn't something you understand or even like very much, but there's no question that it's intricately woven through the fabric of your relationship.

The odd part is that you're never quite sure how the intensity is going to manifest: jealousy, fury, endless questions, or soft and intriguing, but effective passion. Sometimes, the intensity doesn't have anything to do with the relationship but with the personal dramas in the Scorpio's life. Many times, you may even hear from work colleagues that he's a perfectionist and difficult to work with. The word "crazy" may even get into the picture.

Scorpios have a magnetism that is legendary. It doesn't even matter if he's good-looking—it's always there. Consider this: Scorpio is always the sexiest person in the room. Astrologers say that Scorpio is also known for his bedroom prowess: this isn't myth. Unfortunately, other problems can weigh

Scorpio down, so he's got to be clear of mind and calm in order to woo you in his cool, mysterious way.

If your Scorpio is completely direct with you, consider yourself lucky. Chances are, he's got a number of secrets he keeps hidden from the world. It may be something that's happened in his past, or a fetish he doesn't want to let you in on, or even another woman he sees occasionally.

▲▲▲▲▲▲▲▲▲▲▲▲▲▲▲▲▲▲▲▲▲▲▲▲▲▲

A Sign of Lying

You'll always be able to tell when Scorpio is fibbing. You can feel it. The energy around him changes. If you keep insisting that he tell you the truth, he may even get angry. If he does, it probably means there's something he's not telling you. The only way to get it out of him is to get him in a good mood and pretend you don't really care. Then coax the confession out of him.

▼▼▼▼▼▼▼▼▼▼▼▼▼▼▼▼▼▼▼▼▼▼▼▼▼▼

Scorpio's senses are strong, especially those of sight, touch, and taste. If he touches you, you'll feel it down to your toes. He has keen sight, meaning instincts and taste, meaning food. However, there's one sense he lacks: hearing. It seems as if he doesn't hear anything you say. It's not that he doesn't really remember. Instead, he has a mental block against the things he doesn't want to know. Very likely he'll pretend he doesn't know what you're talking about. The truth is, Scorpios have excellent memories. Don't let him get away with this.

Many Scorpios are hidden workaholics. They need to complete the task at hand before they can go on to the next. They're very good, in the beginning, at concealing this fact. Therefore, the thing that will be most important for a Scorpio is to get you. Then, predictably, he'll go back to his normal routine of working crazy hours, complaining about it, and never resolving the problem.

Many Scorpios have obsessive tendencies—whether or not you see them in the beginning. At first it may just seem like you're another obsession. He'll be so bent on getting you that you'll wonder if you've just stepped into a romance novel. Be aware that this may change later. Scorpio can't leave the duties of his job for long—he defines himself by them.

Know, too, that if he's having many problems at work, your relationship will suffer. He needs to resolve work issues before he can think of getting intimate again. He cannot separate these two parts of his life—try as he may.

In this respect, you must understand and be supportive. There's no other way around it.

In the case of Scorpio, before you even think of letting romance get the better of you, ask yourself: Is this person happy with his life? Does he pity himself? If a Scorpio is not happy deep down, he will go into periods of self-doubt and pity—and will bring you down with him. Some Scorpios are emotionally mature and can handle the world around them. Find out first, though.

TIPS

Scorpio will stay in a romantic situation that's not working for longer than he should. If he starts pulling away, or is less jealous or possessive than he was before, you're probably losing him. The worst thing you can do at this point is to chase after him. Let him come after you. Scorpio is a lonely, private soul—but he hates being alone, too.

PILLOW TALK

The best time to approach a Scorpio about something important is after lovemaking. His guard is let down almost completely. Be aware of Scorpio's temper. He bottles things up inside, and then it all comes out at once—in a huff. Don't ever try to convince Scorpio he's wrong at this point. Let him calm down first; then he's more likely to see your side of it.

MATCHES WITH SCORPIO

Scorpio is usually compatible with Taurus, because the signs are polar opposites and balance each other. The water of Scorpio and the earth of Taurus mix well. However, both signs are fixed, which means that in a disagreement neither will give in to the other. Scorpios can be compatible with other Scorpios as long as each person understands the other's intensity and passions. Pisces and Cancer, the other two water signs, may be too weak for Scorpio's intensity, unless a comparison of natal charts indicates otherwise.

Fire signs may blend well with Scorpio, depending on their charts. If a Scorpio is emotionally solid, a Leo may be a good match. Scorpio loves Leo's sunny nature and is drawn to it. If Scorpio doesn't pull Leo down with him, this can work. Sagittarius, especially if Scorpio is near the cusp of Sagittarius, can be the same—but ditto with the "bringing her down with the house." If the two can respect each other and find a good balance, this can be a working partnership. Aries and Scorpio, however, will find that the emotional gap is probably too wide a chasm to cross.

SAGITTARIUS IN LOVE

The individual searches for truth, and the truths two people ultimately find revealed in each other are Sagittarian themes. No matter whom a Sagittarian loves or marries, there will always be a part of him or her slightly separate and singular. Sagittarius is pretty clear in what he wants. He knows if he's in love—or not. Enticing a Sagittarius to fall in love with you can be challenging. Playing hard to get might capture his attention, but he will rely on his instincts and intellect to decide if you are the one he wants and needs, or not.

He's so blunt and tactless with his words that they can sometimes cut you to the bone. But believe everything that comes out of Sagittarius's mouth. If he tells you he's in love, he is. If he tells you he's not, he's not. Sagittarius is not a very diplomatic soul. In his mind, honesty and straightforwardness are everything, and he likes someone who will listen carefully to everything he has to say.

Off by Himself

Strangely enough, Sagittarius sometimes gives the impression that he's lost in another world. He seems quiet—or into himself. This isn't entirely true. In truth, he's probably thinking about work or some problem in quantum physics—he's not thinking about your relationship.

Sagittarius wants everything to go smoothly. In his mind, if things are not moving forward, he's not going to waste his precious time on you. Just don't badger him for his thoughts.

TIPS

Let Sagittarius come to you to ask how you're feeling. He needs to be left alone to experience his space and freedom, and then he'll come search you out.

MATCHES WITH SAGITTARIUS

Other air signs are compatible with Sagittarius. The Sagittarius-Gemini polarity confers a natural affinity between the two signs. But other fire signs might work well, too. It just depends. Sagittarius, above all other fire signs, is the most emotionally secure. Sagittarius is not the most stable (Leo is), but he thinks he is. This can make him a bit of a know-it-all. He doesn't tolerate as much as Leo, but he's not as ridiculously immature as Aries can sometimes be.

He comes off as a natural, quiet leader. And he is. Actually, the best match for Sagittarius is a water sign—particularly Pisces. These two go together so well because Pisces is strong and sensual enough for Sagittarius but is also a master in the art of silent persuasion. Sagittarius needs someone who is loving, sweet, and tender, who will let him do what he feels like doing, and isn't nitpicky. Again, a water sign might do him good because he likes being shown the way; yet, all the while, he's the one who can act in charge of things.

Finding a Soul Mate

When Sagittarius falls in love with "the one," she's set for life. Sagittarius can be the least faithful sign of the zodiac, but she can also be the most faithful. If she finds what she's looking for, Sagittarius will settle down and not look any further.

You can get a Sagittarius to fall in love with you if you are sweet, yet strong. He hates silent passive-aggressive tactics; if he does something stupid, approach him in that moment and just tell him what he's done wrong. He doesn't go for the shy, sensitive type, though. He needs to feel that his mate can do fine without him. Only then will he stay.

CAPRICORN IN LOVE

At times, Capricorn needs a partner who is serious, while at other times he needs a lighthearted mate who will simply make him laugh. The latter will have an innocent quality—a purity—that Capricorn is drawn to. Which mate Capricorn ends up with, though, depends on where he is emotionally and mentally. This is true for all of us to some extent, but it's especially true for Capricorn.

No matter how hard you make Capricorn laugh about himself and the world, his path always leads back to the same riddle. Regardless of how hard he works, how far he climbs, or how emotionally or physically rich he becomes, it's never enough. It only leads back to solitude of self.

Information Is Power

Capricorns respect those who are well informed. If you talk a good game and don't know your stuff, for example, forget Capricorn. He'll smell you out! Make sure to admit it if you don't know what you're talking about. Don't fake it. Capricorn will know anyway.

Capricorns can be very independent. They don't like being told what to do or how to do it. They seem malleable and can get along with anybody, though they don't necessarily enjoy the company of all. A mate must be stimulating, engaging, knowledgeable, and, most importantly, grounded, in order for Capricorn to truly respect him. If Capricorn senses that his partner is off-kilter, he'll run for the hills. He won't try to change her or help her as, say, Cancer would.

TIPS

If Capricorn whispers evocative words of passion, love, and forever after, pay attention. He doesn't spew out or toss around romantic words just to woo you and then leave you cold. He's got to be convinced in order to get involved. True, he's a little better at having meaningless adventures than Virgo is, but eventually he'll want something that means family and future to him. And he takes those ideas very seriously, indeed.

MATCHES WITH CAPRICORN

Virgos may be too literal and spirited for Capricorn. Plus, Virgo in bed can bring out Capricorn's traditional side, which bothers Capricorn, who secretly longs for someone who can open him up, emotionally and spiritually (both in bed and out). Taurus may be too fixed, but because they both have the earth element in common, Capricorn and Taurus can get along well.

Of all the water signs, the intensity of Scorpios may be overwhelming—though Capricorn will get a real kick out of Scorpio's tendency to be jealous. In bed, these two can be smoldering. However, the ambivalence of Pisces will, most likely, drive Capricorn nuts.

Capricorn and Cancer

Capricorns may just get along with Cancer because they're both cardinal signs (that is, signs that initiate a change of temperate zone season) though this could be a possible mad rush to the finish line, too! The two can be competitive. Cancer and Capricorn both have refined senses of humor. A Capricorn must have patience to deal with Cancer's moods (which isn't likely).

Strangely enough, a Leo might be the best bet for Capricorn. If Leo has some earth in her chart—or some balanced air—they get along well. Certainly, the attraction is there. Capricorn mystifies Leo. Capricorn praises Leo the way she needs to be praised.

AQUARIUS IN LOVE

Aquarians need the same space and freedom in a relationship that they crave in every other area of their lives. Even when they commit, the need doesn't evaporate. They must follow the dictates of their individuality above all else. This stubbornness can work against them if they aren't careful. Aquarians usually are attracted to people who are unusual or eccentric in some way. Their most intimate relationships are marked by uniqueness.

Aquarians can be very instinctive, but this doesn't mean they're self-aware. They also try to root for the underdog but sometimes pick the wrong underdog or victim to defend. Their upbeat, positive outlook on life can be tempered by idealistic notions they try hard to suppress. The biggest goal in life, for them, is to remain calm and cool. This is very important for Aquarius because, when he lets loose, he can be a fireball. And, if he gets too wound up, the aggression he exudes can be harsh for other people to cope with. Instinctively, he knows this and tries to temper it, often unsuccessfully.

Aquarians know they're strong individuals and that they can turn the tides to their favor. Luck follows them everywhere—even if they're not aware of it. They may even sense where they're headed before the fact. An Aquarius is not a big mystery, though. If you want an answer about love, just ask. Aquarians will tell you if your relationship is headed somewhere or not. If they're not sure, chances are that the answer is no, but they can be swayed over time.

▲▲▲▲▲▲▲▲▲▲▲▲▲▲▲▲▲▲▲▲▲▲▲▲▲▲▲

The Age of Aquarius

Aquarians are survivors. So, if you want to be with one, know that they're hard-headed with their decisions. Under that cool exterior is a person who must, eventually, follow his heart and mind. This can be difficult, too, because the two forces don't always agree! But sticking with an Aquarius will pay off. They'll trust you and slowly get attached.

▼▼▼▼▼▼▼▼▼▼▼▼▼▼▼▼▼▼▼▼▼▼▼▼▼▼▼

Aquarius also must see a bit of the world before settling down. He may even get married a couple of times before realizing that he wasn't ready for what he thought he was. An ideal partner for Aquarius will show his own mental agility, his independence, and his emotional strength of will. These traits will get an Aquarius to follow you to the ends of the earth, but only if he's ready for something real to enter his life.

SEDUCTION TIPS WITH AQUARIUS

Aquarius loves to shock! He tests people to see how smart and cool they'll be when they realize they've been had. If someone overreacts or is too sensitive to this test, Aquarius will lose interest. It's all part of being fascinating, interesting, and fun for Aquarius. He has to know you'll play the mental games he loves to play—and that you're strong enough to handle them. Therefore, don't get angry when Aquarius tests you. Laugh about it—and do it back. Aquarius will appreciate this!

Aquarius is impressed with bold, aggressive moves. You can grab an Aquarius when you want, and he certainly won't shy away. Just make sure you have the mental connection first, or you'll be wasting your time. Aquarians are capable of having sex or a fling without getting emotionally connected at all. They won't judge you if you sleep with them right away, usually, but if you get overly romantic or clingy when Aquarius isn't quite as into it as you are, Aquarius will definitely back away from the situation.

His Cheatin' Heart

If Aquarius is not getting what he wants out of the relationship, in any way, he's more likely to cheat than any other sign. Aquarians, like Sagittarius, will be faithful only to "the one"—and, even then, it's still difficult for an Aquarius to be completely and utterly devoted.

If an Aquarius has a short fling, or encounter, it doesn't mean his heart will be in it. Aquarians can turn their emotions on and off, but only when they're not in love. When they're in love, it's another story altogether.

TIPS

Like Aries, Aquarius always needs a challenge on some level in all of his relationships—or he won't take you seriously. Remember, Aquarius is a survivor and knows that nothing worth having comes too easily.

MATCHES WITH AQUARIUS

Due to the lack of prejudice in this sign, Aquarians usually get along with just about everyone. They're particularly attracted to people with whom they share an intellectual camaraderie—someone who makes them laugh and makes them feel good about themselves. In this way, Gemini can be a fabulous match for Aquarius, as long as they don't butt heads. This relationship can work only if the two find balance between neediness and independence. Also, Gemini can be extremely jealous and possessive with mates, which Aquarius abhors.

Aries is usually a good match for Aquarius. Together, they have lively, fascinating conversations, plenty of spunk, and mental camaraderie. Unfortunately, the flakiness factor of Aries can be evident to Aquarius, and he's not sure if he can trust her. However, he likes the challenge.

Many Aquarians wind up with Virgos. Virgos have the kind of stubbornness and organized stability that Aquarians secretly crave. But this may also be an ego thing. Remember, Aquarius loves a challenge, and Virgo keeps him squirming with her moral lectures and hard-headed ways. But, mentally and in bed, these two can do very well together.

A Libra or another Aquarius can be a good match—especially if one is more outgoing and gregarious than the other and lets his partner shine. Aquarians are usually secure enough to see bad and good traits in a partner that are similar to their own, and still be able to deal with them and move ahead with the relationship.

A sign that's sextile or trine to Aquarius will also work. And Aquarius's polar opposite, Leo, can be an interesting mate for Aquarius. If Aquarius doesn't get too self-involved and gives Leo her fair due, this can work. But Leo is usually running after Aquarius, and Aquarius can get bored of that—fast. If Leo pulls away a little, this rapport can function well. All in all, Aquarius is a great partner if you've truly won his heart. If not, you'll just be a stop along the way for lively Aquarius, who craves adventure and experience.

PISCES IN LOVE

Through the heart, sensitive Pisces experiences his subjective reality as real, solid, perhaps even more tangible than the external world. For some Pisces, romance can be the point of transcendence—the stage in which he penetrates to the larger mysteries that have concerned him most of his life. To be romantically involved with a Pisces is to be introduced to many levels of consciousness and awareness.

There is nothing weak about Pisces, as many astrologers claim. Instead, Pisces watches from a distance and determines the best point of attack. Pisces, also, many times seems sweet and kind. But know this: when Pisces is in a relationship and feels comfortable, there is no one who can manipulate you and your feelings like Pisces can (except, maybe, Cancer). Pisces know how to play cold and walk away until you follow. A Pisces knows that this tactic always works in human nature and has this move down to a science.

Pisces are ten times craftier than they appear. They're incredibly good at hiding this side of themselves, and they're so adept at playing along with you and being on your side that you won't even know what hit you when they use something—something you've told them—against you, in the future.

Study for the Test

Pisces will test you. All Pisces know how to challenge and how to get the answer they're looking for at the moment. If you're smart enough, you'll recognize this and pass the test. If not, Pisces will turn away without warning and find someone worthier of his affections.

Pisces is idealistic. But also, he is a dreamer with a vision. Most Pisces know what they want and go after it with a kind of slow, methodical gait. Eventually, most of them get what they want, even if it takes time. But Pisces instinctively know how best to get the most out of their astonishingly calm composure and patience.

Pisces includes a little bit of every sign and can usually pull out this grab bag of talents at will. He can be a little mysterious like Scorpio, play the noble like Leo, insert the commanding attitude like Sagittarius, be the charmer like Gemini, and act the part of smooth talker like Aries. The only role that Pisces has difficulty playing is Aquarius, whose sign sits next to Pisces.

In fact, Pisceans have a hard time hiding disdain for those they don't like. Pisces has a regal air about him like Leo. But while Leo is more caring and noble, Pisces has a proud, capable, and studious air, which, try as he may, he cannot shake.

Empathetic, Not Sympathetic

Pisces is intelligent and empathetic. Don't ever confuse sympathetic with empathetic, though. Pisces will not feel your particular brand of sadness, though he seems to. Instead, he's likely to bring you out of the despair by understanding your plight and giving you good advice for it. But the sadness he shows you will never reach his heart.

However, there is no one like Pisces to give you good advice. Aries may be good at it, but he orders you around while doing so. His words are more command than suggestion. Gemini is good at it, but aggressive. Pisces, though, will put the idea into your head and let you come up with the solution.

TIPS

Pisces also has a thing for power. If you're someone he can look up to and admire, you'll win Pisces's heart. Unlike the air signs, Libra, Gemini, and Aquarius, Pisces will be more won over with accomplishment and quiet romantic gestures than by pure physical beauty.

Since Pisces likes the cool and understated, your manners, gestures, and even dress should be tasteful and elegant, not showy or ostentatious. The way someone puts herself together will be more important to Pisces than makeup or any other superficial traits. Pisceans also appreciate directness and fire—gumption and energy. They love intensity and romance, in a grounded and refined way.

MATCHES WITH PISCES

Other water signs seem the obvious choice here. But Scorpio might overpower Pisces and Cancer might be too clingy. The signs sextile to Pisces are Capricorn and Taurus. While Capricorn might be too limited and grounded for the Piscean imagination, Taurus probably fits right in. Gemini, also, because it's a mutable sign like Pisces, can be compatible.

The real shocker here is that Sagittarius may be the best combination for Pisces. Though appearing opposites, they complement each other quite well. Pisces is able to soothe the Sagittarius savage beast; she lets Sagittarius do what he wants, yet always keeps the upper hand with a cool, polished, quietly strong demeanor. This is what Sagittarius likes best. As for the other fire signs, there doesn't seem to be much chance for them, but it really depends on the other factors in the two separate charts.

Sex

If your romantic relationship has moved beyond flirty friendship to a deeper commitment that could include intimacy, you might be wondering if the two of you are as compatible as lovers as you are as friends. What if you desire a slow, sensuous, and tender sexual encounter, but your partner prefers a lightning hot, muscular romp? Or, while you opine that a dreamy sexual fantasy is almost as satisfying as the physical experience, he counters that robust, frequent sex is a healthy tension release. Knowing how each astrological sign approaches intimacy and expresses passion in relationship to your own sign can enhance your understanding and intensify the experience when the moment is right.

ARIES

Sex with impatient, adventurous Aries can be dramatic and happen fast, so don't expect long-lasting foreplay. Aries are aroused by seeing the clothes come off. They love to be pleasured and can even be selfish lovers. Ever the bold trail blazers, they will try anything new at least once. With this sign, expect fireworks. If you want a faithful Aries, try to stay away from those who have their Venus (their love sign) in Aries, Sagittarius, or even Aquarius. They tend to wander. If you're an earth sign, pick an Aries with lots of air in his chart—he'll be drawn to you. If you're a water sign, you'll probably do well with Aries if he has a lot of fire.

TAURUS

If you're into languid, sensual lovemaking, a Taurus is for you. However, if you bed a Taurus too quickly, you'll lose his respect. The sensual Taurus wants to make love—a slow, seductive tango—that culminates in sex. Even if Taurus likes to talk "dirty," he still wants to know that the feelings there are real. Then he'll loosen up and be himself in bed. Taurus is compatible with Virgo and Capricorn and with Water signs. Taureans are fatally attracted to Scorpios, their polar opposites. Although their elements, earth and water, should make them compatible, this tends to be a superficial connection. Instead, beneath the surface, they are at war with one other. But this kicks up the chemistry.

GEMINI

Gemini is the biggest flirt in the zodiac and plays sexy to the hilt. He'll flirt in front of you and exude charm like you've never seen (except perhaps from a Libra). It can make you positively dizzy watching him work the room. He'll be faithful after you've won his heart. Unfortunately, this isn't an easy task. Gemini will always go for the coolest person in the room, unless he's serious about settling down. Then, he'll choose the person who grounds him. Engage him in an intriguing or interesting conversation—then leave and make it appear you are having a wonderful time without him. This may be a game, but it works. When Gemini finally realizes you've bailed on him, he'll come looking for you.

CANCER

In bed, the Cancer lover becomes a knight in shining armor—gentle, thoughtful, and protective. He won't tell you what turns him on during sex; you are expected to intuitively know. He'll try new positions if he thinks it will please you. If you are an outdoors kind of girl, put on a girly dress, some lip gloss, and perfume. Femininity turns up the heat for Cancer men. The erogenous zones for men and woman of this sign are the stomach and breasts. When Cancer gives his heart, expect him to be a sweet, attentive lover. Even if you are the initiator and a little aggressive in bed, don't worry as he'll like it.

LEO

An erotic call at 3:00 A.M., a chopper ride over Manhattan, five dozen roses that arrive at your office; this might just be Leo's prelude to lovemaking. He likes to do things in a royal manner that makes a dramatic statement and gets your attention. He is a sensual creature who likes luxury and believes you get what you pay for. This lover understands the difference between paying for a $300 hotel and a $500 hotel; and if you'd prefer to stay in a mud hut with no air conditioning or heat, you'd better find another Sun sign to share your bed. If you want to turn him on, make him think that you see him as a god (or, if your Leo is a woman, a goddess). Leos enjoy their sexual trysts and pleasure their lovers well because they want to be seen as the best in bed.

VIRGO

Virgos, like Taurus, need to feel some kind of purity and sweetness in order to make love. He'd rather be in love than not, and sometimes won't even have sex unless he's feeling love. You have to make Virgo feel special, or sex just won't happen. He can have adventurous affairs. However, as he gets to know himself, he'll simply want more from you and will despise the thought of getting close if you don't love him as much as he loves you. This is a sign that sees sex as a release from daily tension—a healthy outlet that is necessary for one's well-being. In bed, this sign is sweet and considerate and can get turned on just knowing how much you appreciate him.

LIBRA

Although Libra can be aroused by a little role-playing or sex games, don't try it until the relationship is on equal footing. Libra seeks balance always, and this goes for bedroom activities. He'll eagerly give, and you'll receive, but it has to work both ways. Libra is often idealistic and overly sensitive. Additionally, it takes a Libra a while to reveal himself to you. You may find it difficult to deal with his constant back-and-forth of letting himself go and reining himself in. But ultimately, Libra men and women are charming and make wonderful lovers when you make them happy and meet their needs.

SCORPIO

Suggest smearing his body in chocolate icing from the neck down, and Scorpio might just go for it. His intensity is legendary and that extends to the bedroom. He likes to be very sexy, yet tasteful. Scorpio can be the pleasure-seeking lover with strong fantasies. Both the men and the women of this sign will try new and different things involving intimacy. They'll keep your secrets and expect you to keep theirs. The Scorpio man, however, will negatively judge you for using your sexiness to flirt with his friends—don't do it. Scorpio might keep his rage hidden for a while, but in the end he'll just think you are not the good girl he thought you were. Scorpios will have flings with ultra-sexy women, but they will never marry them.

Forget chasing after him. The Scorpio man needs to woo his woman. He may do it subtly, at first, but eventually he'll invite you for a weekend away somewhere special. If he wants you for his mate, Scorpio will be relentless in his pursuit until he gets what he wants.

SAGITTARIUS

Sagittarius is adept at separating sex and love. He is a passionate fire sign; however, sleeping with you doesn't necessarily equate with being in love with you. Ask him directly (not in a needy way); he will tell you frankly and won't mince words. He's an avid sportsman and that extends to the bedroom. Get him turned on with a pillow fight or a tickling match. This is an ardent lover, more sensitive than he appears. Although he will care for any woman with whom he gets involved, he won't have patience for those who play hard to get. If you lie to him or express neediness, it will only drive him out the door in search of a new lover. The way to keep him is to make him guess. Use direct words, quiet emotions. Sagittarius likes a subtle steering toward love.

CAPRICORN

To arouse a Capricorn, use a three-prong approach—combine sexiness with conservativeness and dress for the occasion. Capricorns appreciate a lover with confidence and know-how. They are often attracted to mature lovers, older than themselves. Such a relationship provides a sense of stability and security that Capricorns prefer over mercurial fireworks. Sex for them is straightforward in keeping with the earthiness of their sign. Above all, Capricorn wants a loyal, stable, solid, and devoted partner. This lover needs to know that you'll be there when he needs you or he'll never consider you for the long term. Once in a relationship, Capricorns have a tough time walking away.

AQUARIUS

Getting an Aquarius hot and bothered might work better from a distance, through sexting or phone sex. Lovers of this sign possess a detachment that can drive you crazy at times. However, if you show the same detachment toward your Aquarian, it might actually serve as an aphrodisiac. For some Aquarians the whole idea of sex and sexual fantasy appeals more than the actual act.

PISCES

Pisces is a sensitive and expressive lover with a seemingly supernatural depth of perception. He will do anything for his mate. Piscean sexual fantasies are richly imagined. They prefer show to tell when it comes to lovemaking. If love is absent, the Piscean can view the relationship with astonishing coldness, even if he finds it difficult to break away. Still, he will love you forever or at least tell you that. Pisces, like Cancer, has a tough time deciding what he truly wants. There's something always in the back of a Pisces's mind that says "I could probably do better." And, because of Pisces's idealism, he'll always wonder what kind of mate he'd have in a perfect world.

Money

What is true about your relationship with money—how you earn, spend, and save it—might not be true for others. Each sign of the zodiac holds a certain attitude toward money, whether it is Aries's tendency to keep it circulating or Scorpio's use of other people's money to make more and hide it. Fiscal responsibility or lack of it definitely impacts the success or failure of any enterprise, so before you enter any agreements discover what astrology reveals about your potential partner and money.

ARIES

There are no two ways about it: Aries people spend money as fast as it comes in. An Aries knows something should be tucked away, but retirement seems such a long way off. Besides, money always comes in when needed! The challenge for an Aries is to develop the habit of saving.

TAURUS

Despite the Taurean need for material security, they enjoy spending money. But the spending is rarely frivolous because Taurean tastes are specific and usually refined. Books, art, travel, and shamanic workshops may offer security for the Taurus.

GEMINI

How a Gemini handles money depends on which of the twins holds the purse strings at the time—the spendthrift or the tightwad. Either way, Geminis enjoy spending money on the things they love, such as books, movies, theater, and travel.

CANCER

Cancers aren't lavish spenders except when it comes to their homes and families. Then, nothing is too expensive. Otherwise, they tend to be big savers. As teens, they stash their allowance in cookie jars; as adults, they stick their money in long-term CDs.

LEO

If Leo wants it, Leo buys it. If he can't afford it, he charges it. If his charge cards are maxed out, then he hocks his Rolex or his collection of baseball cards to buy it. Saving for a rainy day just isn't in the picture because, for a Leo, there aren't any rainy days! There are, of course, exceptions to all these generalities. A Moon in an Earth sign, combined with a Leo Sun, would mitigate the flamboyance, particularly if the Moon were in Capricorn. But these are just details.

VIRGO

When Virgos are big spenders, they usually pull back at some critical point and question what they buy and why. What need does it fill? If they are tight with money, then something happens that impels them to loosen their hold—to spend money for enjoyment. Virgos follow an arc of evolvement toward perfection in everything they do. They analyze patterns in their lives and seek to change those that don't work.

LIBRA

A sense of balance allows Libras to strike the right note between spender and miser. Libras tend to save, but they enjoy spending when they can afford it. Most Libras know their limits.

SCORPIO

Scorpios are masters at using other people's money to build their own fortunes. This is as true of a Mafia don as it is of a Wall Street entrepreneur. Scorpio attaches no moral judgment to it; this is simply how things are. In return, Scorpios can be extravagantly generous in charity work or as anonymous donors to worthy causes. Your Scorpio may even rewrite the last act of your rejected screenplay and get it to sell.

SAGITTARIUS

A Sagittarius has plenty of options about where to spend his or her money—travel, education, workshops, seminars, animals, or books—and that's often the problem. How can they narrow their choices? What should they buy first? More than likely, they will toss all their choices into the air and seize the one that hits the ground first.

CAPRICORN

Thriftiness is the hallmark for Capricorn finances. They build their finances the same way they build their careers: one penny at a time. They do seek status and the acquisition of material goods that reflect what they seek, so they may go through periods where they overspend.

AQUARIUS

Aquarians are generous with their families and loved ones, and that compassion extends to humanity at large. They stash money away, but the accumulation of wealth isn't the point; their freedom is.

PISCES

Pisces is usually less concerned about money and material goods than he is about enjoying what he does to make a living. Can he transcend himself through his work? Does his tremendous compassion find expression through his work? If not, then he will undoubtedly change his work again and again until he finds the job or profession that suits him.

Health

If you are like many people, you desire robust health and fitness and may push yourself hard to achieve that goal. But pushing too hard might not be good for you. Did you know that there are bodily weaknesses associated with each astrological sign? The good news is that by identifying the weakest areas of your body, you can avoid potential problems through self-monitoring and behavioral and lifestyle changes.

ARIES

An Aries requires adequate rest and good nutrition to replenish all the energy he burns. He shouldn't eat much red meat and will benefit from herbs that belong to this particular sign: mustard, eye-bright, and bay. Since Aries rules the head and face, these areas are the weakest parts of the body for him. Common ailments are tension headaches, dizziness, and skin eruptions. In fact, many Aries suffer from migraines and allergies, too.

TAURUS

Taureans tend to have broad foreheads and thick, sturdy necks, and many retain their youthful appearances long after people of other signs show their age. Taureans benefit from a daily regimen of physical exercise and should be moderate in their consumption of fattening foods. This, of course, is undoubtedly true for all signs. But moderation is particularly necessary for the people under the sign of the bull who have slower metabolisms.

GEMINI

Gemini people are generally slender and full of nervous energy. All this energy can be difficult to rein in sometimes, particularly on nights when they work late and their heads race with ideas. Geminis benefit from breaks in their established routines and need physical exercise to ground their thoughts. People of this sign are prone to respiratory and nervous ailments.

CANCER

Cancers tend to hang onto emotional baggage that eventually can create health problems. Cancer people are prone to ill health (for example, depression) from emotional as well as brain-chemistry imbalances. Other health concerns for Cancers include diseases of the liver, pancreas, circulatory system, and digestive system.

LEO

Leos generally benefit from low-fat diets because one of the weakest parts of their bodies is the heart. Exercise, even if on the light side, is needed to channel some of their abundant energy.

VIRGO

Since Virgos fret and worry so much, their physical ailments usually manifest first in their stomachs: colic in infancy, stomach upsets as a youngster, ulcers as an adult. But because Virgos are fussy about their diet and health, they grow into their own bodies with innate wisdom.

LIBRA

Libra tends to have a slender well-formed body. Since Libra rules the lower back and diaphragm, unvented emotions manifest first in those areas of the body. Libras benefit from physical exercise, particularly anything that strengthens the back and maintains general flexibility.

SCORPIO

Due to the unusual will power inherent in the sign, Scorpios often work to the point of exhaustion. Any illness usually has a strong emotional component. Scorpios are prone to medical disorders affecting the sex organs, bladder, and urethra; they also tend to have menstrual problems and ulcers.

SAGITTARIUS

Sagittarian individuals tend to gain weight because they indulge their appetites. Jupiter, the planet of expansion, rules this sign and often expands the physical body as well. Health issues for this sign include liver, cellulite, stretch marks, sciatica, and injuries to the hips and thighs.

CAPRICORN

Capricorns appreciate the benefits of exercise and have something physical that they do regularly. Their knees tend to trouble them. Because the sign is sometimes repressed emotionally, Capricorns benefit by venting what they feel, which in turn improves their physical health.

AQUARIUS

Those born under the sign of Aquarius have a sensitive nervous system and can be easily excited. Their minds are incessantly busy, and they should guard against exhausting their energy reserves. They are prone to injuries to their lower legs and ankles.

PISCES

Pisces tend to have foot problems such as boils, bunions, gout, swelling, and itchy feet. They are also prone to obesity and dermatitis. Addictions can be a problem for Piscean individuals, and they benefit from spiritual practices such as **yoga** that allow them to release emotion and stress while strengthening their feet and ankles.

Work

Are you a born leader or do you prefer to follow one? Do you enjoy being the center of attention or working behind the scenes. Your astrological sign reveals not only the kind of role you might choose to assume in the business world but also what type of work in which you might excel.

ARIES

An Aries excels at anything in which leadership ability is paramount. These people like giving orders, and they're terrific at delegating responsibilities. They have numerous ideas and want to put them all into effect yesterday. As a fire sign, they pour energy into whatever they do.

TAURUS

Taurus excels at work that requires persistence, stability, and relentless drive. They're able to take abstract ideas and make them concrete and practical. This means they're good at behind-the-scenes work, especially if the work is artistically creative—writing, costume design, gourmet cooking, musical composition, or anything to do with nature. You won't find a more tireless worker in the zodiac.

GEMINI

Gemini shines in work that provides diversity. It doesn't matter if it's with the public or behind the scenes, as long as it isn't routine. They make good counselors because one of the twins is always willing to listen. Their love of language gives them a talent for the written word. Acting, politics, libraries, research: all these fields fit Gemini.

CANCER

Cancer enjoys working from home. The intensity of the feeling for individuals of this sign enables them to excel in medical fields where they have direct patient contact. For the same reason, they also make good psychic healers, counselors, and psychologists. Areas of work that match well with the Cancer personality include publicity and marketing, sociology or anthropology, children, or other people's homes.

LEO

A Leo excels at work in front of the public. He's a great actor, orator, Speaker of the House, or CEO—a menial job won't do. Leos are good at teaching because the classroom becomes their stage and their students become their audience. They make excellent writers, editors, and journalists. They also tend to be good with animals and enjoy training, caring for, and loving them.

VIRGO

Virgos sincerely strive for perfection in their work and careers. They do best when working for others—doing social work in hospitals, clinics, hospice programs, or with their children. The challenge in every area of a Virgo's life is to serve without self-sacrifice. Their striving for perfection compels them to evolve and change.

LIBRA

The Libra's obvious choice for a profession is as an attorney or judge because of his finely tuned sense of fair play. Librans excel in any profession that calls for an acutely balanced mind and sensitivities. They make good editors, musicians, accountants, artists, and parents. The work itself is less important than what it teaches Libras about making decisions, in spite of their ability to see all sides of an issue.

SCORPIO

Scorpios make excellent actors, detectives, spies, even teachers. There's just no telling where all that rawness of perception can take a Scorpio. One thing's for sure, though—his work follows his passion.

SAGITTARIUS

Sagittarians are best suited to work in a job or discipline where they have complete freedom to call the shots: an owner of an airline, CEO, small business owner, entrepreneur, actor, writer, or traveling salesman. The point isn't the work so much as the freedom they have doing the work.

CAPRICORN

Capricorns excel in any profession that is structured, such as engineering, medicine, editing, politics, building, architecture, ceramics, and leatherwork.

Their strong desire to succeed is colored by traditional values and a conservative approach. In some Capricorns, these traits make them exceptionally good workers who progress slowly and successfully toward their goals. With others, tradition and conservatism hold them back.

AQUARIUS

Aquarians work best in avant-garde fields: film, the arts, cutting-edge research in electronics, computers, or psychology. Many have raw psychic talent that can be developed into clairvoyance, remote viewing, and precognition, and most are very intuitive. The main element they seek in their work is freedom.

PISCES

Pisces do well in anything that is behind the scenes. Due to their dreamy imaginations and mystical leanings, they excel in the arts, literature, and drama, or as monks, mystics, and even inventors. Piscean Edgar Cayce is probably the best example of what a Pisces is capable of doing in metaphysics. Piscean Albert Einstein is one of the best examples of Pisces as scientific genius.

To Sum Up

Astrology as a field of study is illuminating and comprehensive but also expansive, meaning that there will always be more to learn from this ancient discipline. So far you've gained an overview of the signs and symbols of the zodiac, birth charts, the twelve houses and house cusps, the planets and their planetary dominion, and the Sun signs. Additionally, you've discovered how to apply your knowledge of astrology to your life by reading about how the signs get along in relationship to one another. You've also learned about the astrological aspects of sex, money, health, and work. Now you are in a position to apply everything you've learned about astrology to your life. Your destiny lies ahead. It may be written in the stars, but you have free will; so it will be up to you to decide what you will claim and manifest from that vast realm of potentiality.

Part Two

THE TAROT

The whole visible universe is but a storehouse of images and signs to which the imagination will give a relative place and value; it is a sort of pasture which the imagination must digest and transform.

—Charles Baudelaire (1821–1867), French poet

Draw the card with the magician's image from the **Tarot** deck and you are assured of creating success in all you do. Pick the Hanged Man and you would be advised to let go, surrender for your highest good. As soon as you begin to work with the Tarot, you begin to see how the universal images or scenes represent the grand mysteries of life, and yet as you look deeper, you find a personal resonance. That is the power of the Tarot—to tap into your unconscious where hidden are vast stores of information and memories to use in your quest for greater self-knowledge.

Introduction: What Is the Tarot?

Tarot cards are wonderful tools to use for prediction but also for use in meditative practice for deeper self-awareness. The card images stimulate the intuition, which is the key to the gateway of the unconscious. Further, they illuminate the hidden factors in your life, factors that you may not be aware of that are secretly shaping your existence. They kindle the fire of your creative imagination and spark ideas for new endeavors.

Although theories abound about the origins of the Tarot, the prevailing belief is that they were used in fifteenth-century Italy as playing cards. In fact, one of the most complete early examples of the Tarot—the Visconti-Sforza deck—dates to A.D. 1450. Tradition holds that the symbolism of the Tarot cards derives from ancient secret teachings of Egypt, the Hebrew **kabbalah**, Hermetic philosophy, alchemy, and other mythologies and religious systems. The cards' numerological associations find resonance in the philosophy and mathematics of **Pythagoras**, the Ionian Greek who taught that letters and numbers contain divine essence and extraordinary powers unrealized by the uninitiated. In the view of alchemists and mystics, the Tarot symbols spring from the soul of the world, a vast repository of knowledge, like a cosmic library of universal archetypes and wisdom derived from the dramas of all humankind.

THE BASICS

A typical Tarot deck consists of seventy-eight cards. The first twenty-two are identified as the Major Arcana. The fifty-six remaining cards are called the Minor Arcana and contain information representing a body of wisdom and guidance for your everyday affairs. There are many different ways to lay out the cards for readings, from a simple yes/no spread to the popular Celtic Cross layout, or even more elaborate and complicated spreads.

Handle the cards with the care and respect appropriate for any sacred object. Wrap the cards in a piece of silk fabric, store them in a small box, or keep them on your home altar or tucked inside your bedside table drawer. Don't leave them lying around. Always return the deck to its special storage container and location immediately after you have finished using it.

Handling Your Cards

Impregnate the cards with your energy through frequent handling. However, if you permit someone else to handle your cards, clear that person's energy from the cards after their use. Place the cards in front of you, hold your hands palms down over them, and say, silently or out loud, "I call upon the divine powers to bless and protect these cards, for my intention is to use them for good only. I declare that only good shall come from their use and that all negativity shall be turned away from them."

Choosing a Tarot Deck

Are you a visual person? Do story scenes help you remember symbolic meaning? Perhaps you feel a connection to abstract imagery or are attracted to images of a particular culture. These questions might help you pinpoint which type of Tarot deck will work best for you. The Major Arcana images and symbols are pretty much the same in all decks, even if depicted through different themes such as angel, alchemy, feminist, magic, and myth or by culture such as African, Celtic, and Japanese. In some decks it's difficult to tell immediately if a pip or numbered card is upright or reversed; in others it's obvious. Many stores keep sample packs available for you to examine and test before you buy. See a variety of decks and try a free reading on the Internet at *www.facade.com*.

If you don't want to spend a lot of time sorting through all the options, try the Waite deck. Most books about the Tarot, including this one, are based on the Waite deck's illustrations. Ultimately, the best deck for you will be one that resonates with your own inner sense of symbolism and is compatible with your belief system. If you don't feel a kinship with your deck, get another one. To tap your own inner power using the Tarot, it is essential that you feel an affinity for the cards.

SHUFFLING THE CARDS

How you shuffle the cards is up to you; the point is to imbue them with your energy vibration. The object is to establish a link between yourself and the oracle.

Part Two: The Tarot   69

Hold the pack in one hand. Use your other hand to slide out small groups of cards and reposition them. Repeat this step, moving the cards around with both hands. Alternatively, you can cut the cards into several stacks and restack them, repeating the sequence until you feel you have done enough to thoroughly shuffle them.

Learning to Interpret the Tarot

A Tarot reading, properly conducted, contains a story. As in myths, the images on the cards meld into a meaningful pattern that can clarify the issues confronting you. Do readings for yourself, studying the cards and interpreting their symbols to gain spiritual insights or practical solutions to problems. Always apply your intuitive powers as you use your Tarot deck as a lens to explore vast realms that lie beyond the limits of your conscious mind. Take note of how intuitive information will come like a dream or a flash of inspiration. Give yourself permission to let these flashes inform your interpretation of the cards.

OPENING YOURSELF TO INSIGHT

The Tarot's symbols speak to a very deep, ancient part of you that has been ignored or discounted. By using the Tarot on a regular basis, you strengthen the connection between your ordinary, rational, mundane way of thinking and the other levels of existence—whether you view them as being inside or outside yourself. It's a bit like paying attention to your dreams. After a while, you'll start to understand things you didn't understand before.

When meditating on the cards or doing readings for yourself, you may get sudden, unexpected ideas or impressions that may—or may not—be directly related to a particular card or spread before you. These flashes of insight arise because your work with the Tarot opens a portal between the selves (or between the different levels of reality) so that uninhibited, unimpeded communication can take place. Often these instantaneous revelations that slip in the back door of your mind are as meaningful as the reading itself. Sometimes, while you shuffle the cards, a single card will fall from the deck. Usually this card answers or sheds light on the question you're contemplating at the time.

Tarot Symbolism: What Do the Cards Mean?

Symbols embody the essence of whatever they stand for; they aren't merely a convenient form of shorthand. That's why they have such power, why they appear in diverse and widely separated cultures, and why they have endured for millennia.

UNIVERSAL SYMBOLISM

Symbols that turn up again and again, in all parts of the world, possess universal appeal and resonate in what Swiss psychiatrist Carl G. Jung called the collective unconscious. The symbols mean essentially the same thing to everyone, regardless of age, race, religion, or nationality and get around the limitations of the rational, analytical, left brain. Often we confront these symbols in dreams, where they provide guidance and awaken us to parts of ourselves that we may have ignored in our waking lives. The Tarot works in a similar manner.

The following table shows a number of common, universally understood symbols that you may notice on the cards in your Tarot deck. They can be helpful keys as you examine the cards and learn their significances.

The Symbols of the Tarot

Symbol	Meaning
Circle	Wholeness, unity, protection, continuity
Square	Stability, equality, structure
Triangle	Trinity, three-dimensional existence, movement
Downward triangle	Divine feminine, earth or water elements
Upward triangle	Divine masculine, fire or air elements
Star	Hope, promise
Five-pointed star	Protection, the human body, physical incarnation
Six-pointed star	Union of male/female or earth/sky, integration, manifestation
Vertical line	Movement, heaven, sky, masculine energy
Horizontal line	Stability, earth, feminine energy

Cross	Union of opposites, heaven/earth, death/regeneration, or incarnation, manifestation
Spiral	Life energy, renewal, movement toward the center
Sun	Clarity, vitality, optimism, contentment, masculine energy
Moon	Secrets, intuition, emotions, feminine energy
Dove	Peace, reconciliation, promise
Crane	Wisdom
Rose	Love
Mountain	Challenge, vision, achievement
Ocean/Water	Emotions, the unknown depths of the psyche
Snake	Transformation, hidden knowledge, kundalini energy
Egg	Birth, fertility
Rainbow	Renewal, hope, happiness
Book	Knowledge
Lantern	Guidance, clarity, hope
Bridge	Connection, harmony, overcoming difficulty
Tree	Knowledge, growth, protection, strength
Butterfly	Transformation

PERSONALIZE SYMBOLS

When studying the symbolism in the Tarot, remember that your own responses and interpretations are what count most. Cars suggest movement and freedom to most people, but if you were in a serious auto accident when you were young, cars may represent pain or danger to you. Trust your own instincts and intuition. After all, your Tarot deck and your subconscious are attempting to communicate with you, and they will do it in imagery that you can understand.

CHANGE IS OKAY

Tarot decks that come packaged with their own books or instructional guides generally explain the significance of the symbols displayed on the cards. Even so, if your own feelings about the pictures on the cards don't coincide with the artist's, give your own responses precedence. And if your interpretations of certain symbols change over time, that's okay, too.

NOTICE COLOR'S SYMBOLISM

The vivid, gorgeous colors on Tarot cards embody specific symbolic, spiritual, psychological, and physiological properties. The color hue and shading in Tarot imagery symbolize a mood and convey a message much like imagery in religious icons or the soothing pastel palette of hospital wall art.

In magical practice, colors correspond to the four elements. Red is associated with fire, blue with water, green with earth, and yellow with air. Because each suit is linked with an element, many Tarot artists use the colors connected with the corresponding suits to trigger subconscious responses and insights. Therefore, some decks emphasize red on the cards in the suit of Wands, blue on the Cups cards, green on the Pentacles cards, and yellow on the Swords cards. Other meanings for the colors can add insights to your interpretation of the cards.

The Symbolism of Color

Color	Intention
Red	Passion, vitality, courage
Orange	Warmth, energy, activity, drive, confidence
Yellow	Creativity, optimism, enthusiasm
Green	Healing, growth, fertility, prosperity
Light blue	Purity, serenity, mental clarity, compassion
Royal blue	Loyalty, insight, inspiration, independence
Indigo	Intuition, focus, stability
Purple	Wisdom, spirituality, power
White	Purity, wholeness, protection
Black	Power, the unconscious, banishing, wisdom
Pink	Love, friendship, affection, joy, self-esteem
Brown	Grounding, permanence, practicality

Astrology and the Tarot

One of the most interesting things about the Tarot is the way in which it dovetails with astrology. Astrology has the Sun, Moon, and stars; so, too, does the Tarot. The four elements and directions are cornerstones of astrology and are also common symbols of the Tarot. In fact, many Tarot decks also include astrological elements in their illustrations to reveal celestial influences at work in the Tarot.

ASTROLOGICAL INDICATORS AND IMAGERY

Many Tarot decks have cards that feature a crab on the Moon card. The crab symbolizes Cancer, the zodiac sign ruled by the Moon. The Justice card in many Tarot decks depicts the Greek goddess of wisdom Athena holding a scale or balance, the symbol for Libra.

Tarot artists frequently incorporate illustrations of the planets, constellations, zodiac wheels, astrological glyphs, and other symbolism into their compositions to convey insights and information.

The Tarot in the Renaissance

The link between astrology and the Tarot was evident in some decks that appeared during the Renaissance. The Minchiate Tarot, for instance, featured ninety-seven cards instead of the usual seventy-eight. This interesting oracle included twelve cards for the twelve astrological signs plus one for each of the four elements in addition to the Major and Minor Arcana.

THE MAJOR ARCANA

The Major Arcana, also called trump cards, are considered the most complex cards in the Tarot deck, as they reveal ever-deeper meanings according to the diligence you apply in studying them. The specific symbols or scenes of those cards have remained basically the same for centuries, representing, some say, the dream patterns of all humankind. Each of the Major Arcana cards carries a title or moniker: Magician, Empress, Lovers, Moon, Tower, Wheel of Fortune, and so forth. They are numbered from zero (the Fool) to twenty-one (the World).

The Cards of the Major Arcana

The twenty-two cards of the Major Arcana are believed to hold greater significance in their symbolism, purpose, and meaning than the cards of the Minor Arcana, which relate more to the affairs of daily life. As you familiarize yourself with the Major Arcana, you might discover that a particular card holds special relevance to you for a universal issue that transcends ordinary daily concerns, for example, a life transformation or courage in the face of a life-threatening illness.

THE FOOL

DESCRIPTION

The Fool is a fascinating figure, yet he can be an ambiguous symbol. He is always depicted as unconcerned—or unaware—of any danger lying ahead. Usually the Fool is youthful, but sometimes he is an older traveler who has obviously been on the road a long time.

Like a hobo, he carries all his worldly possessions tied in a small bag on a stick over his shoulder. Behind him, the Sun, symbol of the source of all life, is shining on his enterprise. He may carry a rose, symbol of love, or a traveler's staff. Often he is dressed in bright colors, and the card's general impression is cheerful and sunny. Sometimes the Fool is wearing the parti-colored costume and cap and bells of a medieval court jester, or he might be dressed in the plain garb of a wanderer.

Often he is accompanied by a dog, which is a symbol of our natural instincts. The little dog gambols about the Fool, sometimes pulling him back from the danger ahead, suggesting that our instincts, if followed, do provide us with guidance on our life journeys.

Ordinarily, the Fool is shown as a person full of confidence—often the confidence of youth—and trust in the beneficence of the universe. He symbolizes that blind leap of faith that we all must take upon entering the journey of life itself, especially if that journey is spiritual.

INTERPRETATION

When the Fool appears in a reading, depending on its position in the layout, it symbolizes someone who is about to embark on a new way of life. This may involve a physical journey, moving to a new place, starting a new job, or getting married or divorced. Often, the appearance of the Fool indicates a person who is ready to start on a spiritual path, who has made peace with the need to experience absolute faith and trust in the universe. If such is the case in your reading, you have no sense of worry or fear and feel you are protected and that everything will turn out well. You may be consciously in touch with the intuitive realm of your being, or you may simply be naive about what the future will bring. The Fool represents a state of openness and faith that he'll be supported in his adventure.

THE FOOL AND ASTROLOGY

The Fool is related to Uranus, the planet that destroys old ideologies, concepts, and structures. Uranus represents not only the advanced thinker, modern scientist, and esoteric occultist but also nonconformists of all stripes. Uranus produces sudden changes of all sorts and, like a thunderstorm, often serves to clear the psychic air.

Uranus is exalted in Scorpio, an indication of unusual daring and a willingness to stake life itself on adventures into the unknown—as the Fool is about to do. Uranus rules the sign of Aquarius, an air sign that emphasizes mental activity. The image of the Fool blithely embarking on a solo journey into uncharted territory typifies the Aquarian spirit of adventure.

THE MAGICIAN

DESCRIPTION

The Magician is powerful, representing worldly wisdom and the control of unseen forces that operate in human lives. A deeply complex symbol, he is usually depicted as a male figure who stands alone before an array of the traditional magician's tools. In most decks, these tools are the symbols of the Minor Arcana suits, each of which corresponds to one of the four elements: a pentacle for earth, a sword for air, a cup for water, and a wand for fire. To possess knowledge of these elements is to gain mastery in the world.

THE MAGICIAN.

In the Waite deck, the Magician holds a wand, a phallic symbol, aloft in one hand toward the heavens, or the upper world of divine power, while his other hand points downward to the Earth, the base of life. Above his head floats the symbol for infinity. He knows how to use his tools to connect the two worlds of spirituality, or metaphysics, and physicality, or the mundane plane of existence.

The Magician usually wears a belt. In the Waite deck, this is a coiled snake, the *ourobouros*, or snake biting its tail, an alchemical symbol for wholeness. This represents the power to heal through connecting the two worlds within one's self. In the Waite deck, above the Magician are trailing vines, like grapes, symbol of wine, a sacred drink in many cultures. At his feet is a garden of roses, lilies, and greenery. These represent the vegetable kingdom in general. These symbols tell us that the Magician is in possession of knowledge that enables him to manipulate the material world through aligning it with the spiritual plane to create the desired circumstances.

INTERPRETATION

The appearance of the Magician in a reading indicates latent powers, yet to be taken up and brought into manifestation. Also known as the Juggler, this card suggests that everything in the universe is spread out before us, and if we learn to use the latent powers correctly, we can manifest the results we desire. These are literally the basic materials of creation, and it is the task of the Magician to handle them well, to manipulate and control them for beneficent purposes.

Thus, the Magician shows us that what we consider to be illusion is another form of reality, and what we consider to be reality can be mere illusion. This is a deep understanding of how we must learn to use our intellects, our intuitive abilities, our personal talents, and our practical skills in order to mediate between the two worlds, both of which affect us simultaneously.

Just as a mage, or true magician, stands at the center of the universe with the tools and ability to manipulate it for his purposes, so does each of us create, or recreate, our own universes within ourselves, first in our minds, and then in our manifest realities. This card tells us that our nature is one with the nature of the universe. It suggests that we have the ability to control our own lives, that we can manipulate people, things, and events—so long as we go about it the right way and for the right ends.

THE MAGICIAN AND ASTROLOGY

The Magician is related to the planet Mercury, the planet of the intellect; it represents how the mind works, how you learn, and how you communicate. In astrology, Mercury is linked with cleverness, dexterity, quickness, and change-ability, but it is also the mark of the trickster—all characteristics associated with the Magician.

Mercury is multifaceted, a god of many attributes. He governs all aspects of communication—writing, speaking, learning, commerce, and messages of all sorts. The Magician symbolizes the power of the mind to create ideas that eventually manifest in the physical world, shown by the earth sign Virgo. The Magician's ability to move easily between the two realms, Heaven and Earth, is one of this trump's most intriguing qualities.

THE HIGH PRIESTESS

DESCRIPTION

The High Priestess represents that which has yet to be revealed, secret knowledge, the duality of life on Earth. She symbolizes feminine spiritual power, or the goddess from whom all life comes and to whom all returns in the ever-cycling round of earthly existence.

THE HIGH PRIESTESS

She is depicted as a serene-faced female figure, sometimes seated with a book on her lap, suggesting the Divine Law that underlies the manifest universe. The scroll or book represents the Akashic Records, the divine repository of our lives, past, present, and future. Sometimes, she is standing, holding a staff and pointing toward an unseen object in the distance, another indication of something yet to be revealed.

She sometimes sits or stands between two pillars, which represent the opposites of the dual nature of our world: good and evil, light and dark, truth and deception. She promises reconciliation of these opposites to those willing to follow the spiritual path of understanding **universal law**. In the Waite deck, the High Priestess sits at the doorway to the temple, which symbolizes the body, as if welcoming students to enter and learn her secrets. However, the crescent Moon at her feet warns of the danger of releasing higher knowledge to those unprepared to handle it.

In the Waite deck, two pillars represent a doorway to the interior of life's mysteries, with the High Priestess as the guardian of the entryway. Also in the Waite deck, she sits against a background of pomegranates, a reference to Persephone, daughter of Demeter, who leaves the daylight, or upper world, for six months each year to tend to the dead in the underworld. In some decks, she carries flowers or is depicted against a background of vegetables and vegetation, another reference to the goddess, or Grain Mother.

On her breast, the High Priestess wears a cross, symbolic of the four elements—fire, earth, air, and water—held in balance. She wears a crown, usually a crescent, the horns of the Moon, or a variant of it. In the Waite deck, between the horns sits a sphere, representative of the full Moon, while the horns echo the images of the waxing and waning Moon. The three lunar phases symbolize the three stages of womanhood: maiden, mother, crone.

INTERPRETATION

When the High Priestess appears, she indicates that something hidden, or interior, is preparing to come forth or that you need to pay more attention to your inner world of dreams, imagination, and intuition. She advises you to develop awareness of the totality of yourself, the night side, so to speak, as well as the daylight personality and activities.

The High Priestess may indicate that you are attempting to hide something that needs to be revealed. Or she can mean that you're too much involved in an isolated inner world and need to reconcile the inner life with the outer one.

Psychologically, the underworld refers to the unconscious, or what is in the process of coming into being. In this twilight realm, of which dreams are a component, we encounter our inner selves through intuition and fantasy. The High Priestess is an image representing our potentials that have yet to be discovered and brought forth—our secret selves longing to be recognized.

THE HIGH PRIESTESS AND ASTROLOGY

The High Priestess is linked with the Moon, which governs the emotions and intuition. The Moon is a metaphor for all that is instinctive. Cyclical and constantly changing, the Moon is called the soul of life, mediator between the planes of the spiritual (Sun) and material (Earth), reflecting back the light of the Sun it has received into itself. Thus, the Moon is also a metaphor for receptivity, the yin principle in Asian philosophy, and is emblematic of the container of life, that matrix that nourishes the process of manifestation.

Symbolically, the Moon serves to reveal the nonconscious side of human life, and in that diffuse light you can often see more accurately than in the glare of the noonday Sun. The Moon allows you to shine light into your inner spiritual world, to illuminate what springs naturally from inside yourself. In moonlight you perceive the reality of your inner, spiritual self more fully. As a lunar figure, the High Priestess speaks to your deepest inner needs, your memories, feelings, moods, and internal rhythms.

THE EMPRESS

DESCRIPTION

The Empress is a card of beauty and creativity, the matriarch incarnate, symbolic of the Universal Mother as monarch. She represents the social concept of the feminine in the maternal role: procreation, nurture, the security and comforts of home, and domestic harmony.

The Empress is always a mature female figure, often seated on a throne. In some decks, she is standing in a field, surrounded by flowers and vegetation, representative of the bounty of Mother Nature and her harvest. Full breasted and sometimes pregnant, she symbolizes fruitfulness and earthly abundance.

As a symbol of the Empress's royal position, she sometimes holds a scepter and wears an imperial crown of great magnificence. In many decks, a shield or coat of arms leans against her throne at her feet. In the Waite deck, this shield is heart shaped and bears the astrological symbol for Venus, which also appears in many other decks.

INTERPRETATION

When the Empress appears, a strong feminine energy is at work. As a mother figure and representative of the traditional female role, she is a creative force that works for harmony. She brings disparate things together, reconciling differences, like a mother running a household must do. This is a card of emotional control and making things work congenially toward a common social goal.

The Empress also refers to the person's emotional and physical resources for nurturing, healing, feeding, and supporting other people. Often, there is a situation in the person's life where love and nurturing are required—sometimes by the person herself, sometimes by others in the environment. This card is related to the caretaking process and may refer to the way the person was mothered; the first and most significant relationship you form is with your mother, and this relationship has a direct bearing on all subsequent relationships.

THE EMPRESS AND ASTROLOGY

The Empress is related to Venus, the planet of women, love, beauty, desire, pleasure, and relationships. Venus symbolizes the deeply feminine part of all people, male as well as female, telling of their capacity to reach out to others in a loving way, not just sexually or erotically. She also represents the affections and symbolizes what people value in terms of social natures. Venus functions through relating—to other people, to your own desire, to nature, to the things you love, and to the outside world.

THE EMPEROR

DESCRIPTION

The Emperor is a figure of supreme authority. He is usually shown seated on a throne, sometimes flanked by animals. In the Waite deck, these are rams' heads, symbolic of masculine power. He wears robes over a full suit of armor, holds a scepter in the shape of the Egyptian ankh, and is crowned elaborately. In some decks, his shield, bearing the symbol of the imperial eagle, leans against the throne. Often he appears outdoors, against a backdrop of mountains, another reference to worldly power. His age and position of authority speak of experience and wisdom gained. Although he is depicted as a warrior, his attitude is one of kindness as the beneficent ruler of his empire.

While at rest, the Emperor's attitude suggests he is willing to fight for what is right and what is his duty to protect. He is the executive, or leader, who has reached the summit of authority and achieved worldly power.

Thus, the Emperor is a father figure, as the Empress is a mother figure. He lays down the ideals, morals, and aspirations for the entire family to follow. He is the builder in the material world who strives to make constructions of lasting value and importance.

INTERPRETATION

When the Emperor appears in a reading, look for issues related to authority. Although the Emperor represents worldly power and wisdom, he is not simply a figure who gives commands to others. His achievement is to understand that peace and security require a willingness and ability to defend it.

The Emperor is a teacher figure, and what he teaches is the meaning of power and how to use it in this world. Though not overtly aggressive, he tells us that it is necessary sometimes to take up arms against evil forces. With the Emperor, there is no waffling about what is right and good, no rationalizing that the ends justify the means. As a protective male force, especially of the home and of domestic harmony, he personifies the ideal that what is worth having is worth fighting for.

The Emperor in a reading can also indicate issues concerning one's biological father, or authority figures in general. He can show that the time has arrived to *become* the authority figure, rather than depending on others to provide protection. The Emperor often appears when the person is struggling to achieve personal independence, to overcome the inner parent tapes, to become his or her own person.

When the Emperor appears, he can be an indication that the individual's real father has either recently died or may die soon, a situation that can bring up feelings of being abandoned by a protective father figure. It is important to remember, though, that separation from the parents is a crucial stage in human development and must be accomplished. It's also possible that someone in the person's life is acting as a father figure, perhaps a boss or a husband. Whether this is positive or negative will be indicated by the placement of the card in the layout.

THE EMPEROR AND ASTROLOGY

The Emperor is related to the sign Aries. As the first sign of the zodiac, Aries symbolizes leadership, initiative, action, energy, and new ideas. It is associated with beginnings of all kinds and is the primary energy that gets things going. People born under this cardinal fire sign are self-starters, leaders—not followers. Willful and daring, with a strong desire to be first, Aries people are always looking for the next adventure, challenge, project, or experience.

Aries is ruled by the planet Mars, the exemplar of all the traditional aspects that we esteem in the male of the species: sexual prowess, courage, energy, action, protectiveness, and valor. Though Mars is known as the god of war, he also represents daring and forthrightness. As a warrior, he is both aggressor and protector. Mars expresses the principle of action, in any and all spheres. In mythology, he was first trained as a dancer, then as a warrior. The war dance prepared the spirits of the warriors for physical danger and trial, joining them together as a group—what we today call male bonding.

Mars and the Emperor represent primal male energy, the archetypal masculine, or yang, force that is the counterpart and complement to Venus and the Empress.

THE HIEROPHANT

DESCRIPTION

The Hierophant is a figure with authority and power, like the Emperor, but the Hierophant's power is of a spiritual nature, whereas the Emperor's is temporal. Often, he is shown as a religious leader, such as the Pope of Roman Catholicism. Some decks title him the Pope. He is usually seen seated on a throne, dressed in priestly raiment, crowned, and holding a scepter. His implements will vary according to the religious theme of the deck. His scepter symbolizes the three worlds—the physical, the astral, and the etheric. His free hand is held aloft in a position of blessing. Two or three acolytes may stand before him, either as participants, supplicants, or students, defer-

ring to his wisdom and understanding him as a representative of religious authority.

Like the Emperor, he contains within himself the wisdom of a spiritual calling, and like the High Priestess, the Hierophant frequently sits or stands between two pillars, which signify the duality of matter and spirit.

▲▲▲▲▲▲▲▲▲▲▲▲▲▲▲▲▲▲▲▲▲▲▲▲▲▲▲▲

A Bridge Between Two Worlds

As a spiritual teacher whose task it is to connect the world of humans with that of the gods, to forge a link between the material and spiritual worlds, the Hierophant is a pontifex, an ancient word that meant maker of bridges, and which is used to designate a priest.

▼▼▼▼▼▼▼▼▼▼▼▼▼▼▼▼▼▼▼▼▼▼▼▼▼▼▼▼

In this role, the Hierophant can be seen as a teacher to those who seek the keys to the sacred mysteries. The Waite deck shows two crossed keys below him, representing the intellect and intuition and the need to use them in tandem. He is responsible for making spiritual decisions for others and for blessing them. Unlike the High Priestess, whose world is primarily internal and ephemeral, the Hierophant's influence is of this world, and his spirituality can be achieved through conscious choices made on an intellectual basis.

INTERPRETATION

The Hierophant suggests that the person has chosen a religion or philosophy with which to guide his or her life. In such a case, there is usually a great deal of loyalty to it, whatever the person's concept of God may be. Sometimes the card indicates disentangling yourself from such an association.

In some organized religions, the Supreme Deity does not speak to the individual directly, or to the general populace. Therefore, institutionalized religion makes use of human interpreters who convey the word of God (the Divine Will) to their followers.

The Hierophant symbolizes any organized institution—be it religious, philosophical, educational, spiritual, or temporal—that exerts authority over its followers or participants (a kind of mind control). In such groups, there is always a person, or a group of people, who insist that their way is the *only* way, that theirs is the ultimate truth.

Therefore, when the Hierophant appears, the idea of choice is being presented. At this stage of your spiritual development, you are challenged to remain a follower or to break out and find your own individual truth. This card suggests that you have the opportunity—and often the desire—to choose your own road to salvation, to interpret the word of God in your own way. The Hierophant asks, will you continue to depend on an outside authority, or will you learn to think for yourself? The answer is yours alone, and there may be considerable conflict concerning the issue, but what you decide will affect the rest of your life.

THE HIEROPHANT AND ASTROLOGY

The Hierophant is related to the zodiac sign Taurus, which symbolizes connection to the material plane and, by extension, the accumulation of possessions. Gifted with patience, Taurus lets things happen in his or her own time. Like a good gardener, Taurus is content to wait until the right time comes along, knowing there's no point in pulling up the radishes to see if they are ready to eat. Taurus's patience may seem like slowness, but it is the slowness of certainty and self-confidence. Taurus rests secure in the knowledge that tomorrow is another day and that excess motion will not make the sun rise any earlier.

Rooted in the physical world, Taurus is quintessentially of the Earth. Worldly concerns, material values, and things that are well established fall under the domain of this sign. Related to the second house of money and valuables, materialistic Taurus's natural instinct is to accumulate and preserve both things and institutions. Therefore, both Taurus and the Hierophant are associated with institutions that endure over time—religion, academia, jurisprudence—and the Hierophant represents that which is already established in the social order.

Taurus is ruled by the planet Venus, which also governs material pleasures, enjoyment, and the five physical senses. Though associated with love and pleasure, Venus, as Aphrodite, was a goddess of great power. The Hierophant represents this aspect of Taurus, our grounding in a society or community that allows us to venture forth as individuals and develop our talents, and the powerful institutions of state that both help and control the citizens. Thus, the Hierophant symbolizes the authority represented by social institutions and the security they provide.

THE LOVERS

DESCRIPTION

One popular image on the Lovers card shows a young couple either nude or clothed, standing apart or touching. Above them is an angel-like figure with its wings spread out over them, its hands held above their heads in a gesture of blessing. The Waite deck depicts them as Adam and Eve, standing respectively before the Tree of Eternal Life and the Tree of the Knowledge of Good and Evil. Imagery in other decks suggests choice is involved, as well as the possibility of union.

Some decks include three people, as if the third party—who might be another young person or an older parental figure—were an influence in the relationship. In decks where three figures are shown, a winged, cupid-like figure on a cloud may appear and point an arrow in the direction of one of the women.

INTERPRETATION

Although many readers interpret this card as representing romantic love, it is allegorically a statement about union of opposites, whether those are a man and woman or inner conditions of conflict. The Lovers refers to discrimination in making choices. The male and female figures are symbols not only of human love and marriage but also of the dual nature within ourselves. We all have opposite traits and inner dichotomies that need to be reconciled. Partners of any kind often experience conflict that requires making choices, sometimes tough ones, and effecting reconciliation.

Choice or Partners?

In decks that show one young man and two young women on the Lovers card, the implication is that he must choose between them, another indication that this card is as much about choice as it is about partnership.

When the Lovers card appears, it points to the need to heal an inner rift. Although it can herald a romantic involvement, it most often turns up when a critical life decision must be made, sometimes in connection with a love relationship. There are obstacles to be overcome, both within and without. This card suggests that you are at a crossroads. You have to consider all of the ramifications of the situation and choose carefully in order to further your own development and to accommodate the needs of others in the situation.

In mythology, the Lovers card reflects Eros, the son of the great goddess of love and beauty, Aphrodite. Eros was named Cupid by the Romans, and it is his job to shoot the arrows of love, which was considered a form of madness, at unsuspecting youths. Thus, Eros was often depicted blindfolded to represent that love is blind. But Eros has another role—to guide us toward our true destiny, which is to say, "Do what you love and everything else will follow naturally."

THE LOVERS AND ASTROLOGY

The Lovers card is related to the sign Gemini, which symbolizes the dualistic character of humanity (male/female, yin/yang, left brain/right brain). The third sign of the zodiac, and an air sign, Gemini is associated with siblings, neighbors, and the immediate environment.

The most mutable of the mutable signs, Gemini's nature is to change. Its symbol, the twins, clearly depicts its duality. The speed at which Gemini can change is sometimes daunting—as anyone who has ever been involved in a romantic situation with a Gemini can attest. But the Lovers card is not to be taken at surface value. It describes the reconciliation of opposites, or duality, either with another person or within yourself.

Gemini is ruled by the planet Mercury and, as Lois Rodden comments in her book *The Mercury Method of Chart Comparison*, it is Mercury who "opens the gates between two people," showing a "clear picture of both the attitude and the circumstances" between them. She states, "Mercury is the planet that carries the awareness, or level of communication, from one person to another."

THE CHARIOT

DESCRIPTION

The Chariot is usually depicted as a strong male figure holding the reigns of two sphinxlike beasts, one black and one white. Sometimes the beasts are unicorns or other mythical creatures like Pegasus, the winged horse, or griffins. The charioteer is fully armored and carries a scepter suggesting royalty or that he is in the service of royalty. In some decks, he wears a belt and a skirt decorated with zodiacal glyphs, symbolic of time. On his shoulders are crescent moons indicating emotional factors and unconscious habit patterns that need to be changed.

In some decks, the charioteer holds no reins—he uses sheer willpower to keep his steeds moving together in a forward direction. The beasts pulling the chariot signify the opposing forces, which were reconciled at the stage of the Lovers and represent the person's mastery of these opposing forces and control over inner conflicts. This card suggests that before taking on outer enemies or obstacles, it is essential to be in charge of the inner opposites and stop fighting yourself. The Chariot is a symbol of the self and its direction, as is any vehicle, such as an automobile, that appears in a dream.

INTERPRETATION

When the Chariot appears, there is a need to be in control of competing forces, whether these are inner conflicts, people, or a situation in your life that requires you to take command in order to reach your goals. Like the celebrated but seldom achieved bipartisanship of government, the solution to the problem at hand is to take the middle road between the conflicting elements.

You may feel unequal to the challenge of controlling the multiple factors of a given situation, but if you choose to just go with the flow and make the best of where it takes you, you will succeed. Once you have resolved the conflict within your own mind, even if that requires considerable struggle, you will be able to move forward. To do this, you need firm resolve—*self-mastery*. With a strategy determined by clear thinking and a sense of purpose, you will overcome all obstacles.

The Wheels Go Around

The wheels of the chariot signify the ever-changing life cycles. The animals are pulling in opposite directions, and the charioteer is holding the reins taut to keep the beasts in tandem—a symbolic statement of the need to master and reconcile conflicting forces, both inner and outer.

Receiving the Chariot in a reading, depending on its position in the spread, is generally favorable. It indicates you have the means to triumph over all obstacles and stay the course you have set for yourself. It can also mean that assistance is on the way as a result of your own strength and determination. It may suggest you are in the process of transforming yourself and your ways of thinking and behaving in order to create a firm foundation from which to go forward and achieve your desires. At this time you are keenly aware of how to use your past experience to reach a major goal, and you are in touch with deep inner resources.

At a literal level, the Chariot relates to travel and transportation and could mean changing your mode of transport, such as buying a new car or traveling by rail or some other form of wheeled vehicle.

THE CHARIOT AND ASTROLOGY

The Chariot is related to the zodiac sign Cancer, which symbolizes the sheer tenacity of the life force. The crab, Cancer's image, is known for its ability to hold on. If a crab has something in its grasp with one claw, the only way to get it loose is to cut off the claw. The Charioteer, likewise, holds firmly to his steeds. In the Waite deck, the Chariot depicts a man trying to control two animals that seem to be going in opposite directions. Cancer represents the process of the growth of the soul through the sustaining efforts of the life forces, which are by nature dual (masculine/feminine, yin/yang). Thus, Cancer's primary characteristic is tenacity.

Cancer is the first water sign, and like all water signs it represents relatedness, with other people and with the opposing forces within one's self. Associated with motherhood and family, Cancer is an extremely powerful sign whose energies initiate and sustain life. In the Cancer stage of development, we are required to play a larger role in our own development, to nurture ourselves, to learn to master our own opposite natures, and through that mastery to win victory over obstacles that stand in our way.

Cancer is ruled by the Moon, and it is this connection to the Great Mother that strengthens the inner life force this sign represents. Thus, the Chariot symbolizes the process of self-development through aligning yourself with the creative forces in the universe that sustain us here on Earth. The card also shows the effort necessary to guide the two sides of yourself to move forward successfully in life.

STRENGTH

DESCRIPTION

Most decks depict Strength as a woman in relationship to a lion. Some writers see this as a struggle, but in many decks there does not appear to be any conflict. In fact, Strength seems to be controlling the lion and may even seem affectionate toward him. A few decks show a strong young man wrestling with the lion. The man is bare-handed, which suggests that he needs no weapon.

In the Waite deck, the woman is bending over the lion in a gesture of gentleness, closing his jaws as if she expects no resistance to her touch. She is garbed in a flowing garment and wears a garland of flowers in her hair. Above her head is the symbol for infinity. In other decks, she caresses the lion, rides atop him, or stands beside him.

Although many interpreters view this card as emblematic of the struggle with one's inner animal nature, others see it as symbolic of self-confidence and inner strength, of being in harmony with one's instinctive nature. The woman is taming or making friends with the powerful force represented by the animal nature. Though the lion is clearly the more physically powerful of the two, the woman represents human courage and willpower that masters the instinctive realm not by force, but by cooperation.

INTERPRETATION

When Strength appears in a reading, you are exhibiting moral courage and fortitude. You have learned to work in harmony with your own instinctive nature, to listen to it and hear its whisperings. As in tales of the hero's journey, the seeker often meets with animals, representative of the instinctive realm, who guide and help him on his way. Strength indicates that you have come through difficulties and learned to rely on inner strength to solve your problems.

▲ ▲

The Goddess Artemis

Strength relates to the pagan goddess known as the Lady of the Beasts, who possessed understanding of the ways of nature. In ancient pagan times, this goddess reigned supreme. Later, she was personified by the Greeks as Artemis, goddess of the hunt, and by the Romans as Diana.

▼ ▼

This is a time when faith in yourself will pay off, when your position is strong because you have made yourself strong through suffering trials and tribulations without being defeated by them. It is a time to let people around you know who you are—especially anyone who has been dominating you.

The indication is that it is the feminine principle that does the work of reconciling the mental-rational faculty with that of the intuitive-instinctive nature. The feminine is always in closer touch with nature than the masculine. Whether the reading is for a man or a woman, the same meaning applies. The lesson is that we do not conquer our animal natures by brute force (which is the typical masculine mode of approach to obstacles) but by gentleness and feeling our way into rapport with the instinctive side.

Depending on the placement of the card in the spread and the question being asked, Strength indicates that what is required in the situation is for spiritual strength to replace or overcome physical strength.

STRENGTH AND ASTROLOGY

The card Strength is related to the sign Leo, which, like the heart, symbolizes the center from which the life force emanates, from which all energy flows and returns. Strength shows the creative individual potential that can manifest into reality.

Leo is the sign of the personal ego, with strong needs for self-expression and admiration. A fire sign, Leo displays vital energy, action, and creative talent. A fixed sign, Leo represents the eternal flame that animates all of life.

Ruled by the Sun, Leo is the sign of the natural leader, one who is not easily discouraged and who pursues goals with a great deal of persistence and devotion. The lion, Leo's symbol, has long been an imperial symbol, appearing on the royal coats of arms of many noble houses of Europe. Astrologically speaking, the Sun represents individuality, or the essence of Spirit. In metaphysical terms, it is significant of each person's individual connection to the light source of the Divine. Psychologically, the Sun represents the archetypal father concept.

Strength, therefore, signifies the divine, creative force within you, which is your inner strength. It also describes the process of connecting with Source or Spirit and expressing that powerful, life-giving energy creatively in a disciplined, mature, courageous manner.

THE HERMIT

DESCRIPTION

The Hermit is a guide figure represented as an old man, often bearded, holding a lighted lantern aloft in one hand and a staff in the other. He is usually dressed in the long robes of an anchorite or monk, plain and unadorned except for, in some decks, a knotted or tasseled cord around the waist. He radiates the wisdom of the archetypal elder figure, the sage of myth and legend.

The Hermit is generally standing, sometimes walking, looking ahead at what only he can see—your future. He is an ancient who is experienced on many levels and now functions as a teacher and guide. Mountains in the distance suggest he has reached the heights and returned to our plane to assist us in our development. He is wise in the ways of all the worlds, visible and invisible, material and immaterial.

Alone with His Staff

The Hermit travels alone, a seeker after truth, lighting the way ahead for those who follow. He needs no trappings of rank or royalty, wears no adornment, and carries no baggage. His goal is to search and to show others their true direction. His wooden staff symbolizes his connection to the forces of nature and the instinctual realm.

The Hermit's slightly bent posture and serious expression link him to Father Time, or Saturn—the planet that symbolizes boundaries and limitations, the obstacles and lessons that appear on everyone's life course. His solitude suggests the periodic need to withdraw from the hectic everyday world in order to regain perspective through silent reflection.

INTERPRETATION

When the Hermit appears in a reading, it can mean that a guide figure is at hand, offering help. You must make an effort to connect with this guide or consciously begin a search for the truth. A second interpretation is that you must voluntarily withdraw from contact with the outer world for a time in order to search your soul for the meaning of life. The implication is that the inner work needs to be done *now*, and that Spirit cannot speak to you if you are distracted by the noise of everyday life. The answers lie in silence, and the work can only be done alone.

Whichever interpretation seems to suit you and the question being put to the Tarot cards, the overall meaning is the same: the time has come to reunite with the Source, whether for guidance or inner balance. Sometimes, the guide figure may represent a person, such as a counselor of some sort—a therapist or clergy person—but usually it refers to inner guidance, or getting in touch with a guide from the other side.

THE HERMIT AND ASTROLOGY

The Hermit is related to the zodiac sign Virgo, which symbolizes the quest for perfection. Virgo represents the ideal that resides in the divine essence and the knowledge that can be harvested only from the fields of experience.

The most mental of the earth signs, Virgo's hallmark is work; its canon is duty. Excellent critical faculties make people born under this sign perfectionists. Interested in learning all there is to know about the world, with an emphasis on practical skills and utilizing tools, Virgos aim to be useful to others.

▲▲▲▲▲▲▲▲▲▲▲▲▲▲▲▲▲▲▲▲▲▲▲▲▲▲▲

The Sign of Service

Though Virgo has high aesthetic standards, art for art's sake doesn't interest people born under this practical sign, who always prefer things that serve a purpose. Their concern is what will be effective, not what will be fun. Thus, Virgo is called the sign of service.

▼▼▼▼▼▼▼▼▼▼▼▼▼▼▼▼▼▼▼▼▼▼▼▼▼▼▼

Virgo is ruled by the planet Mercury, which also rules Gemini. In Gemini, Mercury expresses itself by gathering information; in Virgo the information is sorted and analyzed. The Hermit, too, depicts knowledge gained through experience, as well as the process of carefully sorting and analyzing information so it can be used for the good of all. Notice that the Hermit is usually shown withdrawing from the world—for often the only way to gain wisdom is to retreat into solitude. However, he carries a lantern to light the way for others to follow the path.

WHEEL OF FORTUNE

DESCRIPTION

Invariably, the Wheel of Fortune card shows a wheel—often with eight spokes, a reference to the eight pagan holidays that mark the ever-turning cycles of life, death, and rebirth. The wheel is also a symbol for the Sun's path across the sky. Human or mythical figures may also be attached to the wheel.

WHEEL of FORTUNE.

The Waite deck shows a sphinx holding a sword at the top of the wheel, calmly watching as the karmic wheel revolves. Around the wheel are letters that spell "Rota," a reference to the "Royal Road of the Tarot." The ascending figure on the right is a jackal-headed man, called Hermanubis, who is known for keen eyesight. A serpent descending on the left side represents earth and the sexual energy that arises from it. Above and below, at the four corners of the card, are winged creatures holding open books. These correspond to the bull, the lion, the eagle, and the man, symbols of the fixed signs of the zodiac, Taurus, Leo, Scorpio, and Aquarius, respectively. In the Christian tradition, these refer to Matthew, Mark, Luke, and John.

Other decks show monkey-like figures caught on the wheel, or people in flowing robes wearing garlands in their hair, or eight young women between the spokes wearing expressions that range from joy to despair. The suggestion is that the figures are rising and falling through the various life cycles as the wheel turns. Occasionally, the wheel stands alone, obviously turning, or it is a disc decorated with symbols suspended in the sky. Sometimes a blindfolded woman is turning the wheel.

INTERPRETATION

When the Wheel of Fortune appears in a reading, it means that something has been put in motion over which you now have little or no control. You are being forced to accept the action of the forces of destiny, to get in tune with them, and to align yourself with their aims. Generally, however, the outcome is considered favorable.

These forces already set in motion foretell of changing circumstances, usually for the better, beneficial changes that will promote your growth and advancement. Balance may be an issue if you are resisting change, but you now have no choice but to go along with whatever process is working in your life. The Wheel of Fortune is a reminder that every period of intense activity must be followed by a fallow time of rest and inactivity. Where you are in your own personal cycle will be shown by the other cards in the spread.

The Three Threads

The Wheel of Fortune is linked to the three Fates. One spins the thread of life, the second weaves it, and the third cuts it. Thus, the Wheel of Fortune is a reminder of the mysterious cycles of life, death, and rebirth and of the invisible forces that measure them out to each of us.

This card almost always heralds good fortune coming as a result of what you yourself have put into motion, even if you aren't totally aware of what you have done to initiate the process. You may have applied for a new job, met a new person, begun a romance, decided to take a college course, or had a chance encounter that got the ball rolling—or the wheel turning. It means a new phase, possibly the need to make an important decision, or even a totally unexpected circumstance developing that will change your life.

WHEEL OF FORTUNE AND ASTROLOGY

The Wheel of Fortune is related to the planet Jupiter, which marks the point in our solar system where we move from the realm of the strictly personal (represented by the Sun, Moon, Mercury, Venus, and Mars) toward the external world and society at large. Jupiter, the giant among the planets, represents the principles of expansion and growth.

Note resonance between astrology's Jupiter, sometimes called the second Sun and greater benefic, that generally symbolizes blessings of prosperity, success, good luck, honor, and accomplishment and the Tarot's Wheel of Fortune, which likewise represents good fortune and fulfillment.

Jupiter rules Sagittarius, the sign that signifies the interface between the individual and the institutions upon which the social order rests—schools and universities, churches, the legal system, philanthropic and social organizations, government, and the like. Jupiter's association with learning and religion represents the higher mind and, consequently, the development of higher mental and spiritual attributes. Jupiter exceeds the purely rational level of Mercury to seek an understanding of universal principles on which thought is based. Through acquiring and integrating higher knowledge (symbolized by the planet Jupiter), you can improve both your position in the world and your connection with the Divine (symbolized by the Wheel of Fortune).

In astrology, Jupiter represents the ideological basis for systems of thought, be they philosophical or religious, orthodox or unorthodox. Thus, look to Jupiter for spiritual, as well as social, development. Jupiter is exalted in Cancer, which rules the home where the principle of learning is first established. The family is the basic unit of society; therefore Jupiter represents how to grow beyond the personal sphere and how to integrate your personal life with the larger world. The Wheel of Fortune also shows how your family, education, philosophy, and social position influence your ability to succeed in life.

JUSTICE

DESCRIPTION

The Justice card usually depicts a female figure, robed, sometimes armored, and crowned. She holds an upright sword in one hand and in the other, perfectly balanced scales. In some modern decks, she is either a nude figure with arms outstretched in absolute even balance, or she is shown standing between a large set of scales while holding a smaller set.

Unlike the contemporary image of Justice as blindfolded, this Justice is open-eyed, suggesting that divine justice rather than the laws of man are at work here. She stares straight ahead, suggesting that divine justice is not bound by human limitations and that divine law is not subject to error and bias.

INTERPRETATION

When the Justice card appears in a reading, it can indicate that an actual legal matter is pending or being considered. Whatever the situation, you must weigh many factors in order to make a reasoned and factual assessment, i.e., judgment, of the matter at hand. The Justice card warns you to receive guidance from your inner self, not to rely solely on human advisors. Also, it cautions prudence and care, the need to deliberate calmly and carefully before taking action or concluding an outcome.

Reap What You Sow

Justice may describe a matter in which some sort of rectification is necessary, where wrongs must be righted, in a spiritual or personal sense, regardless of whether any laws have been broken. This is a card of karma and suggests you are reaping what you have sown. The card may be advising you to become more balanced or fair-minded.

If other people are involved, you would be wise to take their point of view into consideration, for issues of fairness are paramount now. You can expect legal matters, if a part of the circumstances, to proceed smoothly, fairly, and in a dispassionate manner. Be confident that Justice will prevail as a result of your own temperate behavior and rational thought. Depending on what other cards appear in the spread, a third party could come to your aid and help you get the fair outcome you deserve. This card can also represent anyone involved with the legal profession—a lawyer, judge, witness, law enforcement officer, and the like.

Justice is related to a mythic lineage that stretches back to ancient Egypt. In Egyptian mythology, the goddess Maat—whose name means truth and justice—stood in the underworld. She held a pair of scales upon which she weighed the newly dead person's soul against the Feather of Truth to decide whether the soul was worthy to pass into the realm of Osiris, god of the underworld.

JUSTICE AND ASTROLOGY

The card Justice is related to the sign Libra, which has as its symbol a blindfolded woman holding a set of scales to signify impartial justice. Libra represents striving for balance in all things. By extension, relationships—personal and professional—fall into Libra's domain because you must balance your own needs and desires with those of other people if everyone is to live together peacefully on this planet.

Libra is ruled by Venus, the planet of love and partnerships. Divine love shows itself through human love, and by loving others we discover the path to the Divine—the source of ultimate justice.

THE HANGED MAN

DESCRIPTION

The Hanged Man is a tantalizing figure. Usually a male, hanging upside down by one leg, the Hanged Man's expression is serene, as if he were thoroughly enjoying his state. Suspended as he is by one foot, he appears to be engaged in a bizarre form of meditation or ritual.

In the Waite deck, the Hanged Man is shown hanging from a tree. Its roots are in the ground, and the crosspiece that supports him sprouts leaves. Some authorities say this is the Tree of Life itself. Around the Hanged Man's head is a golden halo, like the rays of the sun. Yellow is the color of Mercury, the planet of the mind. Other decks picture only the horizontal beam, but it too has leaves on it, showing that it is living wood.

INTERPRETATION

Many writers see the Hanged Man as a card of self-sacrifice and martyrdom, but others view this tantalizing card as voluntary surrender to the process of achieving enlightenment. It may require giving up superficial pleasures and trivial activities in pursuit of a more spiritual way of life. The word *sacrifice* derives from the Latin *sacer facio,* which means to make sacred. Therefore, the Hanged Man may represent a sacred pursuit.

When this card appears in a reading, depending on its position in the layout, you have usually received a call to follow a less materialistic way of life. You are ready for whatever personal sacrifice is needed, or you are preparing to make such a gesture. You may need to pause momentarily and suspend ordinary activities to better realize where you are headed spiritually.

Often, the Hanged Man signifies going through a major transformation, perhaps caused by illness or some loss. The result has shaken up your old way of life and made you realize that there is more to life than money, material goods, and physical reality.

This card can indicate that a new commitment to the development of the inner self is demanded. You might need to spend time alone in order to reevaluate just what is and what is not important to you. It may be very difficult to let go of old patterns—a relationship, a job, a worldview, a lifestyle, or a group of other people—but letting go is essential to your continued growth.

THE HANGED MAN AND ASTROLOGY

The Hanged Man is related to the planet Neptune—a planet difficult to define, for it symbolizes all that is unreal, ethereal, mystical, otherworldly, invisible, inspirational, imaginative, and creative. Neptune's negative associations include escapism, drugs and alcohol, avoidance of responsibilities, destructive self-indulgence, deception, fraud, delusions, fascination with celebrities' lives, and involvement in religious cults.

Astrologers view Neptune as the higher octave of Venus. Therefore Neptune's energy is expressed in music, poetry, and the arts in general. In its highest form, it represents the celestial musician who dances to the rhythm of the universe. This cosmic dancer is the progenitor of the seven muses, those spinners of artistic inspiration. Such elevated inspiration may also fuel prophecy and visions, which reveal universal truth impenetrable by the power of reason alone. Through Neptune's vibration, you can contact the universal guides, or master souls, who govern our planet's evolution.

Neptune rules Pisces, the zodiac sign symbolizing that which is most ephemeral in human nature, the desire to unite with the cosmic consciousness. Venus is exalted in the sign of Pisces, but while Venus's energies influence human love, Neptune's energies are concerned with the expression of universal love.

The Hanged Man also represents self-sacrifice or, more accurately, ego sacrifice. This may mean letting go of your own desires to achieve a greater good or to align yourself with the Divine Will. Either way, the Hanged Man often signifies a higher level of vision that requires you to see things in a different way, which is why the card depicts a man dangling upside down—by removing the blinders of the earthly or human realm.

DEATH

DESCRIPTION

The Death card tends to frighten people who see it come up in a reading, but despite its grim depiction it symbolizes the transforming powers of life, death, and rebirth. Many decks picture a skeleton with a scythe grinning toothily and wearing a black hooded robe. The Waite deck pictures Death as a man in black armor riding a white charger, suggesting the perpetual movement of the cycles of life and death.

The knight carries a banner on which is embroidered the mystical white rose, symbol of pure and true love. The rose with five petals represents the five senses of material life, combined with the immortality of the heart, or soul. Greeting the knight with hands outstretched in blessing or supplication is a priest figure wearing a mitered cardinal's hat. Two children look on in awe. In the background, the sun is rising, a sign of resurrection, over a body of water representing the unconscious realm.

Other decks show barren backgrounds; sometimes severed body parts are randomly lying about. One deck features the four horses of the Apocalypse riding through a stormy sky. Another presents a black-robed and hooded faceless figure standing in a woods, who appears to be supporting with one outstretched arm a huge white rose that dominates the card visually.

INTERPRETATION

The Death card in a reading rarely foreshadows a physical death. What its appearance means is the end, or death, of a cycle. Whenever a stage in one's life ends, there is a need for mourning. It is only the refusal to accept that something is ending—trying desperately to hold on to what is clearly over—that causes trouble. Employing cosmetic means to stave off the approach of age, for instance, is a useless effort to avoid the inevitable. What gives importance and meaning to this card is your *acceptance* of the change that cannot be avoided. Thus, in essence, the ultimate message of the Death card is the promise that new life follows disintegration.

DEATH AND ASTROLOGY

The Death card is related to the sign Scorpio, which represents the transforming powers of life and death. In dealing with the process of transformation, Scorpio embodies life's ultimate mysteries—sex and death, rebirth and regeneration. The eighth sign of the zodiac, Scorpio, the fixed water sign, is concerned with the processes of destruction and renewal.

Scorpio is ruled by Pluto. Discovered in 1930, Pluto symbolizes the transformative processes of both the inner psyche and outer world—and the link between the two. Like Scorpio, the Death card shows the breakdown of a previous form or structure and its transformation into something else. Vegetation rots and becomes mulch, from which arises new vegetation. The individual sperm and ovum both "die" to be transformed into the embryo.

Astrologers associate Scorpio (most compelling and most difficult of the signs) with the transformative process that goes on in the dark underworld of the psyche, sending up clues to its metamorphosing work via dreams and, sometimes, in compulsive behaviors.

TEMPERANCE

DESCRIPTION

This lovely card often features a winged angel—male, female, or androgynous. In the Waite deck, the angel is standing in a stream bordered by flowers, with the rising Sun shining in the background. In most decks, the figure is pouring liquid—the elixir of life—from a golden vessel into a silver one in a continuous stream, suggesting the interplay of the material and spiritual worlds and the eternal flow of the waters of life. The word *vessel* is related to the Great Mother Goddesses of antiquity, and the body is often referred to as the vessel of the soul. Thus, both the angelic figure and the cups are symbolic references to the feminine principle of cooperation, balance, harmony, receptivity, and creativity.

INTERPRETATION

Temperance, as its name suggests, is about moderation in all things. When Temperance appears in a reading, depending on its position in the spread, you are being cautioned to have patience, which may be difficult under the circumstances. However, the circumstances of your situation will teach you to wait calmly when it seems like nothing is happening.

The person who receives Temperance in a reading is not in a position to hurry matters along. The only course is to sit and wait for things to move in their own time. The trick is to make the waiting constructive. This is one of the great lessons of the Zen masters. Learning to do nothing mindfully is a milestone on the spiritual path. It's of vital importance to know that there are times when nothing *can* be done and nothing *needs* to be done. Therein lies the state of grace.

TEMPERANCE AND ASTROLOGY

Temperance is related to Sagittarius, the sign of the truth seeker. It is concerned with all manifestations of the higher mind and universal values. The ninth sign of the zodiac, ruled by Jupiter, Sagittarius signifies the religious and intellectual institutions that bind society together and advance learning and morals. Sagittarius is symbolized through the archer. The icon powerfully expresses a love of personal liberty and intellectual freedom. It stands for the absolute truth underlying all causes, for the unifying principle at the center that binds all things into a single whole.

A mutable fire sign, Sagittarius is far-reaching conceptually and intellectually, eclectic in the quest for knowledge, wisdom, and experience. Ultimately, it seeks the inner teacher and guide and is related to the Archangel Michael, who is the angel of fire. Sagittarius is the sign of philosophy, religion, and law, as well as of long-distance travel, for all these endeavors help us to expand our knowledge.

Like the zodiac sign of Sagittarius, the Temperance card of the Tarot describes not only the quest for knowledge and experience but also the qualities of self-discipline, faith, and vision that temper desire and direct it in a purposeful way. Thus, Temperance represents personal will aligned with the Divine Will.

THE DEVIL

DESCRIPTION

Many decks picture a medieval Christian-type devil, complete with horns, hooves, a hairy tail, and a pitchfork. Usually at the devil's feet are two small, humanlike figures, one male and one female, with chains around their necks that are attached to the block upon which the devil sits. However, it is important to note that the chains are loose and the people could easily slip them off, suggesting self-imposed limitations.

Whatever form the Devil takes in various decks, he is usually pretty scary looking. Occasionally, he is bat-like or stylized depending on the theme of the deck and its designer's inclinations toward the figure. The Gilded Tarot portrays him as a muscular young man, whose face is half hidden beneath a helmet-mask. In some decks, he has an inverted pentagram over his head or on his brow. In one deck, there is no devil at all, only two nude figures chained to a symbolically decorated block, straining toward an open doorway at the end of a long tunnel.

The variety of illustrations implies widely differing opinions of the card's meaning. For some, the Devil is a creature of consummate evil; for others the Devil is a mythical creature. Many psychologically oriented people see the Devil as a symbol of human indulgence, ignorance, egotism, greed, and irresponsibility. Thus, the illustration appearing on the card represents a point of view, as well as the traditional meanings associated with the card.

INTERPRETATION

Superficially, the Devil appears to be one of the more alarming cards of the Major Arcana. However, he does not represent satanic forces with evil intent, and it is important to remember this when doing readings. He is the Horned God of pagan times, connected to the fertility rites banned by the Church, which feared the power of pagan rituals, especially those including sexual activity.

When the Devil shows up in a reading, depending upon his position in the spread, he is telling you that you need to reevaluate your relationship to material things, which are keeping you chained. It's time to look at whatever is limiting you and holding you back from personal growth, especially abusive, obsessive, or harmful relationships. You are being called upon to confront your fears about financial security and social and material success—the things of this world. The Devil is a reality check.

The Devil Takes Many Forms

The Devil is related to the old pagan god Great Pan, a god of nature and the natural processes of the physical world, including sex. The Greek form of Pan was Dionysus, who was known for cavorting with satyrs and in whose honor wild and uninhibited rituals, which, included a sexual free-for-all were held annually.

You need to recognize and acknowledge things you don't like about yourself—your personality, body, or temperament. It's time to let go of old fears, hang-ups, inhibitions, and ways you manipulate others to satisfy your needs instead of taking responsibility for yourself in a positive manner. Often there is a sexual component involved that is having a harmful effect on your whole life. Or there could be a nonsexual relationship that binds you and that must end before you can grow further.

Whatever the situation, you are the only one who can change it. The two chained figures on the card represent bondage to the material realm. Their loose chains indicate your potential for attaining freedom by relinquishing obsessive ambition and excessive attachment to the things of this world.

THE DEVIL AND ASTROLOGY

The Devil is related to the planet Saturn, known to astrologers as the Lord of Karma, and as the great teacher. Saturn is the planet of discipline and structure, time and ambition. Its placement in your birth chart represents where you are tested by the universe, where you face tasks and trials in the form of obstacles, which are the lessons you must learn. Saturn is also associated with stability, permanence, responsibility, dependability, endurance, and a capacity for self-sacrifice.

Saturn is sometimes a harsh taskmaster. Once you learn Saturn's lessons, you are blessed with wisdom and an understanding of the earthly realm. During the approximately twenty-eight years it takes Saturn to transit all the signs of the zodiac, Saturn's energy emphasizes the necessary ways a person must develop to achieve maturity. Saturn shows you how to live in harmony with yourself and others, take responsibility for your actions, and to act not only for your benefit but society's as well.

Saturn represents the laws of limitation and conservation. Many people find it difficult to cope with the restrictions and structures imposed by Saturn, which is one reason the planet and the Devil card share linkage. Often, Saturn's influence corresponds with painful circumstances that seem to merely happen, hence the planet's association with karma and fate. Ultimately, though, Saturn teaches you to face your own weaknesses, fears, and doubts (conditions represented by the Tarot's Devil card) so you can become your own authority rather than relying on others to wield authoritative power. The symbol of the Devil is as the dweller at the threshold, the keeper of the keys to the gate, and the conduit through which you achieve freedom through self-understanding.

The Devil also symbolizes your lower instincts, obsessions, and indulgences. When you have freed yourself—no longer enslaved by those instincts—and pass the tests Saturn sets for you to master, you can then claim your secret power and live in tune with your true or authentic self.

THE TOWER

DESCRIPTION

The Tower usually depicts a stone tower of fortress-like construction, such as those still remaining from medieval times in Europe. The tower is in the process of falling down or being destroyed, most often by fire or lightning.

In the Waite deck, and some others, the Tower's crown is being blown off by the fiery impact. The blast catapults human figures out of the windows. The implication is that the forces of heaven are angry and attacking the structure, causing flaming debris to fly out in all directions.

THE TOWER.

INTERPRETATION

Like the Death card and the Devil, the Tower tends to strike alarm and fear into anyone in whose reading it appears, and indeed many writers assign a fully negative meaning to this card. The Tower does not necessarily represent ruin and devastation, although its appearance usually does herald swift and dramatic change—sometimes shocking and extremely upsetting change.

The Tower of Babel

The Tower parallels the Old Testament story of the Tower of Babel, which was a massive structure intended to reach all the way up to God in His heaven. Also known as *La Maison Dieu* (The House of God) and the Falling Tower, or the Tower of Destruction, the Tower corresponds to the number sixteen and to the Hebrew letter Ayin.

It is important to keep in mind that you've usually brought the situation on yourself by ignoring or denying that something is rotten and needs restructuring or deconstructing. Most likely, you're already well aware of a pressing need to make changes, but you're steadfastly refusing to take action. Then along comes a circumstance, such as losing a job or getting a divorce, or having an accident or a financial setback, that forces you to face reality.

There's no question this card signifies the crumbling of an old and outworn structure. It demands that you begin to deal seriously with your life collapsing all around you instead of, like the Roman emperor Nero, fiddling while your house burns. Any number of possibilities exist—breaking off an unsatisfactory or destructive relationship, quitting a stifling job, casting off false materialistic values, confronting long-buried issues of guilt and shame, shucking the social conventions that limit your progress, selling your over mortgaged house and living more simply, or ridding yourself of burdensome possessions. The list is endless, but you nearly always know what the issue is and that you're imprisoned by a self-created fortress, whether for protection, safety, or from fear of facing the unknown.

The message of the Tower is that you must destroy the old structures before they destroy you so you can become free. Otherwise, they may be shattered by seemingly outside influences (which you have actually created yourself). In the wake of the chaos, a new order will grow. What was unsound will come tumbling down. You can pick and choose among the rubble to decide what is worth saving and, from that, rebuild your life in accordance with who you truly are.

THE TOWER AND ASTROLOGY

The Tower is related to the planet Uranus. Many Tarot decks feature imagery that depicts the tower being struck by lightning and destroyed. Both lightning and sudden destruction are associated with Uranus. Astrologers also connect Uranus with change, especially the unexpected kind. In fact, one of the meanings of the Tarot's Tower card is a major change of an unexpected nature.

The first outer planet in our solar system, meaning a planet that cannot be seen with the naked eye, Uranus is associated with transpersonal affairs. It rules Aquarius, the sign of humanity. In this role, Uranus sometimes instigates changes in your life or in society for the good of the whole rather than for the individual. Moving outward from the Sun, Uranus is the next planet after Saturn. Saturn represents structures, institutions, and social systems that may provide stability and security, but whose limits and rules also imprison. Uranus's role is to break up old structures and traditions that have outlived their usefulness, so that a new order can be ushered in.

Many decks show one or more people being thrown from the crumbling tower in a haphazard manner. Indeed, Uranus's influence is often experienced as unsettling and chaotic. You may not be able to see where you are going while in the midst of the changes going on in your life.

The end result, however, is freedom—one of Uranus's most distinctive attributes. Frequently the freedom brought by Uranus and signified by the Tower is independence from restrictive social conditioning and established ideas, which enables you to think for yourself and make your own choices.

THE STAR

DESCRIPTION

This lovely card usually portrays a nude female figure in or beside a pool of water, pouring from two jugs, one held in each hand. In the Waite deck, she kneels and pours the contents of one pitcher into the stream and the contents of the other into the ground, showing the connection between the two feminine elements: earth and water.

The background of this card always displays stars; often, one directly above the figure's head is much larger than the others. Many decks show seven subsidiary stars, sometimes arranged to reflect the portal or two-pillar theme, sometimes set in a circle or a halo-like form around her. The stars sparkle above a pastoral setting: trees, mountains, birds, flowers. If trees appear in the image, they may be configured on either side of her, another echo of the portal or pillars. The colors are usually bright, often with yellow (the color of optimism) predominating, although some decks depict a nighttime scene.

The naked woman represents unveiled truth and purity. The jugs she holds contain the waters of life. Some of the water is being returned to the Source, and some is being used to infuse the land with new life.

INTERPRETATION

The Star is a universal symbol of hope. Its appearance can signal the end of the travails represented by some of the earlier cards, symbolizing that a new and happier phase of life is coming into being. We see shooting stars as harbingers of good luck. From earliest times humans have been awed and fascinated by the star-spangled sky, the constellations, and the apparent motion of the bowl of the heavens.

The Star in a reading is like looking up at the bright starry sky on a clear night and seeing all the magnificence of the universe. It stimulates us to ponder the great potential of each and every human being for growth, inspiration, intuition, inner wisdom, and happiness.

Although the Star does not usually point to any specific planetary transit, as do some of the other Major Arcana cards, it does have a strong connection to astrology in general, for the zodiac signs relate to constellations. When the Star appears in a reading, it is a good time to have your horoscope read or to begin studying astrology yourself. A gate has opened for you to new possibilities. This card portends good fortune, creative inspiration, spiritual growth, help from unseen forces, and wishes come true. It marks a time of fulfillment.

THE STAR AND ASTROLOGY

The Star is related to the zodiac sign Aquarius, which embodies the idea of the individual as a cooperative member of the larger whole, that we are all one big family—a concept that can be grasped only intuitively. Brotherhood or sisterhood is the ideal, for Aquarius sees everyone in the humanitarian spirit of friendship.

Astrology and astronomy are considered Aquarian vocations—an obvious link between the zodiac sign and the Star card. In a symbolic sense, the Star represents hope and a belief that the future holds a brighter tomorrow, a better place. Aquarius is the sign of the future, of all that is new and fresh and promising. Few are more idealistic than an Aquarian.

Aquarius is the eleventh sign of the zodiac, the fixed air sign. Aquarius experiments with all established structures and rebels against those it finds too restrictive. It freely crosses all man-made boundaries to experience the new and unusual. This sign's purpose is to bring about needed reforms by introducing innovative ideas.

THE MOON

DESCRIPTION

The Moon is a magical, mysterious card emblematic of the unconscious and the invisible realm of dreams, imagination, and psychic impressions. Usually the Moon occupies the top half of the card, sometimes shown in both its full and crescent phases with the crescent enclosed in the full circle. In the Waite deck, drops of water fall from the Moon, raining down on two canines, a dog and a wolf, which bay at the Moon. Two towers, one on either side, reflect the portal theme. At the bottom of the card is a pool or pond of water from which crawls a crab (symbol of the astrological sign Cancer, which is ruled by the Moon), crawfish, or lobster. The water suggests the Moon's link with the tides, the Earth, the emotions, and the unconscious realm.

Some authorities say the animals represent our opposite tendencies—the wolf, the untamed inner animal nature; the dog, the domesticated, daily persona we show to the world. But canines and the moon have deep mythological roots that relate to the underworld. In addition, the dog indicates psychic ability, as it is able to follow an invisible trail and locate what cannot be seen.

INTERPRETATION

Astrologically, the Moon represents the soul, which is the link between spirit (Sun) and matter (Earth). The Moon is feminine: It symbolizes what we feel and how we respond. Therefore, it is emblematic of all that is receptive in human nature: the subconscious, the emotions, the instincts, and the automatic functions of the body. The lunar self is the channel for the flow of the universal, or divine, source, and as such, the Moon has great power. It affects everything and everyone on Earth, from the ocean's tides to the moods and reproductive cycles of humans.

Therefore, when the Moon appears in a reading, it suggests that you should be paying more attention to your inner self, your lunar self. It advises you to illuminate your deepest nature. In its diffuse light, we can often see more clearly than in the glare of the noonday Sun. The light of the Sun enables us to see the world around us, but the Moon allows us to illuminate what springs naturally from inside ourselves.

During the hours of night, our subtle senses are more open and receptive to our inner spiritual harmony. When the Moon appears in a reading, it is time to attend to your dreams, feelings, instincts, and intuition.

Although traditionally the Moon card can indicate deceit and self-deception, confinement and undoing, these conditions are usually a result of ignoring your own inner promptings. If you get "taken"—especially emotionally—it's because you were letting your rational mind override your feelings. The Moon card's appearance also notifies you to take care of loose ends connected to the past, especially to your mother or other females.

Take Care of Yourself

The Moon card can point to a need to nurture yourself or to care for your health. For artistic people, its presence in a reading may mark a time of increased imagination and creativity.

The Moon is the symbol for the goddess, whose three aspects represent the three faces of the Great Triple Goddess. As the newborn crescent, the Moon is the maiden, the virgin—not chaste, but belonging to herself alone, not bound to any man. At the full Moon, she is the mature woman, sexual and maternal, giver of life. At the end of her cycle, the waning Moon about to turn dark represents the crone whose years have ripened into wisdom.

THE MOON AND ASTROLOGY

The Tarot's Moon card is associated with Pisces, the twelfth sign of the zodiac. Ruled by Neptune, Pisces is linked with creativity, psychic ability, empathy, illusions, and poetic sensibilities. The astrological sign also represents self-sacrifice for a higher cause and reveals the soul's struggle with the imperfections of the material plane.

Linked Opposites

The symbol of Pisces—two fish swimming in opposite directions—suggests the dichotomy between the material and spiritual realms and also finite consciousness on the one side, and the infinite consciousness of the universe, or cosmic consciousness, on the other side. The connecting point is Earth, where the spiritual and material aspects of being meet. One fish stands for the physical body, with all its limitations and mortality; the other symbolizes the soul and the invisible world without boundaries.

When you study the Moon card, its symbolism suggests turning its light within to illuminate your inner spiritual world. In moonlight, you become more aware of the shadings and nuances of feelings and inner perceptions. Thus, you can tune in more accurately to the spiritual vibrations of others. The Moon card represents the unconscious, hidden side of your nature, as well as the complex, emotionally driven, murky situations in which you perhaps find yourself at times. The Moon also represents the deep well of intuitive knowing that cannot be accessed only through your intellect.

THE SUN

DESCRIPTION

The Sun card features a blazing Sun, sometimes with a face, with sunbeams radiating out from it. Beneath the Sun, in the Waite deck, a smiling nude child is riding a white horse. Behind him, a banner unfurls, held up by a winged staff. In the background, huge sunflowers grow against a stone wall.

Some decks show two children with their arms around each other; other decks picture a young couple holding hands. The child, or children, is clearly very happy. The Sun's planetary ruler is Leo, which is linked with children, pleasure, and creativity. The astrological Sun also rules the heart, the center of the body and the personality. The Sun card represents life itself, for the Sun gives life to everything on Earth. The Sun suggests vitality, confidence, achievement, ego attainment, and success in all endeavors. It is emblematic of the proverb, "May the Sun shine on all you do," the implication being that sunshine brings joy.

INTERPRETATION

When the Sun card appears, it is an indication that your past work is now bearing fruit, a concept that is symbolized by the child or children. Along with the Moon, it implies the union between the unconscious realm of creativity (Moon) and the conscious realm of manifestation (Sun). Whether the birth represented is a biological child or a creative project, the outcome is a happy one. It is a time when good things come into your life—success, optimism, achievement, health, general good fortune, and happiness.

When the Sun turns up, it brightens any negative cards in the spread—no matter where the Sun appears in the spread. His influence is always beneficial, suggesting prosperity, enthusiasm, honors, public recognition, and attainment. You are happy to be alive because you feel it is the dawning of a new day. Any special efforts or ventures, such as taking a test or making a presentation, will turn out favorably.

In the wake of the demise of the Great Mother Goddess as the sole divinity, the Sun, which represents the masculine principle, came to be worshipped as the central deity in many cultures. The ancient Egyptians, after eons of a pantheon of goddesses and gods, under the leadership of the pharaoh Akhenaten, were persuaded, albeit reluctantly, to accept a single god—known as Ra, Amun-Ra, or Aton (all of which were names for the Sun)—which Akhenaten believed was the god of all gods. The Greeks called their Sun god Helios, whom the Romans named Apollo.

THE SUN AND ASTROLOGY

The Sun card finds resonance in the zodiac sign Leo, which is ruled by the Sun. Astrologically speaking, the Sun is the Light of the Soul and represents individuality, or the essence of Spirit. In metaphysical terms, it signifies each person's individual connection to the Divine. Psychologically, the Sun represents the archetypal father image, although it does not necessarily indicate a direct relationship to an actual parent.

In the Tarot, the Sun card symbolizes clarity and vision—the brilliant light of day that illuminates the world and chases away the shadows of confusion. Under its bright rays, you see the path before you. This card signifies a release from a time of darkness, as well as the light of reason burning through emotional fog.

Astronomically, the Sun is at the center of the solar system. In astrology, it is at the heart of the birth chart, showing what you potentially are, not necessarily what you will become. Why you think you are here on Earth, where you are going in your life, what makes you feel important are all related to the Sun in your birth chart. It speaks to your purpose in life—the sense of "I am." In the Tarot, the Sun card symbolizes individuality and self-confidence, your ability to be truly yourself regardless of what others think.

The Sun's glyph, a circle with a dot at the center, signifies the emanation of life-giving energy from the unlimited resources of the Divine. A perfect shape without beginning or end, the circle symbolizes the totality of the entire universe. The dot represents the point of light that comes into the individual. As such, it is the aperture through which divine nature shows the unlimited possibility of growth that can be achieved through conscious attunement to the divinity within each being.

JUDGMENT

DESCRIPTION

The Judgment card visually seems negative. In the Waite deck, a winged figure, whom some call the angel Gabriel, emerges from a cloud and blows a trumpet. Beneath him are several nude figures of men and women looking up, hearing the trumpet's blast. Their arms are outstretched, and they seem to have risen from coffins or the Earth itself. Their expressions reveal awe tinged with fear.

JUDGEMENT.

Of all the allegorical symbolism of the Major Arcana, this is the most purely Christian, suggesting the feared Day of Judgment, when God will judge all souls and apportion out rewards or punishments accordingly. However, this is not a totally Christian idea; the Egyptians and other cultures also expressed the notion of the soul being judged. The goddess Maat, for instance, weighs the soul against her Feather of Truth.

Whether seen from a Christian point of view (which these medieval images represent) or from a universal one, the idea behind the symbols is that of an awakening.

INTERPRETATION

When the Judgment card appears, what is being awakened is a sense of a Higher Self within. Sometimes the card coincides with a person turning away from a traditional set of beliefs toward one that better suits his or her personal philosophy of life. Judgment represents the end of something—an old way of life, a cycle that is finished. It is a time to seek new direction, to make adjustments that reflect who you truly are—perhaps by breaking away from your conventional way of life and beliefs.

Generally speaking, this is a positive card symbolizing regeneration and rebirth into wholeness after a period of confusion and a sense of confinement (shown by the coffins). You may have been feeling "dead" in your old life. When Judgment appears, you have the unique opportunity to relive, to enliven yourself and your environment by making the appropriate changes. What is ending is doubt and indecision, depression and despair, fear and inhibition. It's a time of new freedom to be yourself.

The Judgment card relates to classical Greek Hermes-Trismegistus in his role as *psychopomp,* or guide of souls. The activity of Hermes refers to alternatives of life, to the dissolution of fatal opposites, to clandestine violations of boundaries and laws—in other words, the overturning of the rational world and the discovery of the magical powers of the inner world.

JUDGMENT AND ASTROLOGY

The Judgment card is related to the planet Pluto, which symbolizes the transformative processes of both the inner psyche and outer form. Pluto, recategorized by astronomers as a dwarf planet, has an eccentric orbit that takes it periodically closer to the Sun than to Neptune. One of the important lessons of Pluto depicted by the Tarot card Judgment is how you will use Pluto's power. Both the planet and the Judgment card are associated with fate, or karma—particularly the individual karma that is linked to the karma of the society into which we are born.

Pluto, the planet of death and rebirth, symbolizes the great collective, what Carl G. Jung has called the collective unconscious, the point where we connect with the rest of humanity. As ruler of the underworld, Pluto is a subterranean force to be reckoned with. Judgment, too, shows the inner forces that propel us, the larger societal forces that influence our personal lives, and the results of the interaction of these two forces.

THE WORLD

DESCRIPTION

In many decks, the World card shows a young woman, sometimes nude or wearing a long scarf. The scarf covers her genitals but leaves her breasts bare. In each hand, she holds a double-ended wand that points both upward and downward, suggesting, "as above, so below." In the Waite deck, she is surrounded by an oval-shaped wreath.

As with the Wheel of Fortune card, to which the World is related, the four corners of the card feature a bull, a lion, an eagle, and a man—representing the four fixed signs of the zodiac: Taurus, Leo, Scorpio, and Aquarius. These elemental figures also depict the four directions. In the Waite deck, the wreath is bound at the top and bottom by ribbons in the shape of the infinity symbol, which is found on both the Magician and the Strength cards.

INTERPRETATION

This is the last numbered card of the Major Arcana. It represents balance and support by unseen forces and symbolizes the end of the spiritual journey begun by the Fool. To embark upon the spiritual journey is to invite unseen forces to interact with us. These creative energies manifest in many ways, and often serve as guides. Guides bring us into grace and show the way. To encounter a guide—and they come in many guises—is to enter another realm, a place of great powers and, sometimes, great secrets. This realm belongs to the invisible world, although its denizens can, like angels, assume human or animal form. To interface with this world is to be impacted in a way that is life changing. With guides, we enter a world of supreme power—not the power of the material world but of the invisible order that supports and nourishes our world and our lives here. It is the realm of the sacred.

The World card, with its symbols of the four elements and its joyfully dancing figure, is about balance and completion.

When the World card appears in a reading, it is a signal that you have been guided to the successful conclusion of your spiritual journey. At this, the final stage, you will receive what is rightfully yours because you have earned it. Now you are and feel whole, complete. You are refreshed from your long journey and ready to begin anew at a higher level.

THE WORLD AND ASTROLOGY

The World card finds resonance in the symbolism of the zodiac sign of Capricorn as the world leader, father, authority, the social order, pragmatism, and the slow-but-sure ascent to the top. Ruled by Saturn, the planet of discipline, organization, limitation, awareness, and time, Capricorn's principle is "I use." The tenth sign of the zodiac, Capricorn builds what is practical and useful to society. Then, while meticulously sticking to the rules of the game, Capricorn earns success and glories in its rewards.

Likewise, the World card, too, indicates success as the result of hard work. Rewards that are due to you, often after a long struggle, are represented by this card. Order, knowledge, stability, authority, and achievement are hallmarks of the card. It suggests that things are as they should be, not because of chance or dumb luck, but because the necessary steps have been taken, and the required effort has been invested to bring about a desired result.

Astrologers have always regarded Capricorn as a sacred sign. Within its boundaries the winter solstice occurs. Christmas and the winter solstice are celebrations of continued life amid the darkest, most barren time of the year, marking the return of the Sun and life. The World represents the cosmic order depicted by the cyclic nature of life and the seasons. A card of hope and promise, it also symbolizes light at the end of the tunnel, the sense of satisfaction and fulfillment that comes from knowing you've done your best.

The Minor Arcana

The Minor Arcana cards, similar to an ordinary deck of playing cards, have four suits. Cards in each suit are numbered from one to ten and are thus linked with **numerology**'s symbolism. Each suit also includes a King, Queen, Knight, and Page (referred to as the court cards). These cards often represent people, although they can have other meanings and purposes. Finally, each suit also contains an Ace. In the Waite deck, the scenes or symbols on all the cards of the Minor Arcana represent the card's meaning.

THE FOUR SUITS

The four suits in many decks are called Wands, Pentacles, Swords, and Cups. During the medieval period, the suits represented the four main classes of society—the nobility, the clergy, the merchant class, and the working class. Today, the correspondences remain but are expanded—the wealthy, old-money class corresponds to the medieval nobility class. The clergy category expands to include the professionals and academics; the merchant class now includes people in business and people employed by corporate institutions; and the blue collar or service positions are the equivalent of the medieval working class.

BACKBONE OF THE TAROT

The four suits are fundamental to the Tarot's structure and composition. The suits correspond to the four elements, which are the building blocks of life, the vital and primal forces of the universe. These elements—earth, air, fire, and water—exist everywhere in this world, not only in a physical sense, but also as vibrations or energies. These elements represent or symbolize the four directions, the four seasons, the four Gospels in Christianity, the primary tools used by magicians, and the Four Noble Truths in Buddhism.

Although the suit symbols are most evident on the Minor Arcana cards, they also appear in the Major Arcana. The Magician or Magus, for instance, is usually pictured with the symbols of all four suits before him, indicating his mastery of all the elements. The four suits may turn up on the World card, too, where they suggest a balance of these fundamental forces.

MATCHING SUITS TO LIFE-AREA CONCERNS

These suits help you pinpoint the areas of life that need your attention, because each of the suits represents a distinct realm of activity, experience, and personal growth. When many cards of the same suit appear in a reading, it's a clear indication that the person consulting the Tarot is concerned about a particular area of life—or should be. A reading about a relationship, for example, will usually involve several cards in the suit of Cups, whereas Pentacles are likely to predominate in a reading about finances.

OVERVIEW OF WANDS

The suit of Wands corresponds to the element of fire. Fire is active, outer-directed, linked with Spirit, will, self-expression, and inspiration. It suggests growth, expansion, and personal power. Because fire represents archetypal masculine or yang energy, the symbolism used to depict this suit in the Tarot is distinctly phallic. Some decks use other images for the suit of Wands—rods, staves, clubs, branches sprouting leaves, lances, arrows, torches, or divining rods.

Often the people on the Wands cards (in storytelling decks) are shown as warriors, heroes, leaders, or magicians, dynamic and creative people who charge forth into life with confidence and enthusiasm. They may ride proud steeds, wave flags, or wear garlands. Whatever they are doing, they seem to be enjoying themselves. Even when they face challenges, as the Five and Ten cards frequently show, these courageous and hardy individuals seem fully capable of handling the difficulties placed before them and succeeding at whatever they undertake.

The Number of Decks Is Infinite

You can find a Tarot deck to suit almost anyone's interests. The Baseball Tarot depicts Wands as—you guessed it—baseball bats. The Cooperstown Tarot depicts Cups as baseball gloves.

When Wands appear in a spread or reading, it's usually an indication that some sort of action or growth is afoot. You might be embarking on an adventure of some kind or may be required to muster your courage in a challenging endeavor. Perhaps you could benefit from using your intuition instead of logic to solve a problem. Maybe you need to have fun, take some risks, assert yourself, or be creative.

OVERVIEW OF SWORDS

The suit of Swords relates to the element of air. Like fire, air is a masculine/yang force, so its symbol, too, is obviously phallic. Although usually depicted as a mighty battle sword, the suit's symbol may be represented by ordinary knives, athames (ritual daggers used by magicians), scythes, axes, guns, or spears. Some swords are sturdy and functional, others are ornate, reminiscent of King Arthur's Excalibur. In the Wheel of Change deck, Swords are presented as shards of broken glass. However, the weapon represented by this suit is the intellect. As such, Swords symbolize rational thinking, logic, analysis, communication, and the power of the mind. The Child's Play Tarot uses pencils to denote the intellectual quality of this suit.

Storytelling decks frequently show the characters on the Swords cards as warriors, scholars, sages, teachers, or seekers, serious and dispassionate individuals who pursue answers to life's great questions. The Nine and Ten of Swords, in particular, frequently depict painful scenes of worry, anxiety, and stress, which may be the result of too much thinking or relying too heavily on the intellect.

When Swords turn up in a reading, it often means that mental or verbal activity is a priority. Perhaps you are overworking your mind. Or you might need to use your head and examine an issue clearly and rationally. The King of Swords, for instance, can advise you not to let your heart rule your head. Swords also represent communication, study, or cutting through murky situations with logic and discrimination.

OVERVIEW OF CUPS

The suit of Cups is associated with the element of water. Water's energy is receptive, inner-directed, reflective, connected with the emotions, creativity, and intuition. Because water is a feminine or yin element, its symbols suggest the womb. In the Tarot, Cups are usually shown as chalices or goblets, but any type of vessel can depict the nature of the suit. Some decks picture them as bowls, cauldrons, vases, urns, flowers, pitchers, coffee mugs, steins, baskets, or bottles. Regardless of the imagery, the principle is the same—Cups represent the ability to receive and hold.

For the most part, the scenes that appear on these cards suggest comfort, security, and contentment. Because the suit of Cups represents the emotions, the people on the cards are usually shown in relationships of some kind— romantic, familial, friendship. The Two of Cups symbolizes partnership, and frequently a man and woman appear together in a loving manner on the card. Three women friends often grace the Three of Cups, while the Ten of Cups depicts a happy home and family life.

A reading that contains many Cups usually emphasizes emotions and/or relationships. Depending on the cards involved, you may be enjoying positive interactions with people you care about, or are seeking greater fulfillment in matters of the heart. Perhaps you are suffering a loss or disappointment, or are on your way to recovery and emotional renewal.

OVERVIEW OF PENTACLES

Pentacles or pentagrams (five-pointed stars) correspond to the earth element. Like water, earth is a feminine/yin force that energetically relates to the Earth as the source of sustenance, security, and stability. The suit of Pentacles represents practical matters, money and resources, the body, and the material world. Tarot decks often portray the suit as coins or discs, sometimes as shields, stones, rings, shells, crystals, wheels, stars, clocks, or loaves of bread. Regardless of the actual image used, the suit symbolizes physical resources, values, practical concerns, material goods, property, and forms of monetary exchange—things that sustain us on the earthly plane.

Storytelling decks often depict people on the Pentacles cards engaged in some form of work or commerce, or enjoying the fruits of their labors and the things money can buy. The Three of Pentacles in the Waite deck, for instance, shows a craftsman working at a forge. The Ten of Pentacles presents a picture of domestic security, abundance, and comfort. The Five of Pentacles, on the other hand, portrays a sad image of poverty and need.

When Pentacles appear in a spread, it's a sign that financial or work-related matters are prominent in the mind of the person for whom the reading is being done. In some cases, these cards can also signify physical or health issues, or other situations involving the body or one's physical capabilities. The Queen of Pentacles, for example, can indicate a sensual woman who is at home in her body, who loves good food, creature comforts, and the finer things in life. Depending on the cards, this suit may suggest a need to focus on practical concerns. Or you could be too security-conscious and are putting emphasis on material things at the expense of spiritual, emotional, or intellectual considerations.

NUMEROLOGY AND THE TAROT

The numbers on the pip cards of the Minor Arcana are of primary significance. Regardless of whether the deck you use includes storytelling images on these cards, pay attention to the number and the Minor Arcana suit, for this combination provides the essential information in a reading.

Symbolically speaking, numbers are not merely arithmetic used to denote quantities. According to the ancient, sacred art of numerology, each number also has a unique power and secret significance, applicable both to the spiritual and the material worlds. Cultures with an esoteric tradition have long honored and understood the sacred symbolism of numbers. Each number possesses its own special characteristics. In fact, numbers could be considered our most common and familiar symbols.

When interpreting the number cards of the Minor Arcana, the suit will tell you the area of life to which the number card refers—the nature of the influences and forces at work and on which the specific number is commenting. By combining the meanings of the suit and the number featured on a card, you can determine how the card applies to the particular situation for which the reading is being given.

INTERPRETING NUMBERS ONE THROUGH TEN

ONE (THE ACE)
One signifies new beginnings. It implies something coming into being, the starting point of a whole new cycle. It represents self-development, creativity, action, progress, a new chance, a rebirth.

TWO
The essence of Two is duality. This number depicts some kind of union or partnership, with another person, a spiritual entity, or two parts of yourself. Two also represents the balance of polarities such as yin and yang, male and female, private and public, separate and together.

Two furthers the direction initiated with the Ace. It represents stabilizing and affirming the new opportunity. Sometimes Two shows a need to achieve balance with whatever new factor is being added to the situation that began with the Ace. Whether favorable or unfavorable, this addition will be of importance to you. Depending on the reading, the Two suggests either increased chances for a desirable outcome or greater obstacles involved in achieving that outcome.

Two's vibration can indicate sensitivity to others, perhaps to the point where you consider their needs over your own. "Two-ness" can also mean a state of immersing yourself in another person or in an idea or project.

THREE
The essence of Three expresses the trinity of Mind, Body, and Spirit. It is the number of self-expression and communication, of expansion, openness, optimism, and clarity.

With the Three, you begin to open up and see the big picture, understanding the details of how One and Two combine in your own process of growth and evolution. This is the point at which the project, idea, or relationship you initiated earlier now begins to take form. Three says "Go," but if unfavorable factors are involved, caution is advised.

Three represents movement, action, growth, and development, but in some cases expansion can happen too fast. You may scatter your energies or spread yourself too thin. There is a tendency to leap before you look, or to buy now and pay later. However, properly handled, Three's vibration is cheerful, optimistic, and pleasant, representing a period of happiness and benefits, so long as you pay attention to what you are doing.

FOUR
The number Four equates with foundation. There are four elements, four directions, and four seasons, so Four suggests totality, stability, and security. When Fours appear in a reading, it can indicate a time for self-discipline through work and service, productivity, organization, and pragmatism to establish a sound foundation.

Clarity is important now, so that you can work effectively to make your situation turn out positively. If you are in a place you want to be—a home, job, relationship—you might have to work to maintain stability; if you aren't where you want to be, drawing Fours suggests it's time to plan and work to make appropriate changes.

At this time, life can seem to be all work and no play, but sometimes that's necessary for you to accomplish your objectives. If your goals and purpose are clear, you won't mind doing the work, for you see the end result as beneficial. When Fours turn up in a reading, the message is to take slow, steady, determined steps and move patiently to bring your dreams to fruition.

FIVE

Five is the number of freedom, instability, and change. Its vibration is active, physical, impulsive, impatient, resourceful, curious, and playful. Drawing Fives in a reading suggests excitement, adventure, movement, and challenges afoot.

Although Fives encourage you to take initiative, embark on a journey, or start that new project, consider the risks, too. When Fives appear in a reading, you are willing to take risks because you love the excitement involved in the situation. The cards around the Five will indicate whether there is real danger or if things will work out to your advantage.

Five's energy can be too much to handle at times, especially if you tend to be a quiet, sensitive person. When excitement and change seem to be happening too fast, you might feel as though you've been caught in a whirlwind. Thus Fives are often connected with stress and instability. You might need to move more slowly and gain perspective before continuing on the course.

SIX

Six is the number of service and social responsibility, caring, compassion, and community involvement. It signifies peace and quiet after the storm of Five. This is a time to keep it simple and attend to everyday needs, to rest, and to get into harmony with yourself and your surroundings. Any misunderstandings that occurred during an earlier period of upheaval can now be resolved harmoniously.

When Sixes appear in a reading, it's time to stop and catch your breath, realizing that you have created a comfortable pattern and can reap the rewards of your previous planning (Four) and risk taking (Five). You feel centered and at ease with yourself and your circumstances. Unfavorable cards in the reading may indicate difficult circumstances yet to be faced, but Six cards rarely show anything negative themselves.

Six's vibration is cooperative; it can represent working with others or providing service of some kind. Just remember to take care of your own needs, too. In some cases, Sixes in a reading can show a tendency toward reclusiveness—just vegging out at home to enjoy a time of ease, especially after a period of intense activity or stress.

SEVEN

The number Seven symbolizes the inner life, solitude, and soul-searching. Seven is a mystical number depicting wisdom and spirituality; there are seven heavens, seven days of the week (the seventh being holy), seven colors in the visible spectrum, seven notes in a musical scale, and seven major **chakras**.

When Sevens appear in a reading, it indicates a time of turning inward to discover the meaning of life, what has been happening to you, and why. You may be searching, on a psychological or spiritual level, for answers. Perhaps you feel an intense need to be alone. Seven often refers to birth and rebirth, religious inclinations and spiritual resources. Some people retreat from the busyness of everyday life at this time, take vows of some kind, or begin to practice ritual as part of their inner development. Emblematic of the path of solitude, analysis, and contemplation, Seven marks a time when you are exploring your own individuality in your own way.

This is not a time to begin projects related to the material or financial world. Your energy is focused on the inner rather than the outer realm. Now is a good time to create a sanctuary for contemplation, a private place where you can examine your past experiences and evaluate the present. You might wish to study or research metaphysical subjects, start paying attention to dreams and ESP experiences—whatever will help you to find your own true path in life. In some cases, Sevens in the reading may indicate that you are spending too much time alone and need to socialize.

EIGHT

Eight represents abundance, material prosperity, and worldly power or influence. It is the number of leadership and authority. On the spiritual level, Eight symbolizes cosmic consciousness; infinity's symbol is a figure Eight turned on its side. This powerful number indicates you possess the organizational and managerial skills that contribute to material success—or that you need to develop them. If you have been devoting much of your time and energy to spiritual progress, the appearance of Eights in a reading indicates it's time to get your financial or worldly affairs in order.

The Wholeness of Eight

As the infinity glyph symbolizes wholeness, the number Eight points to the development of multiple aspects of your life—physical, mental, and spiritual.

Eight's vibration is linked with honor, respect, equality, awards, public recognition, power, and abundance in all areas of life. When you draw Eights, the potential for achieving these benefits is likely, but sincerity and dedication are needed.

The Eight cards also caution you to consider the welfare of others as well as yourself. If there are unfavorable factors in the reading, you may need to be careful with money or possessions. Eights reversed can indicate that you have many issues around abundance—or the lack of it—yet to be resolved.

NINE

The number Nine equates with humanitarianism. It represents universal compassion, tolerance for the many differences among peoples, and the attainment of wisdom through experience. Drawing Nines suggests you have reached a level where you are comfortable dedicating your life to others' welfare, or to some worthy cause. The challenge is to avoid getting so caught up in the big picture—the greatest good for the greatest number—that you neglect what is closest to you.

Nine symbolizes integration and, in a reading, shows that you have established your life priorities—you know what you want and how you intend to get it. You feel a flow of vitality between all the different parts of yourself. You understand the interaction between you and the world as a continuing process of living, being, moving. The Nine vibration allows you to see beyond the boundaries of the self into the totality of the universal. You are able to give freely of yourself because you feel complete within yourself.

The last single-digit number, Nine represents the end of a cycle. It's time to tie up loose ends. In most cases, the Nine cards depict fulfillment, completion, wholeness, and the sense of satisfaction that comes from having reached a peak after a long, arduous climb.

TEN

Ten represents both an ending and a beginning, the point of transition from the completed cycle to the new cycle, which has not yet manifested. When Tens show up in a reading, whatever you have been working on or involved with is over. You've got whatever you are going to get out of it, and now it is time to bring in the new cycle that's been waiting in the wings.

Whether the cycle that's ending has been good or bad, you know it's over now, which is especially gratifying if you have been experiencing rocky times. If you have become complacent during a good period, drawing Tens tells you the time has come to challenge yourself and reach for a higher level. As a compound number, Ten, though a form of One, has more impact and therefore adds an extra dimension in a reading. Like ascending to a higher level of a spiral staircase, you can look down at precisely where you began and chart your progress. Now you have a choice to either stagnate in familiar and comfortable territory or to take a chance and start something new and different.

As happens in any period of transition, you may experience discomfort about making the decision to stay put or move on. Both options are available; both require thought and consideration. You might feel you are sitting on the fence, with one foot on either side, not sure whether to jump all the way over. Transitions are like that, and sometimes it takes quite a while to get both feet on the same side of the fence. However, you know that he who hesitates is lost, and though you have the luxury of postponing both decision and action for a little while, when Tens show up in a reading it's a signal that a decision must be made.

How to Do a Reading

Now that you've absorbed the interpretations of the various cards of the Tarot, it's time to learn how to put this knowledge into practice to discover your inner strengths and your true path. It's worth stressing that the more readings you do, the better you'll get at it. As well, remember to treat your cards with respect and love—this will lead to truer readings and a deeper self-knowledge through use of the Tarot.

There are numerous ways to do a reading. Each deck of Tarot cards usually comes with a book or booklet detailing one or more of the more common ways of laying out the cards for a reading. But if you have one issue or situation for which you desire insights, determine which of the four suits best represents that area. Then, pick the card within that suit that speaks most directly to your objective. For example, if your goal is to rekindle love and affection in a romantic relationship, select the Six of Cups from your deck. This card (called the Significator) is sometimes removed from the deck or left in, depending on what layout (or spread) you're using. Note that if you leave the Significator in the deck, the position in which it turns up will be extremely important.

With the cards in your palm, hold your intention for what you want from the cards in your mind. Then pick a card or lay them out in a spread, choosing a spread that's most appropriate to your inquiry (for a list of possible spreads, see *The Everything® Tarot Book, 2nd Edition*, Adams Media, 2006).

Study each card in turn and meditate on its interpretation. The location of a card within a spread is important, too. Sometimes a location or position of the card reveals something about the past, future, or present. Also notice whether or not a card is reversed (that is to say, upside down); reversed positions change the card's usual meaning.

Grow with Your Readings

As you work on specific areas of your life, you'll see your growth reflected in the cards you draw. For instance, you might pick the Ace of Pentacles when you start a money-making venture. As the project bears fruit, you might draw the Seven of Pentacles, which shows you are beginning to see the results of your efforts.

Use the Tarot to Unearth the Power of You

Although the Tarot has long been used to predict the future and provide advice on practical or mundane matters, you can use it as a personal empowerment tool. Think of the Tarot as an oracle of wisdom that can profoundly deepen your understanding of your personal power, enrich your relationships with other people, and unveil your most powerful connections with your Higher Self and divine potentiality.

In her companion book to *The Sacred Circle Tarot*, Anna Franklin suggests you approach the card as if you were going to enter it, like walking through a doorway, and interact with the scenario depicted there. Don't just see the images; try to experience them. Allow your senses to come into play. Feel the Sun on your face, the grass under your feet. Witness the murkiness and mystery connected with the Moon or the burning sensation of anger, jealousy, obsession, and fear depicted by the Devil.

Write down what you glean from your study—your insights, questions, impressions, and feelings. Notice how the energies represented by the cards are playing out in your own life—or how you would like to be able to express them. Because the trump cards are quite complex, it's probably best to limit your study to one card at a time, until you understand it—even if it takes several days or weeks.

GETTING PRACTICAL

Use the Tarot the way it has been employed for centuries—to predict the future or to gain insights into practical matters, such as a job or career, relationship, family, financial, sexual, or health issues. Pull a card each morning and see how its symbolism and meaning is reflected back to you throughout your day in people you meet, circumstances you encounter, and synchronous events you notice.

DEVELOP YOUR INTUITION

Devote some time to developing your intuition as it plays a vital role in the accuracy of your readings. Meditation is a time-honored practice for deepening your sense of your inner self and strengthening your intuitive powers. Dream work, too, can enhance your intuitive abilities. Through your intuition you gain access to a vast body of knowledge stored in your unconscious mind. Before you do a reading sit for a moment with the cards in hand as though tuning in and energizing them.

For your spiritual growth and empowerment, you might consider doing a single, complex reading that allows for repeated in-depth analysis, as though peeling back the layers of an onion, to arrive at interpretations gleaned from weeks or months of studying that reading. The Tree of Life spread is an example of a spread that is more complex, comprehensive, and mystical.

THE TREE OF LIFE SPREAD

Based on the kabbalistic Tree of Life, this spread provides insights into the querent's spiritual nature, as well as the outer conditions that are related to the matter at hand. The card positions correspond to the ten *sephirot* (which represent the ten characteristics of divinity) on the tree. (Note: The Tree of Life spread is read from the bottom up, from card 10 to card 1.)

Card 1: Light (outcome)
Card 2: Wisdom (goals, changes, power)
Card 3: Understanding (receptivity, creativity, limitations)
Card 4: Mercy (abundance, generosity, memories)
Card 5: Severity, strength (struggle, activity, destruction)
Card 6: Beauty (love, compassion, new insights)
Card 7: Victory (romance, emotions, desires)
Card 8: Glory (knowledge, analysis, discrimination)
Card 9: Foundation (sexual issues, illusions, fears, the unconscious)
Card 10: Kingdom (physicality, money, practical matters)

KEEP A TAROT JOURNAL

A Tarot journal or log of your daily readings will reveal your progress. Note the date, what's going on in your life, and any particular concerns or areas of interest. Write down insights or questions that come to you in connection with the card or cards you draw each day. Periodically, you may wish to look back at the cards you drew previously to see how a matter has evolved or how your knowledge has grown over time. Something that was unclear to you before might make sense now. In this way, you can follow your progress and understand how the Tarot is guiding you along your path.

DO DAILY AFFIRMATIONS

Let the Tarot inspire you to pursue personal growth. Write out and say an **affirmation** (a short, positive statement that describes a condition or change you wish to produce). An affirmation may be a phrase you coin yourself, a quote by someone you respect, or a sentence from a book. The key is specificity: "I am truly blessed with _____. Fill in the blank with words like "more money than I need," or, "vibrant health," or, "emotionally healthy relationships."

REPEAT YOUR AFFIRMATION OFTEN

By repeating the affirmation regularly, you reprogram your subconscious and, in time, bring about the desired result. Be aware, however, that you cannot lie to your subconscious. If you proclaim an untruth, your conscious will know it and the affirmation won't work. Instead, find language that expresses the truth.

SEE TAROT CARDS AS VISUAL AFFIRMATIONS

If you want to find a romantic partner, select the Two of Cups or the Lovers from your deck and gaze at it while you contemplate your intention. If you like, you can display the card where you will see it often. Each time you look at it, you'll be reminded of your objective.

You can work on developing inner qualities in the same way. Choose the High Priestess if you want to improve your intuition. Strength can help you increase your personal power and confidence. The Queen of Cups is good for encouraging flexibility and acceptance.

COMBINE VERBAL AND VISUAL AFFIRMATIONS

Although you can work on more than one goal at a time, it's usually best to limit yourself to a few that you consider most urgent or important. Choose cards that represent the end results you desire. Spend at least a few minutes each day contemplating the cards you've chosen, allowing the symbols to imprint themselves on your subconscious. If you wish, you can combine the cards with verbal affirmations—stare at the card while you repeat your affirmation aloud. You're more likely to get fast, effective results if you combine the two techniques.

Some Tarot decks are designed specifically for this purpose. The Tarot Affirmations deck, for instance, combines the imagery of the Universal Waite pack with selected affirmations and sayings. Each card is printed with several inspirational thoughts that relate to the meaning of the card.

THE SIGNIFICANCE OF A SIGNIFICATOR

The Significator links you (or other person for whom the reading is being done) to all the other cards in the spread. When you read for yourself, the Significator brings you into the reading; it serves as your representative for the duration of the reading. Court cards (King, Queen, Knight, and Page) are often chosen as Significators because they depict people. Often the Significator you choose relates to your sex, age, and astrological sign. It may also tie in with your profession, interests, physical characteristics, and other personal factors. For example, if you are a fire sign man over the age of thirty-five, who holds down an executive job or is active in the arts, and/or has light or reddish coloring, you would choose the King of Wands to represent you. If you are a sixteen-year-old Capricorn girl, you'd probably choose the Page of Pentacles as your Significator. The following list includes astrological signs and other information about the Minor Arcana's court cards.

Astrological Significators

King of Wands	A mature man, born under the zodiac sign Aries, Leo, or Sagittarius
Queen of Wands	A mature woman, born under the zodiac sign Aries, Leo, or Sagittarius
Knight of Wands	A young male, born under the zodiac sign Aries, Leo, or Sagittarius
Page of Wands	A young female, born under the zodiac sign Aries, Leo, or Sagittarius
King of Pentacles	A mature man, born under the zodiac sign Taurus, Virgo, or Capricorn
Queen of Pentacles	A mature woman, born under the zodiac sign Taurus, Virgo, or Capricorn
Knight of Pentacles	A young male, born under the zodiac sign Taurus, Virgo, or Capricorn
Page of Pentacles	A young female, born under the zodiac sign Taurus, Virgo, or Capricorn
King of Swords	A mature man, born under the zodiac sign Gemini, Libra, or Aquarius
Queen of Swords	A mature woman, born under the zodiac sign Gemini, Libra, or Aquarius
Knight of Swords	A young male, born under the zodiac sign Gemini, Libra, or Aquarius
Page of Swords	A young female, born under the zodiac sign Gemini, Libra, or Aquarius
King of Cups	A mature man, born under the zodiac sign Cancer, Scorpio, or Pisces
Queen of Cups	A mature woman, born under the zodiac sign Cancer, Scorpio, or Pisces
Knight of Cups	A young male, born under the zodiac sign Cancer, Scorpio, or Pisces
Page of Cups	A young female, born under the zodiac sign Cancer, Scorpio, or Pisces

Keep in mind that you aren't limited to the Court Cards. You may prefer to select a Major Arcana card, such as the Hermit, the Empress, or the Fool to represent yourself. Or you might feel a connection to a card that depicts your state of mind at present—perhaps the artisan, shown by the Three of Pentacles, or the bored homemaker, depicted by the Four of Cups.

Choose a Significator who will represent you in all readings, or change Significators periodically based on the circumstances of the reading. If you've recently given up your job to travel the world, you may decide the Knight of Wands describes you better than the King of Pentacles.

TYPES OF SPREADS

The simplest way to start reading the cards is to stick to simple spreads such as one-card or three-card spreads. As you feel more confident and know the meanings of the cards, proceed to spreads involving more cards such as the Celtic Cross. This popular and versatile card spread requires a Significator. Place it on the table to bring you (or the person for whom the reading is being done) into the reading.

(Place the next card on top of the Significator.)

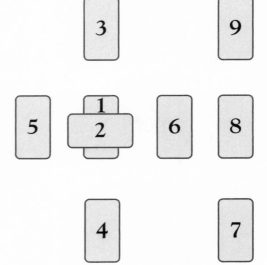

Card 1: This covers you and describes your immediate concerns.

(Place the next card horizontally across Card 1 to make a cross.)

Card 2: This crosses you and describes obstacles facing you.

Card 3: This crowns you and describes what is known to you objectively.

Card 4: This is beneath you and describes the foundation of the concern or past influences affecting the situation. It can also show what is unknown about the situation.

Card 5: This is behind you and describes past influences now fading away.

Card 6: This is before you and describes new circumstances coming into being—the near future.

Card 7: This is your self and describes your current state of mind.

Card 8: This is your house and describes the circumstances surrounding the situation.

Card 9: This is what you hope or fear, perhaps what you both want and fear.

Card 10: This is what will come and describes the likely future outcome.

Relationships

For questions about financial relationships, watch for cards with pentacles (money), wands (growth), or swords (strife). Those same cards and also cups (emotion) might appear in readings involving family relationships. For romantic relationship questions, take note of the suit of Cups and the Major Arcana cards of the Lovers and any Aces (symbolizing new beginnings) in the Tarot spread. Let's say you've recently met a man who interests you, and you are curious about the possibilities of a relationship with him.

If you want to know whether you should consider him as a prospective partner, you could use one of the yes/no types of readings that relies on your first assigning yes to certain cards (for example, the even-numbered cars) and no to others (to the-odd numbered cards).

DRAW A SINGLE CARD FOR INSIGHTS

Pull a single card for clues to the man's character. A positive card suggests pursuing things further; a negative card says don't waste your time. If initial indicators are good, and you'd like to know how to proceed with this man, lay out a more complex spread.

USE THE FOUR-CARD SPREAD

The four-card spread is easy to do. The four cards are laid in a horizontal line. The first card describes the situation. The second reveals an obstacle or opportunity you may encounter. The third card points to what action you should take. The fourth card reveals the likely outcome to the relationship.

THE IMMEDIATE SITUATION (THREE-CARD SPREAD)

Give the three-card spread a try if you are interested in the nature of the present situation (first card), understanding your attitude about what is happening (second card), or what the key element you need to consider might be (third card).

Once you've entered into a relationship with this man, you might feel a need to get more advice or information about him and your situation, and thus you might want to try more complicated spreads.

USE AFFIRMATIONS FOR RELATIONSHIP GOALS

Consider how you might use an affirmation to further your relationship goals. For example, "I am now attracting an emotionally healthy, fiscally responsible kindred spirit as my romantic partner in my life." Or, for a relationship that is ending, you might focus on your own empowerment. "I am letting go of a relationship that has come to its natural karmic end, and I am healing and moving toward balance and wholeness in this new phase of my life." Visually affirm your romantic feelings for your partner with a meditation on the Lovers card.

Sex

Relationships and sex questions often overlap. Use the three-card spread or the simple yes/no spread if you want verification that your timing is right or whether or not to enter a sexual relationship with someone. If you want to understand sex, study the suit of Wands. Many Tarot readers say wands symbolize sexuality, passion, fertility, and issues pertaining to fidelity (although cups are usually a stronger indicator of emotional bonding). The Ace of Wands can represent sexual attraction, arousal, and stimulation. Like the aces of the other suits, the Ace of Wands can also indicate the flowering of a new relationship based on a strong sexual attraction (when the reading is about sex).

Of the cards of the Major Arcana, take note of the Wheel of Fortune card if it shows up in a reading about sex. The imagery of a serpent descending on the left side represents the earth and the sexual energy that arises from it. This card almost always heralds good fortune coming as a result of what you yourself have put into motion, even if you aren't totally aware of what you have done to initiate the process. You may have initiated a new romance or had a chance encounter that got the ball rolling—or the wheel turning.

Money

If you are unsure about your economic or income picture for the future, you might try the general life-conditions spread. This spread can be used to answer just about any question. It provides insight into the querent's psychological state while shedding light on practical matters.

GENERAL LIFE-CONDITIONS SPREAD

Card 1: Who you are right now?

Card 2: What is affecting you?

Card 3: What is it you value?

Card 4: What's bothering you?

Card 5: What does the short term hold?

Card 6: What does the long term hold?

QUICK SPREAD FOR AN AREA OF CONCERN

Alternatively, you could decide to position the cards in a quick-answer spread (a single, horizontal line) involving money. Notice especially when Pentacle suit cards show up (as that suit represents coins, money, and material gain). Major Arcana cards to watch for include the Emperor (prosperity), the Chariot (financial success), and the Wheel of Fortune (money and success).

Card 1: Concern

Card 2: Immediate past

Card 3: Immediate future

Card 4: Querent's state of mind

Card 5: Obstacle

Card 6: Help

Card 7: Outcome

To attract money, you might say an affirmation such as, "I am a wealth magnet and in the process of attracting into my life money from sources both known and unknown to me." Notice whether or not the suit of Pentacles (money) shows up in your personal readings even as money begins to manifest in your life. Take visual cues from the Wheel of Fortune or the Emperor to remind yourself throughout the day that you are in the process of attracting more money, using it wisely, and growing your wealth.

Health

Use the Tarot to help you get to the bottom of your state of health. If you feel like something is out of balance in your body, do a reading to see what the problem might be. Perhaps your heart hurts but the pain is originating from emotions rather than a physical cause. You might see cups (emotion) or swords (strife) as the source. Perhaps you are just tired from your life tasks or work responsibilities. Or, possibly something is out of balance but remains hidden—an illness or disease that has not yet declared itself.

You can find out a lot about what might be affecting your physical, emotional, psychological, and spiritual well-being through a horoscope spread.

WHAT DOES THE HANGED MAN REVEAL?

Look also for the Hanged Man as the card frequently denotes transformation that is the result of disease or illness. If you get this card in a reading, it may be telling you it is time to pause and suspend ordinary activities. Use such times to nourish your body, mind, and spirit.

A Life-Changing Event

Often, the Hanged Man signifies going through a major transformation, perhaps caused by illness or some loss. The result has shaken up your old way of life and made you realize that there is more to life than money, material goods, and physical reality.

The Death card in the reverse position would indicate illness, injury, and immobility, but the card seldom means a physical death. More often, it represents an ending of a cycle or something else in order for a rebirth or renewal to take place.

Use the three-card spread to signify health in body, mind, and spirit. Meditate on the cards' imagery. See the cards as icons through which information goes from the eyes by way of the mind to the heart, thereby in communication with your Higher Self who already knows what must be done. Allow your intuition to bring forth that information.

THE HOROSCOPE SPREAD

In this spread, twelve cards are laid out in a circle, and each card corresponds to one of the twelve houses of the astrological chart. Place a thirteenth card, a Significator, in the center if you want. The first house begins at the nine o'clock position, and the cards are dealt counterclockwise. Each house refers to a specific area of life; thus, the cards are read in reference to the house in which they fall. This spread is not generally used to answer specific questions—it can provide an overview of your life at the time of the reading. Your Sun sign or birth chart are not factors in a reading that uses this spread.

THE FIRST HOUSE: THE SELF

The first house refers to the physical body and appearance, as well as your vitality, identity, sense of self, and the immediate impression you make on others.

THE SECOND HOUSE: PERSONAL RESOURCES

The second house shows what you consider valuable. This includes money, personal possessions, resources, earning ability, and your identification with what you own.

THE THIRD HOUSE: THE NEAR ENVIRONMENT

The third house covers three areas of life that at first may not seem related, but taken together represent normal daily life or what astrologers call the near environment: communications related to the routine of everyday life; involvement with your friends, neighbors, siblings, and the community at large; and short-distance travel in your near environment.

THE FOURTH HOUSE: ROOTS

The fourth house represents the foundation of your life—home, family, parents (especially the mother), tradition, heritage, the past, your homeland—in short, your roots.

THE FIFTH HOUSE: SELF-EXPRESSION

The fifth house shows your creative and self-expressive side, which may play out as artistic endeavors, romantic relationships, hobbies and amusements, or children.

THE SIXTH HOUSE: HEALTH AND SERVICE

The sixth house relates to health, health-oriented routines including nutrition and exercise, and the link between your work and your health. It also describes your daily work or chores, duties, job-oriented relationships, service to others, and the capacity for self-sacrifice.

THE SEVENTH HOUSE: ONE-ON-ONE RELATIONSHIPS

Traditionally the house of marriage and partnerships, the seventh house represents all one-on-one relationships—business and personal, including relationships with your enemies.

THE EIGHTH HOUSE: TRANSFORMATION

The eighth is the house of the past, transformative change, death, inheritance, and other people's resources. In this case, death usually refers to the end of something old so that something new can emerge. The eighth house also shows how another's resources affect you.

THE NINTH HOUSE: HIGHER KNOWLEDGE

The ninth house represents the higher mind, philosophy, religion/spirituality, the law, and advanced education, as well as long-distance travel, especially to foreign lands. This house shows your search for meaning and how you go about expanding your horizons and knowledge of the world.

THE TENTH HOUSE: LIFE TASK

The tenth house represents social or professional status, career, public image, and parents (your father especially). Authority, responsibilities, honor, and reputation are tenth-house matters, too.

THE ELEVENTH HOUSE: FRIENDSHIPS

The eleventh house refers to your friends and groups with which you're affiliated. Your goals, hopes, and wishes are shown by this house, too.

THE TWELFTH HOUSE: THE HIDDEN REALM

The twelfth house represents that which is hidden, or not yet revealed, including your dreams and fantasies. It also reveals your latent talents, as well as fears, weaknesses, secrets, and unknown enemies. Because matters associated with this sector are often unknown to us, the house is sometimes connected with self-undoing.

Work

Information and insights are forthcoming in spreads about your work, job, or career issues when you ask your question of the cards after a brief period of reflection about your greatest concerns. Sometimes, however, an unresolved work issue becomes more complicated the longer it continues. The thirteen-card spread describes the evolution of a situation over a period of time. After shuffling and cutting the deck, lay out thirteen cards in three rows.

THE THIRTEEN-CARD SPREAD

Card 1: Shows the origin of the issue at hand.

Cards 2 through 11: Show development of the situation—positive and negative conditions, opportunities and obstacles, progress, and setbacks. The linear pattern lets you see how each step has led to the next and how it influences the current concern.

Card 12: Reveals the near future.

Card 13: Indicates the more distant future.

Summary

Now that you've learned what each card of the Tarot's Major and Minor Arcana cards represent, how to interpret them for insights, and how to do several spreads, it will be up to you to set aside time to work with the cards and deepen your understanding. Remember, the Major Arcana cards are akin to the lens of a telescope to study your life's distant, far-reaching, and universal issues, while the Minor Arcana cards more closely typify the lens of a microscope through which to view basic areas of your daily life. So whether you seek big-picture revelation about your life's spectacular potential or up-close insights for day-to-day occurrences, you have a potent and powerful tool for wisdom in your Tarot deck.

Part Three

PALMISTRY

If you look deeply into the palm of your hand, you will see your parents and all generations of your ancestors . . . alive in this moment . . . present in your body. You are the continuation of each of these people.

—Thich Nhat Hanh (1926–),
Vietnamese monk, activist, and writer

It's often said that the eyes are the windows of the soul, but in many ways, it's the hands that offer the greatest insights into who you are and what you can become. As distinctive as the genetic code that sets you apart from every other individual on the planet, your hand contains unique lines that tell a personal story. No two individuals are the same when it comes to palms and fingerprints, including identical twins. Find out what your hand reveals about you by delving deeper into the power of hand reading and use what you learn to embark on or continue your process of self-discovery. See how **palmistry** can guide your ambition, lead you to helpful people and meaningful relationships, and enrich your life with practical pointers and revelatory insights.

Introduction: What Is Palmistry?

Prized as a sacred art in ancient Egypt, India, Italy, and Greece, palmistry has evolved into a powerful intuitive practice that focuses on reading and extracting meaning from the lines, textures, shapes, and idiosyncrasies of the hand—not the palm alone, but also the fingers, knuckles, wrists, mounts (fleshy areas), joints, and the overall hand shape. Palmistry can reveal the past, but as one of the oldest forms of divination (predicting the future), it also reveals possibilities that lie ahead. Through palmistry, you can discover the blueprint for your life and gain insight into the lives of others around you. From the lines on your hand you will be able to correlate paths you've already chosen and discover others that you might choose to take. In the palm creases and other markings, you will discern a vast world of potentiality.

As it is practiced today, palmistry offers a complete personality profile of an individual, including his or her major life choices, challenges, and opportunities. And it isn't only palmists who study the hands. Because hand and fingerprints are so unique, they are invaluable to criminologists and law enforcement experts, who must rely on evidence to solve crimes. The palm reader assists in developing criminal profiles to be used along with other pieces of forensic evidence from crime scenes to build a case. While some palm readers rely on their own intuition in reading the marks on a criminal's hands, others call in specialists known as investigative psychics in order to develop fuller, more complete pictures of those involved in criminal investigations.

▲▲▲▲▲▲▲▲▲▲▲▲▲▲▲▲▲▲▲▲▲▲▲▲▲▲▲▲▲

Your Hand Reflects Your Mind

Your palm holds your secrets, too. Carl G. Jung, Swiss psychiatrist and founder of analytical psychology, believed that palmistry is the outward appearance of secrets we try to keep under lock and key in our subconscious minds. Another noted psychologist, Charlotte Wolff, believed that "the hand is a visible part of the brain." She even diagnosed many of her patients using hand-reading techniques.

▼▼▼▼▼▼▼▼▼▼▼▼▼▼▼▼▼▼▼▼▼▼▼▼▼▼▼▼▼

THE BASICS

Each person's palm has six **major lines**, although these lines vary tremendously in their shape, texture, and length. These are the **heart line**, **head line**, **life line**, **Mercury** (health) **line**, **Apollo** (creativity) **line**, and **Saturn** (fate) **line**.

HEART, HEAD, AND LIFE LINES

- The heart line can tell you about your emotional life, complete with your insecurities, fears, and passions. It also indicates potential for love or marriage and is sometimes incorrectly referred to as the marriage line.
- The head line can provide you with a clearer picture of your mental abilities, career or business acumen, and potential for success.
- The life line is more than just an indicator of how long you will live. This line speaks to your personal longevity, stamina, and vitality.

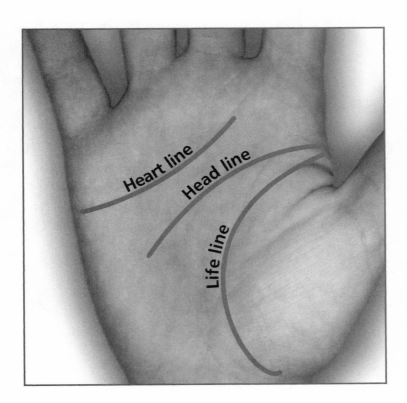

MERCURY, APOLLO, AND SATURN LINES

- The Mercury line carries information about your health (and especially your central nervous system, which is the "messenger" system in your body). This line may also show your spirit of adventure and a healthy curiosity.
- The Apollo line demonstrates your potential for successful development of special talents, creativity, and life energies.
- The Saturn line is your **fate line**. It can tell you what fate has in store for you, and whether you are willing or able to accept the responsibilities that will come with whatever fate deals you in life.

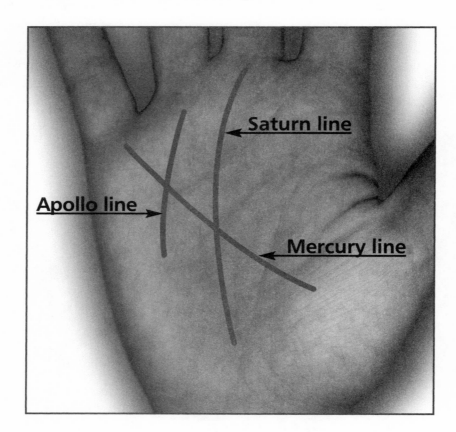

SPECIAL MARKINGS

Special hand markings that carry meaning in palmistry also vary quite a bit, and each marking has a particular interpretation that relates to a challenge or obstacle you may face. First, lines are examined in terms of their depth; then, the palm reader evaluates their unique characteristics. For instance, your life line could have several crosses or tassels around it; this is not an inherently bad thing but could definitely point to some major life obstacles you've had (or will have) to overcome.

Time is determined in specific increments along each line, and these imaginary markings (documented on palmistry charts) could well be called "mile-markers along the highway of life." These markers, too, are not hard and fast—there could be a variance of a year or more in some areas of your life. The important thing is to realize that your opportunities in life come in increments or units of time rather than on specific dates. If you're looking for a reading that says you will find the perfect mate on Thursday in January, ten years from now, you won't find what you're seeking through palmistry. Rather, palmistry will tell you during which period of your life you have the greatest chance to find lasting love and happiness.

A TWO-HANDED PROPOSITION

During a palm reading we also consider the overall size, shape, and texture of the hand. For instance, long, thin hands generally indicate that a person is creative and intuitive, while shorter, stubbier hands typically connote a hardworking or athletic type of person.

Both hands must be read to achieve the fullest picture of where you've been and where you're going in life. Your primary or **dominant hand**, often the first to be read, is the one you use more often (usually the one you write with). This hand will reveal how well you've been able to meet the challenges or opportunities presented in your minor hand. You'll notice lots of similarity between the hands, with slight to moderate variance on the lines.

Right Brain, Left Brain

Your right brain, that part that recognizes patterns and understands the relationships between objects or ideas (lateral thinking) controls your left hand. Your left brain, the part involved with reason, logic, and language (linear thinking), controls your right hand. Some palmists associate the left hand/right brain with the feminine and receptive aspects of your personality, while your right hand/left brain reflects the masculine and extroverted aspects.

Many palmists agree that the lines on your palms change as you go through life even though your fingerprints do not change. For that reason, you might choose to read and record the changes in your palms over a long period of time as you age, achieve personal and career goals, and evolve spiritually.

FINDING A GOOD READER

If you want a personal and insightful palm reading, find a professional palmist—someone who is passionate about the work and who truly knows what he or she is doing. Be aware that there are three types of palm readers: the expert, the novice, and the charlatan. While you may decide to visit the expert or the novice, you want to stay away from the charlatan.

What to Watch For

Avoid establishments that advertise palm readings, as they seldom provide analysis of good quality. Instead, ask for recommendations from friends who have sought psychic guidance through palm reading. Check with the Better Business Bureau for recommended readers; or locate palmists through reputable sources, such as a metaphysical bookstore or a palmistry society or local association of psychics, as some may read palms.

THE EXPERT

An expert palm reader likely will have conducted numerous readings, possibly for many years—perhaps for celebrities, high-profile clients, or even law enforcement. While these readers can be quite accurate, they can also be very expensive—with some charging $100 or more for a single session. Choose an expert only if you can afford it and are looking for a high-quality reading.

THE NOVICE

The novice reader likely will be fairly new to the art of palm reading. Although his or her service can be priced more appropriately, such a reader may lack the skill necessary for an in-depth, intuitive, and interpretive reading. Still, novices can provide accurate readings of your life overview and potential. Novices typically charge anywhere from $10 to $40 for a reading that lasts between fifteen and thirty minutes. More often than not, these readers can be found at local psychic fairs and in the phone book.

THE CHARLATAN

Sadly, there are charlatans everywhere who are more skilled at *pretending* to read palms than actually reading them. They know enough to skim the surface of the topic and offer a few meaningful details, but their intent and focus is to constantly request "donations" for candles, additional prayers, and the like. Initially, this type of reader might charge a small amount to start the reading, and then hike the cost by telling you that you have an "evil eye" or some kind of curse on you. To remove it, they offer a veritable laundry list of other psychic services they want you to purchase—naturally, there's a fee for each.

Another hallmark of charlatans is that they typically read only one hand and only the three major lines (heart, head, and life) as opposed to a legitimate reader, who will examine all of your lines to give you a comprehensive look at your life, accomplishments, and potential.

READ YOUR OWN PALM

Why not do a reading of your own palms? Just like any other arcane art or discipline, regular practice gives you greater understanding and helps you gain proficiency. As you progress along your chosen path of personal growth and empowerment, palm reading can richly reward you for the time you put into it. Knowing your personal life challenges and opportunities can propel you to action—to determine the best way to meet those challenges and to improve upon or capitalize on the opportunities to create a happier and more meaningful life.

AVOID PITFALLS OF COMMUNICATION

Reading the palms of friends, family members, and others around you can greatly improve your communication skills. For example, you can modify the way you communicate with others based on what you see in their palms and discover about their personalities, thus avoiding problematic communication areas and issues.

Trial Self-Reading

Try this simple tip for a self-reading. Make a copy of your palms using an inkpad or a photocopy machine. Then study the image, using a good palm reading diagram (on the Internet you can find many images showing and explaining the lines, mounts, and other markings). Use your intuition for insights; however, be prepared to separate fantasy (your desire to see something specific and special) from the reality of what the markings truly reveal.

You don't have to be a psychic to become a palmist—all you need is a receptive mind and the willingness to be honest with yourself and others. Don't fear acknowledging what you see. If it's challenging, explore that challenge. Remember that the future is all about potential and choice. There is nothing to fear.

Look at Your Hand

The first step in any palm reading begins with an overall assessment of the entire hand. Your examination necessarily would include size, color, thickness, texture, and movement. Take your time so you don't miss anything that might have relevance to your reading. The following characteristics should be noted in the initial part of the reading.

- **Size.** In general, people with small hands tend to act quickly and perhaps impulsively; those with very small hands are generally free, independent-minded thinkers. On the other hand, those with larger hands tend to be more methodical and thoughtful about their big decisions in life. People with average hands are easygoing—they react according to each situation and its own unique circumstances and are not as predictable.
- **Color or consistency.** Color represents life or vitality. If the palms are pale—white, gray, or even bluish—there are definitely health challenges (most likely circulatory in nature); red hands mean you are quick to anger; yellow, jaundiced hands mean you have a pessimistic outlook; and pink hands mean you are well-balanced and have a healthy outlook.
- **Thickness.** Tilt the hand sideways and look at its width. Is it thin or thick? Thick hands belong to easygoing, noncompetitive people; thin hands belong to goal-oriented, driven, or ambitious people who are on a specific mission in life.
- **Texture.** Fine, soft skin indicates refined tastes and usually belongs to the culturally or artistically inclined. Firm skin shows a healthy blend of physical and intellectual pursuits. Coarse, rough, or scaly skin indicates a more adventuresome, outdoorsy type for whom gloves (and personal well-being) are an afterthought.
- **Movement.** How does the hand move? Does it seem flexible? If it is, the person is also likely to be flexible in his or her thinking and general demeanor. A general rule of palmistry is that the stiffer the hand, the stiffer the demeanor. Have you ever noticed a person with hands so stiff they almost seem mechanical? People with hands this stiff typically have mental or emotional difficulties, or have a hard time trusting others.

Make a note about each of the characteristics you've observed. As you get deeper into the lines, ridges, and mounts of the hand, you'll want to look back at your initial assessment to see how developed it's become.

The Meanings of Hair

Hair on the back of a man's hand affirms his masculinity, whereas male hands that are soft and hairless frequently belong to a man more meek and introverted. Women with hair on the backs of their hands tend to be highly assertive, even aggressive. The women with hairless hands often are mild mannered and may have a weak constitution.

Look at your fourth (the pinky or little) finger as it relates to your hand. Is it farther apart than the other fingers? Usually, a little finger that points outward and is spaced significantly apart from the third finger means that you have a quick temper and are not to be reckoned with when upset. If your index finger seems to be spaced farther apart from the other fingers on your hand, you have strong leadership potential and can be a trendsetter.

CHECK OUT YOUR HAND'S SHAPE

The general shape of your hand tells a palm reader a lot about your general character. The easiest way to get a quick read on someone is to look at the shape his or her hands form—and to correlate each shape with a particular personality type. In palmistry, there are four basic shapes and one hybrid or mixed shape.

THE CONICAL OR ARTISTIC HAND

Conical shaped hands are round and have a sensual, feminine appearance. If you have this hand shape, you have a deep appreciation for the arts. If your hands feature lots of curved lines, you are an artist. Quiet, sensitive, and imaginative, you seek solace through music, art, literature, and love. The conical hand is called the **air hand**, since this element most closely captures the free spirit of individualism associated with this hand shape. If you have this hand type, you enjoy having many friends but will be quite selective when seeking a partner. Also, you likely stick to the moral high ground.

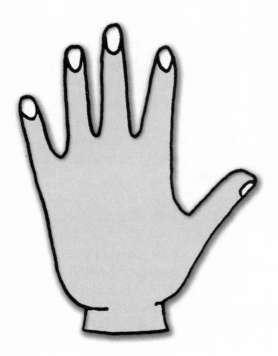

Hands and the Elements
Each type of hand represents one of four elements that the ancients believed composed all matter of our world: Conical hands are said to be air hands; **pointed hands** are **water hands**; **spatulate** hands are **fire hands**; and **square-shaped** hands are **earth hands**.

▼▼▼▼▼▼▼▼▼▼▼▼▼▼▼▼▼▼▼▼▼▼▼▼▼▼▼▼▼▼▼▼▼

THE POINTED OR PSYCHIC HAND

The long, delicate, and tapered fingers that characterize pointed or water hands are memorable if you think of those fingers pointing to spiritual truths. This is why the pointed hand is always referred to as the psychic hand—and the vast majority of those who have pointed hands possess psychic or intuitive ability. If your hands are pointed but you feel you lack psychic ability, perhaps you have psychic powers that remain as yet undeveloped. Nevertheless, if your hands are shaped like the psychic hand, it is likely your intuition and creative energy lie dormant, awaiting a clarion call to manifest. Tremendous compassion or empathy for others, as well as deep sensitivity and intensity characterize pointed hands. If you have water hands, you are highly romantic, responsive to aesthetics, fond of gifts, attracted to sensuality, and bored by routine.

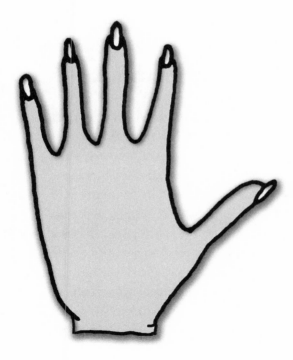

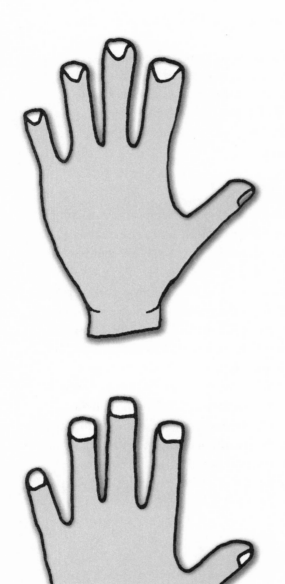

THE SPATULATE OR ACTION-ORIENTED HAND

If your hand is narrow at the wrists, but wider toward the fingertips, you have the spatulate or fire hand. This hand shape indicates you are action-oriented and love unusual adventures; it's not unlike you to pack your bags and head to India for a spell at an **ashram** and the next week traipse around the market towns of Italy's hill country. You like variety and excitement in all areas of life, including the bedroom.

An explorer of people, places, and ideas, you are daring, energetic, and fearless, often challenging the ideas or positions of others who aren't as open-minded as you. Your energy is boundless; you tend to leave others breathless, unable to catch up with you. Spatulate hands are called fire hands since that element most closely captures the personality traits of vitality and dynamism.

THE SQUARE OR PRACTICAL HAND

A square hand appears to form a perfect square from the finger bases to the wrists. If your hand is square and smooth, you are easygoing, have a practical nature, and possess a realistic outlook on life. You are rooted in the routines of your daily life. Friendly and outgoing, you have a tendency to evaluate every situation as black or white, with little left to interpretation. Still, because you are so sensible and level-headed, family and friends regularly seek your help to mediate or settle volatile situations. You, like other square-handed people, are most often drawn to careers that require hard work and persistence, since you excel in tackling large and difficult projects.

Because you are practical and down-to-earth, you are said to have earth hands. The well-padded earth hand also symbolizes a warm, passionate, energetic nature—someone who enjoys the earthy pleasures of food, drink, and passionate indulgences. A thin, square hand, though still an earth hand, suggests less passion and lower libido, while a hard hand often belongs to those who are less flexible and demand more of others.

THE MIXED HAND

Although it's quite a rarity, every once in a while you'll see a hand that has elements of two or more of the five shapes and types. Palmists call these hands mixed. For an accurate reading of a **mixed hand**, you'll need to look for the dominant feature of the hand.

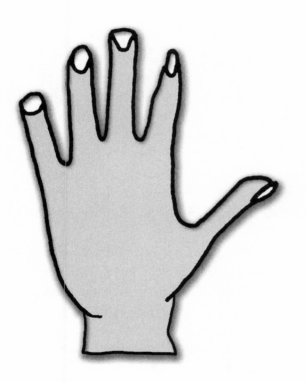

For instance, if you see that the palm itself is basically square but the fingers are long, it could mean that the person seems by outward appearance to be dreamy and intuitive, but that inwardly they are actually strong, practical, and even minded. If all seems balanced in the hand, your mixed-hand person is completely versatile and has a steady, go-with-the-flow kind of attitude. Both temperaments have their positive and negative sides, but there is much to learn from the mixed-hand balanced individual.

KNUCKLES AND ANGLES

Make a fist and closely examine the ridges of your knuckles where they form peaks. A full "mountain range" with peaks and valleys shows a person who has good health, is adventuresome, and fights for his or her beliefs.

If your knuckles are smooth and even, you are intuitive, impulsive, and dreamy. If they are knotty and rough looking or heavily ridged, you are extremely decisive and not easily swayed by hard-luck stories. Tiny bumps on the knuckles connote a shy, introverted personality.

Right or Left?

Remember, if you are right-handed, the right hand represents life as it is and the left represents your potential. Naturally, the opposite is true if you are left-handed!

INSPECT THE PALM LINES

Once you've examined the general shape of the hand, take a look at the palm. The first things you should notice are the main lines. Lines basically come in four different varieties: deep, clear, faint, or broken.

- Deep lines indicate a person who is full of life and who is certain or direct about her needs and desires. These people have absolutely no difficulty in attaining their goals in life—and they don't let anyone or anything get in their way!
- Clear, easy-to-read lines that are plain to see but not exceptionally deep typically belong to peace-loving, even-tempered people. These individuals are often the peacemakers in their families, and others look to them for their fair and objective insights.
- Faint lines appear in individuals who frequently have lots of nagging health problems caused by years of worry or indecision. Often timid and reserved, these people would rather have others lead them in particular situations; they hate having to take action, especially for their own well-being—they prefer others take care of them.

- Broken lines indicate abrupt or traumatic changes in life. A broken line coming off the life line can mean a major shift in lifestyle or personal well-being. A broken line off the heart line may mean a dramatic change in relationship status, such as divorce or separation.
- Long lines on the palm mean that you have well-developed interests and pursue them with a passion, while short lines generally mean that you have many different interests and can be intensely involved with each one—until the next opportunity presents itself.
- Horizontal lines on the palm generally mean conflict or separation, while vertical lines point to a tendency toward people pleasing. Double lines mean that you have spiritual guidance in the form of an ancestral spirit, spirit guide, or angel—and this guidance pertains to the area of your life that the double lines are closest to (either heart, head, or life line).

While not completely conclusive until the rest of the palm reading has been complete, palm lines can tell you a lot about the basis or foundation of your life.

OBSERVE PALM MARKS AND PATTERNS

In addition to major lines, the palm contains lots of smaller lines and other markings. There may be tiny crisscrossed lines, loops, and other lovely little patterns. No matter how incidental these shapes and patterns may seem, your hands have carried all of these markings since about the third month of fetal development inside your mother's womb.

NOTICE THE RIDGES

First, take a look at the overall texture of the palm in order to get a suitable starting point for reading the ridges and patterns contained in the palm. If the ridges in your palm are smooth and soft to the touch, you likely have refined tastes and are the quiet and sensitive type. If your ridges are wider and deeper, creating a rougher texture, you are athletic, action-oriented, and sharper psychologically because of your positive, outgoing attitude.

While it's possible for your hand to have no visible patterns, most hands have at least one type of pattern and a high percentage of hands have several.

The Meaning Behind the Lines

The study of the finely carved lines and patterns in the palm is known as "dermatoglyphics." Here, you are specifically looking for the meaning behind each row of ridges and patterns etched into the palm of your hand by heredity, time, and experience.

LOOK FOR SHAPES IN THE PATTERNS

Now that you have a good sense of the feel and texture of your palm, take a deeper look at the skin patterns on it. Do they form any particular shapes?

There are thirteen basic markings that can appear on the palm of the hand, and each has a special meaning:

1. Chains: Someone who is "bound" by worry.
2. Islands: Loss through difficulty or challenge.
3. Dots: Indication of a surprise or a shocking event.
4. Branches: Rising branches are a sign of good fortune; branches falling toward the wrist are a sign of potential failure.
5. Broken lines: A shift or change in life, or an inability to see things through.
6. Forks: Choices pertaining to whichever major line is closest (heart, head, or life).
7. Circles: Usually, circles predict great fame and fortune; however, you will rarely encounter them.
8. Triangles: Portend great psychic or spiritual abilities.
9. Squares: Ability to teach, motivate, or inspire others.
10. Crosses: Obstacles or blockages on the way; burdens that may hold you back from achieving your dreams.
11. Tassels: Not typically seen on the hand; can represent scattered energies or unmanifested ideas.
12. Grilles: Represent lots of starting and stopping with respect to life's endeavors.
13. Stars: The most auspicious markings on the palm; people with **stars** usually achieve tremendous fame—or lasting notoriety.

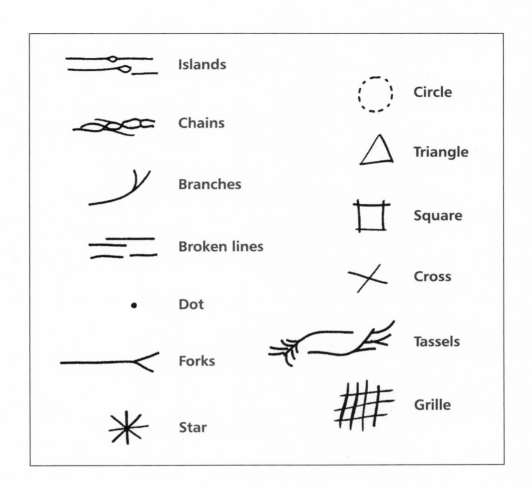

The Patterns Change

Ridges and **patterns** can often change over time and they often do. If you look at hand prints that are ten years apart, you'll see slight variations in the lines as the person has grown or evolved emotionally—proof that you can change your destiny.

TAKE NOTE OF LOOPS

Loops or palm markings are typically found on the webbing between fingers and on finger mounts (the puffy underside of the knuckles of your hand). Loops of vocation or career, found between the ring and the middle finger, show how dedicated you are to your career. If they are large and open, you are probably open to others' input. If small and refined, you are likely an entrepreneurial spirit who prefers solitary work.

Loops of bravery or courage are found just above the joint area of the thumb, near the thumb webbing. If you have one of these, you are fearless in your life's pursuits.

Loops of humor or good cheer occur between the index and middle finger and point to a healthy sense of humor that draws others to you, while a loop on the **Luna mount** (the outside part of the palm between the pinky and the wrist) shows a marked ability to communicate with animals and nature.

Crowds to Watch For

Check your hand for the "crowd factor." If there are lots of lines and patterns crowded together, it means you have an active imagination and like to learn. Having fewer lines is a sign of a more evolved soul.

FIND SHAPES PREDICTING CREATIVITY

If you have several skin ridge patterns that seem to flow into each other to form a triangular shape, that shape is your focal point for creative energy. If you have a "tri-radius" mark on your index finger mount, it typically means that you focus your creative energy on leadership; if it occurs near your third finger mount, you are much more intellectual.

Whorls (unusual circular skin patterns) indicate your future greatness in creative endeavors. If you write, create art, or perform for audiences, search for the unique markings that signal intense artistic talent; for example, the whorl of music (typically found on the **Venus mount**, which is the padded section near the thumb) or a whorl of Luna (on the Luna mount). (See the following for a discussion of mounts.)

Loops or Whorls?

The most common ridges and patterns in the palm are loops—the same pattern we are all used to seeing in fingerprints. Whorl shapes are the least common to appear on the fingers or palms.

CHECK OUT THE PERCUSSION AREA

Turn your hand sideways and examine the outer lateral edge (the area between the wrist and the pinkie). This area is known as the **percussion**, and it is wide enough to span three major mounts of the hand.

When the percussion is tapered, it sticks out just below the little finger and then tapers off until it reaches the wrist. If your percussion area is tapered as just described, you possess an overly active mind. Relaxing and going with the flow might be difficult for you. If your hand features a curved percussion, you have lots of creative ability although you might choose to use it in practical professions such as engineering. Straight percussions are rare—connoting someone who doesn't waste time on artistic pursuits.

Mounts of the Palm

The palm contains nine mounts (the fleshy raised areas on the palm), such as the mount of Luna and the mount of Venus. Palm mounts reveal personal characteristics, natural abilities, and traits. If you are interested in where your dominant energies are directed, look for the largest raised area on your palm. Identifying **zones** of the hands will make finding these mounts easier. Additionally, pinpointing the zones will help more easily correlate aspects of your psyche and personality to be found in these zones. There are several ways to read the mounts and the rest of the palm, based on an analysis of the palm zones.

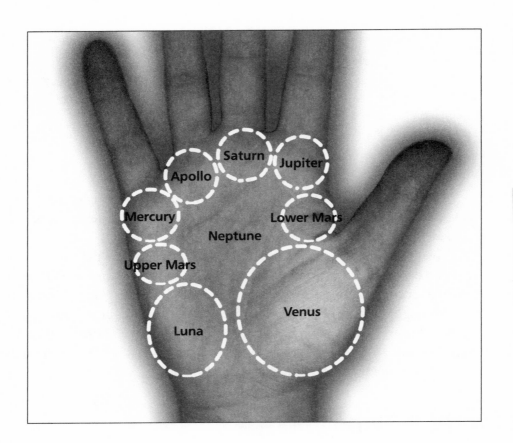

TWO-ZONE ANALYSIS—CONSCIOUS AND SUBCONSCIOUS

Hold your hand in front of you, palm facing the ceiling. Imagine a line that reaches from the center of your wrist to the middle finger, cutting the center of your hand in half. When divided this way, the section of the hand with your thumb contains the conscious zone, and the percussion side section of the palm near the pinky represents the subconscious zone.

The conscious zone corresponds to the physical energies you consciously expend going after the things you want in life; the subconscious zone relates to the passive energies of the imagination and creative thought that you use, without being aware of using them to achieve your goals.

THREE-ZONE ANALYSIS

Instead of dividing the palm into two zones, some palmists prefer three horizontal zones. Here's how it works: Imagine two horizontal lines, right to left, crossing your palm. The top area is closest to your fingers. The bottom area is adjacent to your wrist. The middle lies between the two.

THE FIRST ZONE

The zone nearest to your fingers—the emotional zone—represents your higher aspirations and goals in life. When this area is well developed (fleshy rather than flat) and in close proximity to the head line, it suggests your approach to life is through your mind or intellect.

THE SECOND ZONE

The zone nearest your wrist—the physical zone—represents your physical needs and desires, as well as the energy you willingly expend to satisfy them. An overdeveloped (puffy) physical zone means you will stop at nothing to get what you want—perhaps even selfishly putting your own wants and needs over those of people in your life important to you. An underdeveloped physical zone means you are passive, too weak to fight for what you want. Take assertiveness courses to rebalance this tendency.

THE THIRD ZONE

The middle area—the practical zone—touches your emotional and physical zones. If this area is firm and without numerous mixed lines, it suggests that you are adept at balancing emotional and physical energies.

Significance of the Mounts

The mounts of your palm correlate with definite personality types, as well as distinct physical characteristics. Although the hands of all humans are unique, your personality will have much in common with others who share your type of palm mounts.

FOUR-ZONE ANALYSIS

Draw an imaginary cross over your entire palm, dividing your hand into four distinct zones.

1. The rational zone includes your index and middle fingers and their mounts. When overly developed, this area indicates that you are a strong and ambitious leader. If not well developed, you suffer a lack of self-esteem or confidence.
2. The practical zone includes the mount of Venus—the puffy area of the palm connected with your thumb. The practical zone is ruled by the pleasure principle. If you have a predominant practical quadrant, you likely enjoy physical pleasure and creature comforts. Conversely, if you have an underdeveloped practical area, you lack enthusiasm and energy.
3. The instinctive zone includes your last two fingers and their mounts. Many writers and artists have predominant instinctive areas on their palms; this is entirely appropriate, since this area represents creativity and communication. However, an instinctive area that isn't well developed or noticeable indicates you likely have difficulty in communication, perhaps finding it easier to make your point through figures, charts, or a scientific study.
4. The intuitive zone includes the **Lower Mars mount** (the area underneath your index finger). A well-developed intuitive zone marks psychic powers and spirituality, as well as the gifts of humility and sensitivity. If the intuitive area isn't well developed or is completely flat, the individual could be atheistic and generally prefers an intellectual approach to matters of spiritual belief.

THE MOUNT OF VENUS

Because the mount of Venus represents your capacity for love, affection, desire, and romance, it is the most popular area for palm readers to scrutinize for clues about your love life. The mount of Venus, located at the base of your thumb indicates how deeply or passionately you love others.

PHYSICALITY AND MEANING

If your mount of Venus is overly puffy, it can indicate a fear of commitment and possibly a proclivity for promiscuity. Recognizing the tendencies means you can make conscious choices for dealing with them.

When the head line and the thumb are both strong and steady, your passionate nature is tempered by a sound, moral ability to size up each sexual situation. In that case, you likely focus your physical passions into material gain with tangible, achievable goals.

Of course, love of material pleasures has a price: You might discover that you are too occupied with creating a wonderful life (with all the material trappings of success) that you don't have the time or inclination for small romantic gestures. If that's the case, you will have to work harder at balancing material and physical pleasures.

If you don't have a well-developed head line or thumb configuration, an exaggerated mount of Venus can indicate a callous, uncaring penchant for instant gratification.

The mount of Venus represents love, home, family, sensuality, and morality, as well as passionate emotion and physical energy. The mount of Venus relates to your drive and zest for life.

MOUNT OF VENUS PERSONALITY TYPE

Venus represents the forces of love, peace, and beautiful aesthetics. Generally, people with a predominant mount of Venus fall into a physical type with round faces dominated by large doe-shaped eyes and voluptuous lips, while other facial features tend to be smaller than average. They usually stand slightly taller than other types, and most often have a very robust, healthy outlook on life. Venusians are, of course, the most sensual and socially outgoing of the mount types. They know how to live and love with great passion.

A predominate mount of Venus suggests that you love the finer things in life—from luxury items to special works of art. Your understanding of emotion indicates you would likely excel working in education, politics, or psychology.

A nearly smooth, flat Venus mount can indicate a calculating and overly critical disposition. You tend to be a kindhearted lover rather than overtly passionate. The best match for you in a romantic partner would be someone whose mount of Venus is similar to yours. There's a good chance you will find lasting love because neither of you sees physical passion as a requirement of the relationship.

The Solitary Mount of Venus

When the other mounts are flat, smooth, and undeveloped and the mount of Venus rises alone, it suggests all the areas of your life are well-balanced. You are someone who would make an excellent diplomat.

THE MOUNTS OF MARS

There are two mounts associated with Mars, the planet of action, notable for the energies of aggression and courage. The **Upper Mars mount** is located on the outside area of your palm, just under your little finger. The mount of Lower Mars is found in the area between your thumb and index fingers. These mounts indicate whether or not your primary response to challenging situations is to fight or flee (show courage or seek safety).

Lower Mars shows your capacity for physical strength or endurance, while Upper Mars indicates your moral values. The mounts of Upper and Lower Mars are sometimes referred to as the mount of Mars Positive (Upper) and mount of Mars Negative (Lower).

UPPER MARS PHYSICALITY AND MEANING

A well-developed mount of Upper Mars indicates that you are somewhat confrontational, which can be a positive attribute in a crisis. An overdeveloped mount of Upper Mars can mean that you are a bit of a bully—someone who uses physical force to get a point across. The overdeveloped mount of Upper Mars indicates you are especially competitive when playing games or participating in sports. Balance the competitiveness with meditation or yoga. Remember to temper your language, as well.

A smooth, flat, or otherwise undeveloped Upper Mars mount reveals that you dislike confrontation and seek to escape stressful situations. However, since your strategic and survival skills are superior, you excel at defending others and would make an excellent defense attorney. Fighting injustice suits your personality and mount type well.

A weak or flat mount of Upper Mars suggests you likely have a difficult time standing up for your rights; however, a well-developed mount indicates you are always ready to take on other people's causes and battles.

LOWER MARS PHYSICALITY AND MEANING

If your mount of Lower Mars is not well developed, you likely have a fear of confrontation and lack of courage. Inherently not a bad thing, it makes you much more cautious than you need to be in certain situations and definitely less assertive. When your Lower Mars mount is overdeveloped, you may have an overly confrontational, even combative, personality. Ideally, your mount of Lower Mars is well developed and more evenly balanced than these two extremes.

Balanced Mars

When the two mounts of Mars are developed to the same degree, rising to the same level from your palm, your personality is well-balanced. Otherwise, you either possess tremendous courage and conviction but aren't motivated to use them in a positive direction, or you have the energy to act but little conviction or belief, thus unable to decide how to proceed.

MOUNT OF MARS PERSONALITY TYPE

In general, if your palm sports a predominant mount of Mars (whether upper or lower) you have a forceful personality that can easily dominate heated discussion or debate. But you are intelligent, social, and fun loving—especially enjoying lengthy discussions about any hot topic of the day. You excel in business and commerce; however, you need to have a predominant upper mount of Mars (rather than a lower mount of Mars) to have an easier time climbing the ladder to success. Physically, Martians are distinguished by their long, angular bone structure, combined with a large mouth and a beak-like nose set between strong cheekbones.

PLAIN OF MARS

Located between the two Mars mounts, in the middle of the nine palm and finger mounts—in the very center of your palm, you will find the plain of Mars. Run your finger along this section of the palm and notice whether the flesh feels thick; if so, it suggests a hot temper. Alternatively, a hollowness of this area reveals you might have trouble communicating your ideas to others. If the plain of Mars is neither thick nor hollow, you maintain control and balance of your emotions and tend to see things clearly.

THE MOUNT OF LUNA

Find the mount of Luna located next to the percussion area (base of your hand) and opposite your thumb and mount of Venus. This palm area relates to your imagination, intuition, and creativity.

When this area is normally developed (neither flat, nor too fleshy), you possess a creative imagination and a passion for nature, travel, poetry, art, and literature.

If your mount of Luna is overdeveloped, you might have some difficulty in dealing with reality because your imagination gets in the way. Look at your head line to determine whether it is strong enough to handle your vivid and active imagination—can it ground you enough so you can clearly assess situations? Or is your head line too weak (faint) to have any equalizing effect?

If your Luna mount is underdeveloped, you tend to process every new experience purely from a sensual, feeling standpoint—eschewing logic and decisiveness. The ideal Luna mount is of average development, indicative of a healthy balance of imagination and reality.

If your mount of Luna increases in size toward the wrist area (as opposed to near the thumb), you possess strong intuitive sense, seeing beyond physical reality. You seem to know things before they happen and are adept at planning your life accordingly.

MOUNT OF LUNA PERSONALITY TYPE

In general, people with strong Luna mounts on their hands are dreamy, imaginative, creative, and giving. They are very compassionate and helpful to others; often, they are protective of the people they care about. If your personality fits with the mount of Luna type, you love to share your creative gifts as writer, painter, or public speaker. You would make a terrific psychic, artist, writer, or composer. If a large Luna mount is coupled with a prominent Venus mount, you are destined for world renown and acclaim.

The predominant Luna mount in your hand suggests that you love water and anything associated with it. You may even live near the ocean or frequently travel there.

If your mount of Luna is not well developed or is smooth or unnoticeable, you prefer to stay near home and have a tendency to live in your own little shell. If you do have any imagination, it's a secret that only your private diary will reveal.

The Mount of Neptune
Some readers include the Neptune mount in their readings. Located in between the mounts of Venus and Luna, near the wrist, a thickly padded Neptune indicates charisma, while a deep crease shows an inability to look within for answers.

OTHER PALM MOUNT MARKS

Mounts of the palm, like clouds, suggest shapes (for example, squares, **triangles**, circles, **crosses,** and **grilles**), but the shapes aren't usually exact in their rendering or proportions. Although these shapes can form all over the palm, it's important to note that, on the mounts of the palm, the shapes or marks have distinctly different meanings.

There are five main markings that typically occur on the mounts of the palm. Generally speaking, crosses and grilles represent negative signs, while stars can indicate good luck (especially with money) and squares lessen the impact of negative signs. Mounts containing a triangle indicate wisdom.

Read Clockwise
Just as you read the more general characteristics of the palm mounts in a clockwise manner, so you should do when reading the marks that occur on the mounts of your palm.

GRILLES ON VENUS
Most often, grilles (hash lines, both vertical and horizontal) that appear on this mount represent lots of misguided or splintering energy. Are you passionate about too many things? Grilles warn you that too many passions can lead to stress, tension, and an unhealthy intensity in your emotions. Balance this intense energy with peaceful, restorative walks; meditation; or prayer.

STARS OR CROSSES ON THE LUNA MOUNT

Stars and crosses on the mount of Luna symbolize a travel warning to be extra diligent when traveling. If the star or cross on your Luna mount is encased in a protective **square mark**, then you can safely let your guard down.

OTHER MARKS ON THE MARS MOUNTS

A cross on the mount of Lower Mars is common and symbolizes possible harm directed at you by your adversaries. Their intention might be to undermine your credibility or perhaps something more drastic. Regardless, use caution.

Alternatively, if your palm has the lucky triangle on the mount of Upper Mars, you will be able to outwit any potential adversary, as you possess the skill to circumvent or diffuse such negative energy. Military or political strategists, as well as athletes and salespeople, frequently are born with this mark.

On the plain of Mars, the most common symbol is the cross. Look carefully at your plain because it is easy to miss symbols that might be present because many lines shoot out in all directions. A cross in this area of your hand means that likely you are interested in studies such as alternative medicine, spirituality, or the occult.

Crosses, Stars, and Squares

Each cross, star, or square will tell you something about an area of your life that you need to know more about. For example, the cross sign indicates accidents. If it appears on the mount of Mars, it suggests an accidental death might occur on a battlefield, but a cross on the mount of Luna (Moon) could signify widowhood.

Finger Mounts and Meaning

The finger mounts lie on the palm at the base of each finger area and incorporate the lowest part of the finger. These mounts indicate interests, talents, and skills. Also, when reading the fingers, look for their characteristics and shape, the spaces between fingers, the length of the fingers, and the relationship of the fingers to the palm.

Finger Mounts and Their Planets

The mount of each finger is known by the same name as the finger to which it belongs. Also, the mount is ruled by the same mythical god associated with the finger—Jupiter (first finger, closest to the thumb), Saturn (second), Apollo (third/ring finger), and Mercury (fourth/pinky finger). Thus, in interpretation, each mount shares the same qualities as the finger of which it is a part.

MOUNT OF JUPITER (FIRST FINGER)

The area below your first or forefinger, also known as the Jupiter finger, denotes the **Jupiter mount**. It indicates your public persona (aspects of yourself you reveal to the world), as well as your idealism, honor, courage, and boldness.

A well-developed mount of Jupiter suggests you are optimistic and have an innate sense of justice; however, a mount that rises higher than the other finger mounts means you desire to control and dominate others and might have a tendency to be arrogant and possibly greedy. A flat, low mount suggests lack of ambition, scattered leadership energies and focus, and a generally weaker personality type.

MOUNT OF SATURN (SECOND FINGER)

Your **Saturn mount** is located underneath your second or middle finger. If yours is a predominant mount, you may know only too well Saturn's gloomy influence, making you conservative, distrustful, and unyielding. A large fleshy mount of Saturn engenders solitary, introverted, and aloof behavior in you— you might even be pensive and introspective, as well as cynical and untrusting.

A level mount of Saturn offers a better prognosis—you are friendly and optimistic. Independent enough to think for yourself, you balance the polarities of trust and suspicion, new ideas and old values, the love of solitude and the love of friends. If you have a midsized mount of Saturn, you exhibit just the right amount of common sense and responsibility. You are excessive or obsessive and moody. You are a leader, capable of bringing leadership qualities into any organization.

If your mount of Saturn is flat, hollow, and otherwise weak, you may be flighty, irresponsible, and disorganized.

MOUNT OF APOLLO (THIRD FINGER)

The **Apollo mount**, located at the base of the ring finger, rules those attributes given to Apollo, Roman god of the Sun, who represents light and truth, poetry and art, healing and beauty. A raised Apollo mount suggests you are outgoing, enthusiastic, talented, creative, lively, and positive. You possess versatility, logic, and understanding and like to lead others, which may at times make you unpopular. Your love for beauty, creativity, and self-expression may also be seen in your skills in crafts, cooking, and fashion, if not in the high arts, or at least by a deep interest in aesthetic subjects.

An extreme mount of Apollo brings out negative characteristics. You can become opinionated and ostentatious, too easily impressed by power, position, and fame.

If your mount appears flat or hollow, you will shun the spotlight, cling to your clique, and be willing to settle for a lackluster life; or, you may lack energy due to illness. A weak mount of Apollo makes you more secretive.

Lines in the Finger Mounts

The Saturn mount is hardly ever seen with a large number of lines, but the Apollo mount often has a great many lines on it, indicative of the creativity that is believed to reside there.

MOUNT OF MERCURY (FOURTH FINGER)

The mount at the base of your pinky finger takes its name from the winged-foot messenger god of the ancient Romans. Mercury ruled over commerce and business. This **Mercury mount** represents your ability to express and communicate ideas. It indicates your interest in travel, business, teaching, and practical matters. The mount of Mercury reveals your aptitude for science and the healing arts, as well as meaningful relationships with friends and children.

A well-defined mount of Mercury suggests you have many interests and are confident, quick-witted, and an excellent communicator. When action is needed, you take charge, whether attending to an emergency or closing a deal. You find it easy to read others.

If your Mercury finger mount is excessively large, you tend to be chatty or gossipy, possibly embellishing the truth. Regardless, you will use your skillful communication to advance in life.

A flat mount indicates you are a quiet, shy individual, unable to quickly assess what is going on around you. Or, you might be preoccupied with your own life, with little interest in the lives of others. Also, you might find it difficult to communicate with your mate or lover.

▲▲▲▲▲▲▲▲▲▲▲▲▲▲▲▲▲▲▲▲▲▲▲▲▲▲

A Mount Between Two Fingers

When a finger mount is not clearly at the base of any particular finger but is between two of them, the characteristics are interpreted as a combination of the qualities of those two fingers. A misplaced finger mount may either strengthen or complicate your reading.

▼▼▼▼▼▼▼▼▼▼▼▼▼▼▼▼▼▼▼▼▼▼▼▼▼▼

MERCURY'S NOD TO OTHER FINGERS

Lucky are you if your Mercury mount veers toward Apollo. There's a good chance that you are an astute artist who understands the business side of art. You would excel at owning a gallery. You enjoy the little rituals of life and have an innate curiosity and varied interests. A mount of Mercury that veers toward the edge of the hand, however, suggests you are fast-thinking, fast-talking, fast-acting, changeable, and totally absorbed in what you do.

Major Lines of the Hand

The three major lines—the life, head, and heart lines, in that order—are formed even before you are born, and they change throughout your life in response to stress and illness and according to your actions, which in turn create life changes.

LIFE LINE

The life line, located close to the head line makes a loop around the thumb. It speaks to your personal longevity, stamina, and vitality. A curvy line indicates a lot of energy, whereas a long, deep line suggests a healthy, long life imbued with energy. Or, if there are two or more life lines, you are surrounded by positive energy and abundant vitality.

Because it lies so near to the mount of Venus, the life line can provide many hints about your love life. The life line represents health, so a strong one shows you have much passion to give, while a weak one points to a limitation in the amount of energy you have to give to your physical nature.

LIFE-LINE INDICATORS FOR LOVE

If you have a life line that makes a wide sweep across the palm, leaving room for a large mount of Venus, you have a great deal of love to give and energy to put to use in the sexual arena. You are likely an extrovert and outwardly directed. On the other hand, a life line close to the thumb constricts the mount of Venus and shows a lower sex drive.

HEAD LINE

The head line, located between the first finger and thumb, crosses the midpalm horizontally. The head line can provide you with a clearer picture of your mental abilities, career or business acumen, and potential for success. A straight line indicates deep, clear thinking, while a sloping curved line suggests high creativity.

HEAD-LINE INDICATORS FOR ROMANCE

The head line will also give you clues about your romantic relationships. First, compare the head and heart lines. If the head line is heavier than the heart line, you will look for a partner who can be a good companion and who gives you mental stimulation. You will think before you act on sexual feelings. If the heart line is heavier than the head line, it is just the opposite. You will be ruled more by feelings and your need for passion.

If your head line is straight across the palm, you are practical and realistic about love and you have a less romantic view of things. You also tend to be more traditional about the social mores. If your head line drops downward to the mount of Luna, you are more romantic about love, and the bigger the dip downward, the more imagination and illusion play a role in your hopes and dreams.

HEART LINE

The heart line is located on the little finger side of the hand where it crosses the palm on its way toward the first finger. The heart line reveals aspects of your emotional life such as your insecurities, fears, and passions. It also indicates your potential for love or marriage and is sometimes incorrectly referred to as the marriage line. A feathered heart line can suggest a fickle, flirtatious individual. A heart line that originates under the middle finger indicates that you tend to be materialistic and selfish in the affairs of the heart.

The heart line is a good place to start when looking at your palm to see what your relationships will be like. This line describes both feelings and libido, and shows how well a person manages to bond emotionally with others. If your heart line is long, deep, and without blemishes, you are a devoted friend, secure in relationships, and have an affectionate and loyal nature.

HEART-LINE INDICATORS FOR LOVE

Here are the features that you should look for when reading the heart line for love potential:

- **Chains and islands:** Your feelings are changeable and short-lived. You want intimacy but fear commitment, so you waver and are insecure. Other people may see you as cold and unapproachable.
- **Shape of the line:** If you have a straight heart line, you are very cool and rational, attuned to the mental image of what you want and willing to wait for it. Generally, you are the type of person who makes decisions based on what makes sense. If you have a curved heart line, you are more emotional, moved by your thoughts and desires, and willing to move more physically and aggressively toward goals.
- **Space between head and heart line:** If the space is wide, you are tolerant and willing to live and let live. If the space is narrow, you are secretive and ill at ease in many social situations because you find it hard to say how you feel.

Also check where your heart line ends. If it tapers off under Saturn, you are a very physical person but one who is controlled by the rationality of Saturn rather than by sheer romance. If your heart line ends under Jupiter, your love life will have a strong component of an idealized view of your partner (or your love affair may be with all of humanity). You are loyal, but this may veer over into possessiveness.

Balance Head and Heart

If your heart line ends between Jupiter and Saturn, you can balance between the forces of your head and your heart. You are warm and loving but also can be logical and practical about your partner.

LINE OF DESTINY OR FATE LINE

Your **destiny line** stretches from the bottom of your palm to the base of your middle finger (the Saturn mount). Remember that the mythical god Saturn ruled duty, work, and security, so it makes sense that the line of destiny (also called the Saturn line) reveals the role of career and responsibility in your life. It shows the direction of life and indicates your ability to exert control over it and your ambition to achieve your goals. Your fate line also discloses how the public views you.

Fate and Relationships

The fate line also has another role to play—it shows relationships that affect our lives. Relationships are seen in the lines of influence that rise up from the mount of Luna to meet the fate line, and they can be marriages, important friendships, and business partnerships. (Lines of influence are any lines that run parallel or across major lines.)

Your line of destiny mirrors the effort you put into creating your ideal life. It imparts information about your career, ambition, material well-being, personal success, and fulfillment of goals. The line of destiny is the central element of your hand, supplying stability to the other lines because it connects the intuitive and practical zones of your palm. It shows how you act, use your abilities, control your environment, and deal with the influences around you.

SECONDARY LINES AND PATTERNS

Your palm reveals information about you and your life in other lines and in patterns. The Mercury line, for example, runs from the thumb side of the midpalm across to the little finger. It discloses information about your health (and especially your central nervous system, which is the messenger system in your body). This line may also show your spirit of adventure and a healthy curiosity. The Apollo line runs up from the midpalm to the ring finger and demonstrates your potential for successful development of special talents, creativity, and life energies.

THE STORY OF YOUR FINGERS

Your fingers in palmistry are known by their individual, more esoteric names, which correspond with the gods of Roman mythology for the attributes of those divine beings:

THE JUPITER (YOUR INDEX FINGER) DESCRIBES YOUR LEADERSHIP ABILITIES AND ASSERTIVENESS

If the Jupiter finger extends from your palm out to end at the base of the nail of the neighboring Saturn finger, you are someone who loves power and desires to lead others. If your finger of Jupiter is as long as your finger of Saturn, your egotism shows; you may even feel the need to control others. A crooked or bent Jupiter finger reveals a tendency to dominate other people, while a short Jupiter finger indicates an aversion to personal responsibility.

SATURN HOLDS THE SECRETS OF DARK MOODS

The Saturn finger is your middle finger; it describes your moods, as well as responsibilities. A Saturn finger noticeably longer than the others connotes a tendency for depression. A shorter than normal Saturn finger indicates you tend to fear responsibility and pressure, whereas a crooked or bent finger suggests you have a chip on your shoulder. This is the finger where palmists look for indications of a persecution complex.

APOLLO PROCLAIMS FAME

Fame and happiness could be within your reach. Take a look at your ring (Apollo) finger, as it reveals the potential for you to achieve those things. It also suggests your interest in the arts or sciences. A long Apollo finger reveals your desire to be a celebrity in the creative arts; if the finger is excessively long, however, it indicates a craving for notoriety at any price. A short Apollo finger indicates that you shun any kind of notoriety or publicity, preferring instead to keep a low profile, often working behind the scenes. A low-set Apollo finger means that while you may have an interest in pursuing an artistic career, you may not have been born with the talent to make it happen.

MERCURY BALANCES

Mercury, your fourth finger, points to your balance or abuse of power. A long finger means you have the shrewd ability to exploit the skills and talents of others for business purposes. If it is extremely long, extending past the base of the nail of Apollo, there's a tendency to be a bit of a fraud. A short Mercury finger means that despite your inability to use your own talents to the fullest, you don't like to capitalize on the talents of others. If your Mercury finger is set low, you are the imaginative, dreamy type. This isn't a bad thing—dreaming begins the process of manifesting; however, when you dream but lack grounding (don't set goals or take action) you could face challenges trying to earn a decent living.

FINGERTIPS REVEAL GLANDULAR HEALTH

Vertical lines along the fingertips disclose the overall health of the endocrine glands. For particular glands, consult:

- Jupiter finger (first fingertip): Pituitary gland
- Saturn (middle fingertip): Pineal and adrenal glands
- Apollo (ring fingertip): Thymus gland, the cardiovascular system, and your blood pressure
- Mercury (baby fingertip): Thyroid gland

THUMBS

The thumb, one of the most important character divulgers on the hand, reveals the fortitude of your will and the soundness of your judgment. Your thumb is an indicator of your degree of self-control and personal willpower, as well as your disposition. Note the length of your thumb. A long, well-formed thumb indicates a strong will and sound judgment. A short, thick thumb means you can be quite contrary or stubborn. If yours is a supple-jointed thumb, you tend to be reasonable and adaptable and are generally more tolerant, open, and giving than those with a firm-jointed thumb. Such a thumb connotes compassion and empathy—you give your thoughts, time, and cash more freely to the needy. More concerned with intention rather than hard-and-fast rules, you lobby for change for causes you strongly support.

One Thumb Is as Good as Another

One specific type of thumb is not better or worse than any other. Your thumb's shape can give you information about your potential for ambition and talent, but you should remember that you can overcome any limitations you have inherited in this life.

Does your thumb appear to have a waist line? Such a thumb looks as though it has a waist, formed by the narrow joint that connects the second phalange to the top of your thumb. This type of thumb represents an unwavering tact and the ability to understand lots of different viewpoints. Your empathy enhances your ability to relate well to others. You probably volunteer and support others, and your empathy is nothing short of profound. Your personality's creative and practical aspects are perfectly balanced.

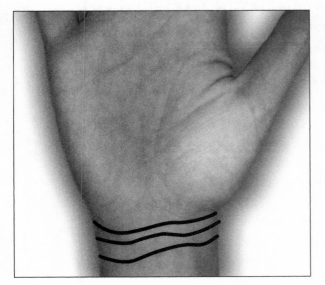

READING WRIST LINES

The wrist lines loop around the bottom of the wrist like **bracelets** and mark the entryway to the hand—the place where the skin patterns begin and the reading of the palm can commence. Traditionally, wrist lines were thought to be an indication of longevity, but there are many other pieces of information that they can tell the palm reader.

Each person in the world has some form of wrist lines on the hand, and they are considered one of the nine sets of minor lines that bring extra interpretive information to a hand. Collectively, the wrist lines are known as the **rascette**, and there are generally three of them (though in some cases there may be four). They are sometimes called the bracelets of life because in the Eastern tradition of palmistry they are used to determine whether the owner of the hand will have a long life. Each of the lines of the wrist is thought to represent about thirty years of life, so a rascette with three complete and clear lines represents a substantially long life.

EVALUATE HEALTH AND VITALITY

A clear and deep first line of a rascette shows that you are in good health and physically fit. If your first line is poorly formed and unclear, it means that you are indulgent and reckless, and that your problems may be more of your own making than you admit.

If the first wrist line curves upward into the bottom of the palm or is broken up to a large extent, it can mean gynecological troubles for females—from barrenness or menstrual problems to difficulty giving birth. In males, it signals urinary, prostate, hormonal, or reproductive problems. Remember to also consider the life line when evaluating what you notice on the wrist lines.

READ LIFE LENGTH AND QUALITY IN THE WRIST LINE

The first rascette (the one closest to the palm) indicates the quality of the first two decades of life, the second the next two, and so on. Other palm readers assert that the length of line indicates the length of life, so if that first line stretches across the entire wrist it means a lifespan of about twenty-five years of good life. Additional lines add to that length.

Although the wrist lines are read as an indication of longevity, they can also reveal other information, such as the inclination to travel. The **travel lines** that often appear on the Luna mount actually begin on the rascette. There are three things to keep in mind when reading the rascette for travel:

1. The lines don't extend toward the Luna mount but rather move upward.
2. The length of the travel line will tell you how long the journey will be and how far you will go.

3. The straighter the wrist lines, the safer the passage on your journeys through life will be.

LOOK FOR MARKS OF GOOD FORTUNE OR TROUBLE

The lines of the wrist can have various types of marks—crosses, **chains**, **breaks**, stars, and so forth. When you are examining the rascette, don't read further than where your wrist bones meet the radius bone on your arm. When reading rascettes, you always want to stay focused on the major lines around the wrist.

- A chain around the wrist symbolizes a life of struggle and hard labor. However, the effort will eventually result in monetary gain.
- A star on the first line of the wrist in the midsection of the line means that you will inherit money early in life.
- A cross on a wrist line means that you will have trouble early in young adulthood when you set out on your own. Your family of origin may intrude on your independence, keeping you from individuating into healthy adulthood.
- A break in any one of the rascette lines shows an untrustworthy and self-centered aspect. A lack of control over your behavior could mean your downfall.
- If the rascette is crossed by an angle, you will be rewarded near the end of your life by financial or career advancement.
- A rascette with a triangle brings you good luck, financial gain, honor, and prestige.

DERIVE MEANING FROM WRIST-TO-FINGER LINES

The lines that extend from the wrist to the base of your fingers have meanings that relate to fortune, fame, and travel, with specific interpretations based on the general symbolism of the finger.

- **Rascette line to Apollo.** A line that travels upward from the rascette to below the Apollo finger means your trip will be a success and lead to honor and renown and wealth. Even if you are a "prophet without honor in your own country," your trip abroad will lead to fame that continues after you return home.

- **Rascette line to Mercury.** A line from the rascette to the Mercury mount will result in a fortune granted in an unexpected manner as a result of the trip.
- **Rascette line to Saturn.** The line that extends from the rascette to the Saturn mount indicates your trip has trouble and could end in catastrophe.

Your Wrists Can Show Your Potential

The rascette marks the beginning of your fate line (or line of destiny), an extremely important area, and the closer this line is to the base of your wrist, the sooner you will learn to be independent and directed. As with the other major and minor lines of your hands, be sure to read both wrists for the best assessment of whether you're meeting your life's true potential.

NOTICE THE MARRIAGE INDICATORS IN THE RASCETTE

If you are interested in prospects for marriage in your future, take a look at the lines that rise from the rascette. A branch to the Jupiter mount on your hand is a sign that you will marry into wealth and power. A branch to Saturn would mean marriage to an older person. A line that extends from the rascette to the Apollo mount represents a marriage to a person with creative talents and artistic tastes. Finally, a line to the Mercury mount means, as you might expect, a union with a businessperson or merchant, or a marriage as a result of commercial activity, for instance, to someone you met on a business trip.

Use Palmistry to Unearth the Power of You

Palmistry, one of the oldest forms of divination, has been used for thousands of years. Ancient peoples perfected the art of palmistry, or **chiromancy**, as it is also called, believing it would enrich their knowledge, from the practical to the metaphysical, and empower them to have mastery over their lives. Like those ancient predecessors, you can use palmistry to become all you were born to be. The future you hold in your hands—or more correctly, in your palms—belongs to you, and only you.

GETTING PRACTICAL

Palm reading is an easy, simple way to help you see what you have done with your talents and abilities so far in your life and how you can claim the power of your destiny, whether it be through a rewarding career, robust health, world travel, marriage to your soul mate, selfless service to humanity or a special cause, or something else. You alone get to decide whether to read palms strictly for self-edification or to share your new knowledge with others. You can use palmistry as a personal empowerment tool for achieving life goals or for spiritual attainment. The practical application of your knowledge of palmistry means you can look into the hands of others for information about them that even they may not know.

RELATIONSHIPS

If you want an instant take on the personality of a potential boss, friend, client, or lover, take a look at the lines, mounts on the hand, and the fingers. The major lines of the palm—head, heart, life, fate—all reveal something about relationships. Perhaps you are eager to find your soul mate. It's possible through your knowledge and use of palm reading that you'll know before your lover does that deep, long furrows in the marriage line on both your palms suggest you are meant for each other or at least you are destined to share a bond that will endure. Of course, as you have now learned, if the line is broken, it indicates separation or divorce.

A cocky new coworker is proving challenging as a team player and you wonder why until you look at his palm and see the telltale whorl surrounded by a loop (the distinctive mark that looks like the eye in the tail of a peacock). It confirms that your new, overconfident, arrogant coworker is an individualist, more likely to excel when self-employed than when working with others.

You've noticed lots of loops on the fingertips of several friends in your inner circle—a sure sign of why they are so congenial—people with a lot of loops get along well with everyone.

The fate line can't be beat as a place to look when you want to learn more about the companions that life will offer you. A line of influence or attachment can arise from the mount of Luna to join the fate line—an excellent indicator for a business partnership or marriage. The lower that the line of influence joins the fate line, the earlier the relationship will be formed.

SEX

There's sex and then there's sensual, passionate, romantic sex. Take a look at your palm's mount of Venus. If it's overly puffy, it can indicate a penchant for promiscuity. You might recall from what you've read so far that individuals with the personality of a Venus mount type are the most sensual and socially outgoing of them all. They know how to live passionately—and well. As you've already learned, the mount of Venus represents love, home, family, sensuality, and morality, as well as passionate emotion and physical energy. This is a good line to check out in the hand of your new guy or gal. Also take a look at their heart line. In your own palm, if the heart line is heavier than the head line you will likely overrule your head to act upon your need for passion.

Don't overlook the shape of the hands when sizing up a potential bedroom partner. You can't go wrong with the square or earth hand, as they tend to have a healthy libido and are warm and passionate, with a zest for life. Equally important, this lover is emotionally healthy. Even better if the life line sweeps across the palm in a way to give lots of room for a large mount of Venus (more than a third of the palm) and the presence of the **girdle of Venus** (the circle between the bases of Jupiter and Mercury), for this represents an exuberant and exhaustive amount of energy to be used in hot and heavy, sizzling sex.

MONEY

Use palmistry to assess your relationship with money and your potential for manifesting it. You'll likely want to check out your partner's palm as well. You might discover that the two of you working together can create wealth better than independently, or that one of you spends while the other earns. Regardless, the indicators for wealth are right there in your palm.

Does your heart line (or that of your lover—take a look at his or her palm for wealth potential) merge equally and gently with your fate line. If so, you will have it all—wealth, love and affection, power, honor, and fame. If your fingers lean toward your Apollo finger, you are passionate in your pursuit of an artistic or creative profession and that passion can translate to income streams. If all of your fingers incline toward your Jupiter finger, you are a highly ambitious person with your heart set on becoming well known for your talents.

A line rising from the mount of Venus to the Saturn mount shows wealth gained through your own hard work. A line rising from the mount of Venus to the mount of Jupiter is a sign of financial success, especially when it ends in a star. If you have a line from the mount of Venus to the Apollo mount, look for a lottery win or other cash explosion. Just remember, if you see the potential for winning the lotto in your palm, you'll have to play the game to manifest that potential.

HEALTH

Doctors say they can tell a lot about what's going on in the body by looking at your nail beds. Now that you know how to read your palm and fingers for your health status, you can make a doctor's appointment as soon as you detect signs of an illness, even before symptoms appear. You have learned that your fingers carry "vital signs" of their own, and their appearance can change from time to time—so check them regularly to know whether your health picture has changed too.

Take a look at your fate line. Does it abruptly terminate at the heart line? If so, a heart condition could be declaring itself. The presence of vertical lines on your fingers can correlate directly with health issues. On the Jupiter finger, vertical lines suggest the thyroid is affected; on Saturn, it's the pineal gland that's the problem. Vertical lines on the Apollo finger relate to the thymus, which can in turn mean that the cardiovascular system is somehow impaired, with blood pressure too high or too low. Also have your thyroid gland checked if you have vertical lines on your Mercury or little finger. Vertical lines can also point to issues of poor circulation or high blood pressure. If there are white blotches on otherwise healthy-looking fingers, take it as a sign of possible circulatory problems.

Now, when you notice lots of short, horizontal lines on your fingers—a sure sign of too much stress and worry—begin some relaxation techniques or meditation to calm your nerves, fully oxygenate your lungs, slow your heart beat, and find peace. If there is an abundance of vertical lines, consider hormonal health issues. Hormonal imbalances and the symptoms of premenstrual syndrome are revealed in an abundance of vertical lines on the fingers.

Now when you look at your nails, it won't be to judge whether or not you need a manicure. You'll be able to access aspects of your health picture. If your nails are unduly pale, your body may be deficient in iron or suffer from anemia; a bluish tint can indicate lack of oxygen; cracking and brittle nails suggest thyroid disease. In all instances, your reading of your nail beds should conclude with a commitment to see your physician and have your health checked out.

After examining your nails, take note of signs of health or lack of it in your fingertips. Vertical lines along the tips reveal the health status of your endocrine glands: Jupiter correlates to the pituitary gland; Saturn, the pineal and adrenal glands; Apollo, thymus gland, cardiovascular health, and blood pressure; and Mercury, thyroid gland. Robust health is a blessing just as ill health is a curse. Your body has its own wisdom and will show you all through your life how well it is functioning if you take the time to read the signs in your palm.

WORK

The fate line through your life will reveal the degree to which you are using your unique abilities and talents to realize your work and goals. Reading that line, you can see how it records the challenges and rewards you meet along the way. A double fate line can mean many things: a close business partnership or career supported by a marriage (perhaps in a dual career such as husband and wife working side by side as farmers or entrepreneurs in a family business), especially if it begins on the Luna mount. However, a double line could also mean that you have simultaneously undertaken two disparate careers, sustained protection from career problems, or have enjoyed great success in a career.

A line that flows alongside the fate line for a short time reveals that outside forces and interests will affect your career for a time, supporting it or adding more pressure. If your fate line begins near the life line but not within it, you will make your own way in life and determine your own priorities. Your success will rely on your ability to work and accomplish things for yourself with no outside influence. Notice whether or not your fate line begins on the other side of the hand in the mount of Luna, which represents the social element. If it does, it means that your career will put you before the public as a politician or actor—in some way that obliges you to gain public approval in order to have success. Your career might also be in the musical arts or in an area where you are dealing with the public (for example, as a social worker); in any event, it will be in a field in which you demonstrate a skillful ability to affect and influence others.

A fork or branch to the Apollo mount, or an ending of the fate line in that mount, is a sign of personal fulfillment in your career and artistic or intellectual success, usually with accompanying financial rewards. A similar fork or branch structure from the end of the fate line that ends near the Mercury mount means success in business or the sciences.

You can take a secret delight if all your fingers point toward the Mercury finger, as it signals your incredible business acumen; you should pursue entrepreneurial interests, especially if your Jupiter finger is long and slender. A whorl on the Apollo finger can validate your choice to be an artist or designer. An **arch** there suggests your incredible abilities will excel if you apply them to working in crafts involving wood, metal, glass, or ceramic. But if you seek a sign that you should pursue a writing or speaking career, seek out a whorl on the Mercury finger.

Perhaps you haven't yet decided which career path to embark upon. A reading of your palm can guide you and clarify the right direction. Venus mount types have such a keen understanding of human emotion; they make exceptional psychologists and teachers—fields you'll want to steer clear of if you have a smooth or undeveloped Upper Mars mount. Such a configuration reveals your dislike of confrontation and stressful situations. However, since you have a keen intellect and the ability to strategize, you could excel in law as a defense attorney.

Summary

You truly hold your destiny in your hands. Through free choice, you alone decide how to manifest your fabulous future. You now know where to look in your palm for assurance that you are on track. Also, you have discovered your special talents and the potential for using them to claim your best life now and for all your tomorrows.

You have learned to read emotional energies in the palm mounts and see the energies you can use to achieve life goals. Your fingers truly do point to the stores of energy you have available to put your unique traits and special characteristics to work for you. You have gained insights into how the major lines of your hands showcase your health and well-being. And that all-important line of destiny, as you'll recall, mirrors the life you are creating, as well as indicates your ambitions, goals, and alliances. You've discovered where to look for endur-ing romance and business partnerships. Finally, you've also discovered which lines around your wrist portend a future of travel or a vibrant, long life.

Through free choice, you alone decide how to manifest a spectacular future from your potential. You now know where to look in your palm for assurance that you are on track. Also, you have discovered your special talents and how to step forward into your best life now. And when you claim all the power you are meant to have, you also claim it for all the generations of your ancestors still present in you.

Part Four

NUMEROLOGY

Numbers rule the universe.

—Pythagoras (circa 572–497 B.C.),
Ionian Greek mathematician, philosopher,
and father of numerology

If you are like many people, you might think of numbers the way accountants, mathematicians, and scientists think of them—as inanimate figures used to calculate or manipulate quantities of things. But to the ancient Egyptians who studied numbers in the context of numerology, the digits were alive, imbued with energy and animated by a life force. Their perceptions didn't stop there. Numbers were not only even and odd but also active and receptive, and male and female in their characteristics.

Although ideas about the mystical aspects of math permeated the ancient world, it took Greek mathematician Pythagoras to organize and popularize those esoteric ideas into what would become the art of numerology. Numerology can help you find the right date to launch an important project, get married, or start a new venture. Once you know how to access the power inherent in numerology, you will be able to enhance your own life, making it richer, fuller, more meaningful, and easier.

Introduction: What Is Numerology?

Numerology is the metaphysical study of numbers and their occult significance. The most important numbers in your life, according to numerology, aren't your bank account balances or how many houses you own but rather your birth name and birth date. The reason is because from those numbers, you discover your purpose in life, your special qualities, and your life lessons—in short, information that will empower you to have the life meant just for you.

THE BASICS

Everything in the universe is made up of some form of energy. Energy never dies; however, it can and does change forms. In numerology, the numbers one through nine, eleven, and twenty-two are special core numbers, significant because of the energy values, symbolism, and meaning associated with those values.

In the material universe, each thing that exists vibrates, and the vibration has a frequency. Once you know the frequency at which an object vibrates, you can assign certain characteristics, energy values, qualities, and the like. The same is true for people. Your birth date, for example, can be expressed as a number. By assigning numbers to the letters of your name, it too can be expressed as a number. These numbers have a symbolic meaning and an energy value that numerologists use to describe you—your personality, strengths and weaknesses, life purpose, relationships, talents and abilities, and more. Before you learn your personal numbers, how to access and manipulate the power of them, and use numerology to further your knowledge of your true self, you might find helpful a little background information about this art.

NUMBERS AS TOOLS

Numbers are the most perfect and pure form of communication. Numbers gave humans the tools to expand universal understanding of what had always been and to impart that knowledge to future generations. As numbers have become the journey of creation both in the physical and metaphysical world, they have never lost their earliest values.

MATHEMATICS VERSUS NUMEROLOGY

The energy of numbers is used in two basic ways: physical mathematics and metaphysical numerology. The related fields of mathematics and numerology both rely on the use of numbers to produce information or to manipulate the environment. But while mathematics is employed in the construction of conceptual systems for understanding Earth's physical laws, numerology expresses metaphysical insights about numbers as they pertain to your life and the mysteries of the universe.

By using numerology, you learn to relate to numbers as living forces, flowing through all of life. Seeing them as energy carriers, you can manipulate them in ways to benefit your life. You can also apply the power of numerology to further your spiritual comprehension and evolution.

Oil and Water

Mathematics and numerology, like oil and water, never occupy the same space. They touch on all surfaces and can exist side by side, but never mix. In math, the numbers are stationary and physical; in numerology, they are lively and movable. However, both mathematics and numerology build and change reality, whether that means you are building a new bridge (using mathematics) or cultivating a new attitude toward life (using numerology).

MIMICRY OF NATURE

The early architects of civilization learned to use numbers as tools to replicate what they saw in nature. Their attempts could only succeed with the intelligent use of numbers. For example, the ancients observed that a river in its natural course made six bends before narrowing to become a natural dam.

From the area of the dam, animals and humans could drink more easily. Plentiful, easy-to-access water meant herds of animals gathered regularly, making hunting easier.

COMBINATIONS, COORDINATES, AND EQUATIONS

The ancient observers recorded the number of bends, the distance between the bends, and the varying depth of the river as it progressed to the natural dam, and made accurate measurements of the dam itself. The numbers were combined, coordinated, and organized into a system, which could then be duplicated. Through trial and error, they further refined the numbers until they achieved an accurate mathematical duplication of nature. Thereafter, human ingenuity working with the mathematical formulae of nature ensured a supply of water. The reliable water source was soon seen as the key to agriculture, one of the earliest signs of settlement and civilization.

NUMBERS IN NATURE

Nature imparts knowledge of numbers through problems you face. Perhaps you know about dining alone or being the only person in a dark parking lot at midnight. One is truly a lonely number—think of the inherent vulnerability. When a number of other individuals stand with you, there is a sense of power and strength in your numbers. Earliest humans learned the value of numbers in their lessons of survival.

Simpler Is Better

Life's complex problems are often solved by the solution that is overlooked because it is the simplest. The ancients found answers and solutions in the numbers they discovered in nature; the process works just as well for humankind today. Shift your energy by going out into nature. Keep your problem close to you as you take the time to observe and reflect—look at angles and pitches of planes and try counting objects. Expect the answer to come and give it time to emerge.

Nature does not hold the same threats to security issues that it did for your ancestors. However, nature still can help you when you are stumped by a problem. For example, suppose you face a challenge you cannot mentally resolve. The solution simply evades you. You take a walk to get out of your mind and into your body. Perhaps you count the petals on a daisy, note the angle of the afternoon sun against the horizon, or kick ten pebbles into the pond. During your meandering in nature, you hit upon some insight. A simple adjustment in your thinking enables you to arrive at a solution.

ANCIENT PROBLEM SOLVING GAVE RISE TO NEW IDEAS

Through intimate interaction with nature, early humans solved their problems: physical problems (how to survive) and metaphysical ones (how to find one's place in life). Both systems approached and solved problems through observation; people looked to the Earth for physical solutions and to the heavenly bodies of the universe for the metaphysical answers. In both scenarios, numbers played an essential role.

SOLUTIONS LED TO NEW PROBLEMS

When humans learned how to manipulate nature, they unwittingly caused a breakdown in the system: depletion of herds from overhunting, dried grasslands from impeding or redirecting water flow, and the like. The environment, so necessary for survival, faced destruction because of human hands. People realized that their knowledge was incomplete; they had trouble coordinating numbers in a positive manner that neither harmed the environment nor threatened human survival. That's when the concept of supply and demand emerged in human thought.

UNCERTAINTY GAVE RISE TO SPIRITUALITY

Luck, chance, and the environment dictated the turning points of life during ancient times. Luck meant being in the right place at the right time to find food—a rabbit darting by while you had a rock in your hand. Chance meant tripping on a boulder while you were overcome with thirst, only to find beneath the boulder, water in an underground spring. The environment, always exerting tremendous influence over every aspect of human life, was unpredictable. In the face of uncertainty, in ancient times as now, people turned to ideas of the existence of a power greater than themselves.

The Rise of Spirituality

Spirituality appeared when early humans temporarily had satisfied the conditions of survival and felt the relief of safety. For example, bringing home six antelope to feed the tribe inspired rejoicing; knowing you were one of those hunters who brought home the bounty inspired self-satisfaction. Such feelings led to primitive forms of spiritual expression such as awe and gratitude. A vertical rock mound or a circle of stone might mark a spot of spiritual significance.

Humans experienced a spiritual leap as they progressed from primeval mating to pair bonding based on personal choice, not chance. The most successful among them were able to dominate the gene pool by conquering other tribes, establishing bases of power, and building human societies.

SPIRITUAL IDEAS EVOLVE

Ideas became more complex as people began to build a civilization. No longer obsessed with how to stay alive, people could engage their minds and imaginations in creative thought. Thus the Hellenistic world produced amazing magicians, alchemists, and astronomers—adepts known as the **magi** who could understand the secret symbolism of numbers and manipulate the fates they read in the stars.

Be Your Own Magi

As you begin to use the teachings of numerology, you consciously choose to become a part of the lineage of wisdom known and practiced by the magi. They believed that not only did each number have a profound role to play in the universe but the placement or alteration of the numbers could effect change and influence outcomes in a person's life. The magi guided people to build better, more successful lives. You, like those ancient seers, can redirect aspects of your life to claim the fullest and richest expression of it, once you understand the language of numerology's numbers and symbols.

The Gift of the Magi

It was the magi who discovered that the language of the numbers exists in nature and is manifested through the numbers' forms, or their geometric format. The square, the triangle, the cone, and the star are the most common forms.

SYMBOLIC LANGUAGE

You might have noticed that in nature, certain symbols are common. Early humans noticed that, too, and used symbols such as circles, semicircles, and triangles in their numerical language. Later, within the art of numerology, numbers and symbols became endowed with rich, esoteric meaning and energy value.

- **Circles.** This symbol is a line with no end and no beginning. It can be started anywhere from a point of contact, and it completes itself. The circle is a constant flow line of wholeness and completion, simultaneously flowing and completing. The circle in nature can be seen in fruits and berries, the midday Sun, or full Moon.
- **Semicircles.** A semicircle is exactly one-half of a complete circle. Imagine one semicircle faces up. Next to it, the other half faces down. The one-half that faces down is enclosed and gives the symbol form. The other half is open; it symbolically receives the energy of life and experience. You might think of the Moon's crescent that occurs during a cycle of waxing and waning or how its lunar form seems to change during an eclipse.
- **Triangles.** A triangle is made up of three straight, intersecting lines. When you think of images of the triangle in nature, consider a towering mountain peak.
- **Straight lines.** A straight line is not really common in nature. It is a singular oddity in the otherwise rounded world of organic shapes, so its special character marked it as a singular occurrence. A straight line had no center and extended seemingly endlessly upward and downward. That characteristic and endless potential in numerology aptly describes the number 1.

These forms in nature needed no further description to clarify the form. Furthermore, they were commonly understood among various cultures; in written form, they were common to all despite language barriers. Simple, consistent, easily replicated, they varied in size, but their meanings remained the same.

The use of these symbols, so organic in nature, opened the way for nonverbal communication that encouraged intuition, inspiration, creativity, ingenuity, and imagination for useful, happier lives for people. Gradually, as people developed the ability to move from symbols to numbers, each number took on a specific meaning, and numerology was born.

Communicating Through Symbols

You can use simple symbols and numbers as a means of communication that will not lose meaning in translation. A woman in Africa and a man in Alaska will both agree on the form of the symbol they are both seeing (for example, if they are both shown a circle or a square). Also, they will agree on the number (say, three circles and two squares). This communication is clear regardless of how the symbols or numbers are being used.

INTUITION

Your intuition plays a vital role as you work with numbers and symbols within the context of numerology just as logic does when you manipulate numbers in math. True intuition is not a guessing process. It is your deep inner conviction that something is correct. Although what you intuit may seem illogical and not provable using facts, reason, or logic, the insight can nonetheless guide you, especially at the turning points of your life and as those turning points relate to numerical information. Give your intuition free reign as you now begin to explore the core numbers of numerology.

THE NINE PURE NUMBERS

The numbers 1 through 9 are considered pure numbers. Each represents a pure quality or, in other words, a characteristic that is unaffected by any other quality. All the other numbers come from a combination of pure numbers.

Just as red, blue, and yellow are the primary colors, and all other colors are a combination of the primary ones, so are 1, 2, 3, 4, 5, 6, 7, 8, and 9 the primary numbers, with all other numbers being formed from them (through reduction by adding them together). Hence, the number 10, a compound number, may be expressed as 1 + 0 = 1.

The number 10 is different from the other compound numbers; it *contains* all the qualities of 1 through 9 and *becomes* all of them. The difference between a 10-derived 1 and a pure 1 is that a pure 1 is like a beautiful tree in your backyard, complete in itself, while a 10-derived 1 is like your backyard. The number 10 expands the singular 1 as it absorbs of all life's experiences.

The Earth's a 10

Ancient numerologists assigned the number 10 as Earth's vibe number. Everything on Earth, according to numerology, happens in groups of 10. You might already know that many ancient calendars had 10 months, which makes sense according to numerology.

NUMBER QUALITIES

In general, each number has three qualities:

1. The constructive quality, which is the positive evolving use of the vitality of the number
2. The quality of avoidance, as when one turns toward behaviors that deny true contact from occurring
3. The third quality is energy that turns into destructive (masculine) or devouring (feminine)

Moreover, with every number you have a choice about how to interact with the options the energies of that number bring:

- To improve your quality as a person
- To compromise your quality as a person
- To wound beyond easy repair your quality as a person

FLOW-LINE ENERGIES

Math is mental and physical energy; numerology is mental and spiritual energy. When you mentally decide to draw a line, any line, you are also leaving a "flow line"—a line of energy that flows along the shape of the line you are drawing. Therefore, the shape of the flow line is the line's essence. This flow line is a stream of energy that is drawn from the force of life, infinity, energy, *Wu Chi*, the collective, time, love, the source, the void—it is known by so many names because each culture or belief calls it something else.

The Power of Flow Lines

In numerology, the energy of the flow line may be called infinity. It is a vast, limitless, spacious energetic force. It is the embodiment of potential, the focus of meditation, prayer, spiritual dance, faith, the arts, great sex, deep trust, and so much more.

FLOW LINES ARE NUMEROLOGY

A flow line starts with your intent. You draw a symbol. The symbol is thereby distinguished from infinity. As the flow line expresses itself as the individual symbol, it separates, or flows from infinity into distinction. The flow line, as it flows onward, expresses its nature through the form it takes and also expresses its unique attributes, separate from and yet part of the whole.

NUMBERS EXPRESSING THEMSELVES

The energy nature of the flow line of 1 is different from the flow line that creates 2, 3, and so on. The individual personality of each number comes through the process of its moving out from infinity into its own existence. In other words, when you are writing a flow pattern, out of necessity it excludes all other options afforded in infinity. By the nature of its exclusion, then, the pattern comes into being. Each pattern becomes a singularity in its form and in its content—and then it returns to infinity.

As you make 0 (zero), the circular flow line is created with the pen, pencil, or brush mark. As the flow line completes, the circle is the living vitality of completeness. Create another flow line for the numerical 1 (one), and although you have followed exactly the same process, you have created a symbol that is singular, without a center, and that stretches upward and downward.

If you attach the vertical line to the circle, you do two things. You create a center at that juncture, and, at the same time, you redirect the vertical flow line into the flow line of the circle. Now the two flow into each other, and what has emerged as a result is a heavenly sphere grounded into Earth, or the number 9 (nine). Try it yourself: Draw a straight line and attach the circle at the top to make the nine. This number 9 symbolically stands for the humanitarian who draws from spiritual awareness and then shares it with humanity.

The flow lines relate to the Earth and the universe. "Up" is upward and universal. "Down" is downward, in contact with Earth. The left side is the intake side. The right side is the outflow side. Roundness is feminine, flexible, open—as in a semicircle, or complete, as in a circle. Straight lines are masculine, direct, and focused.

Masculine or Feminine?

When flow lines are designated as feminine and masculine, the terms do not signify gender but rather an aspect or a characteristic. Numbers 1, 4, and 7 are said to be masculine because they carry aspects of focus, action, singularity. Numbers 3 and 6 are said to be feminine because they carry aspects of receptivity, balance, connectedness, and comfort. Numbers 2, 5, 8, and 9 carry both feminine and masculine characteristics.

THE FLOW LINE OF 0

- Form: A perfect circle and its own center.
- Gender: Feminine.
- Energetic flow: Starts at any point in its circumference, finishes precisely at the same point, creating a continuous flow line.
- Characteristics: whole, complete, filled with endless life of the Earth.

THE FLOW LINE OF 1

- Form: A straight line, no top, no bottom, no center.
- Gender: Masculine; describes the mental.
- Energetic flow: The flow line goes up and down limitlessly because it has no center.
- Positive characteristics: Singular, contained, seeking, reaching, exploring, independent, willful, and courageous.
- Negative characteristics: Egotistic, dominating, and aggressive.

THE FLOW LINE OF 2

- Form: A perfect semicircle in connection at its base with a single horizontal line; its center is where the semicircle and the horizontal line meet.
- Gender: Feminine and masculine; intuitive.
- Energetic flow: The left side of the flow line gives form and protection to the open, receptive, curved container it forms on its right. The semicircle flow line connects to the strong, grounded, horizontal contact with Earth, two very different symbols in firm alliance and balance.
- Positive characteristics: Cooperative, understanding, relationship seeking, balanced.
- Negative characteristics: Timid, self-conscious, and depressed.

THE FLOW LINE OF 3

- Form: Two connecting semicircles, one above the other; the center is in the middle, where they touch.
- Gender: Feminine; emotional.
- Energetic flow: Rounding to its left, forming two receptive containers on its right, rocking connection to both the universe and the Earth.
- Positive characteristics: Self-expressive, creative, ebullient, fun.
- Negative characteristics: Self-centered, lacking in focus, and moody.

THE FLOW LINE OF 4

- Form: A number made up of four connecting straight lines at right angles to one another; the center is where the square meets the line.
- Gender: Masculine; physical.
- Energetic flow: Receives from the universe, structures it, and grounds it.
- Positive characteristics: Structured, disciplined, reliable, and stable.
- Negative characteristics: Opinionated, argumentative, and overly serious.

THE FLOW LINE OF 5

- Form: Two straight lines and a semicircle. One straight line reaches into the mental plane, supporting heaven; the other connects the mental and the semicircle, which rounds on its left and forms a container on its right. The center is where the vertical line meets the semicircle.
- Gender: Feminine and masculine; physical.
- Energetic flow: A reaching for and a focusing of mental energies, drawing direct, focused movement down to connect the rounded, protecting container rocking on Earth.
- Positive characteristics: Curious, adventurous, and industrious shaker-mover.
- Negative characteristics: Impatient, discontented, impetuous.

THE FLOW LINE OF 6

- Form: A larger semicircle with a smaller circle curled into it at its base; its center is where the line touches itself.
- Gender: Feminine; emotional.
- Energetic flow: The flow line curves to the left, containing and securing the smaller circle on its left.
- Positive characteristics: Nurturing, comforting, a number that represents the home and hearth.
- Negative characteristics: Stubborn, meddling, and obstinate.

THE FLOW LINE OF 7

- Form: Two straight lines joining on the top at an angle; the upper line is one-half the length of the lower line and horizontal, connecting into the diagonal flow line. The center is where the two lines meet.
- Gender: Masculine; intuitive.
- Energetic flow: The flow line connects into the mental energies and after taking a sharp turn, runs a downward diagonal course to no apparent end . . . to the devil, if not restrained.
- Positive characteristics: Spiritual, analytical, and still.
- Negative characteristics: Secretive, reserved, and sarcastic.

THE FLOW LINE OF 8

- Form: Two complete circles, one on top of the other; the center is in the middle, where they join.
- Gender: Feminine and masculine; mental.
- Energetic flow: The flow line is two flows moving in two complete circles, joining in a flow of unification (notice that an 8 flipped on its side forms the infinity symbol).
- Positive characteristics: Complete, unified, represents the giver and receiver, and expects success.
- Negative characteristics: Impatient, workaholic, stressed, and overly materialistic.

THE FLOW LINE OF 9

- Form: A full circle on top, connected to a line going straight down; the center is where the circle and the line meet.
- Gender: Feminine and masculine; a blend of emotional and intuitive.
- Energetic flow: A sphere in heaven connects to Earth through a downward-focused flow.
- Positive characteristics: Universal, humanitarian, intuitive.
- Negative characteristics: Financially irresponsible, self-adulating, and possessive.

Two-Digit Numbers

In addition to pure numbers, numerology also singles out the compound number 10 and the mastery numbers 11 and 22. The qualities of mastery numbers supersede their compound qualities—that is, they are not added up to a pure number. Instead, they remain double-digit numbers with their own unique meanings.

THE FLOW LINE OF 10

- Ten is a compound number.
- Ten is made up of each of the preceding numbers—1, 2, 3, 4, 5, 6, 7, 8, and 9.
- Characteristics: collectively numbers 1 through 9.

THE FLOW LINE OF 11

- Form: Two single, parallel straight lines; no center.
- Gender: None.
- Energetic flow: Flow lines are extending up to infinity and down (to the core of the Earth or to the devil). But because the balance of reaching up and down is maintained, imbalance with the dark doesn't happen like it does with the 7.
- Characteristics: Spiritual mastery.

THE FLOW LINE OF 22

- Form: Two semicircles connected to horizontal baselines; the center is where each symbol connects the semicircle to the base and the synergy that is created.
- Gender: None.
- Energetic flow: Two very different symbols in a perfect reflective match.
- Characteristics: Relationship mastery on Earth, where everything is in relationship; spiritual mastery.

In numerology, every number is equal. Every number is compatible with every other number. Every number has its own path to all the following qualities: compassion, love, equanimity, unity, and acceptance. Every number is completely distinct and in harmonic balance with the others. This ability to be distinct and remain in symphony with the group is called *syntony*.

THE POTENTIALS OF COMPLETION

You can see from the following list what the flow lines would be expressing if the pure symbols were completed like this:

- 1 would remain the same flow line—singular, limitless potential in either direction.
- 2 would become a sphere on a horizontal line—grounded completeness.
- 3 would become the 8, the power of life found through a light and open heart.
- 4 becomes a square with a single line connecting to the earth—stability is still the expression and the challenge is to not get closed and rigid like a poorly grounded square.
- 5 would become a triangle on a circle, a representation of great strength and special gifts—the triune resting on a circle of completion.
- 6 would become a circle containing a smaller circle—that which is complete, protecting, nurturing.
- 7 would become an isosceles triangle—perfect strength, perfect form.
- 8 stays complete.
- 9 stays complete.

So with the flow lines extended, the full personal growth potential that each symbol represents becomes clearer. The numbers 1, 8, and 9 start complete and work on expressing this completeness in harmony and balance with their life experiences. They're experiencing rest within the structure of the form; much of the experience is spent keeping the flow structure strong, so containment of the pattern is possible.

The others—2, 3, 4, 5, 6, and 7—are evoking more through experimentation in life to discover aspects of completion. With these numbers comes more movement, more seeking from without, an engagement with life on various levels.

FLOW LINES ARE GUIDES

Flow lines are indicators, markers, and our guides in life. They existed before we existed, and we harnessed their powers in the numbers we use, both in mathematics and in numerology. Numbers have the power of the flow-line energy to help you know yourself—physically, mentally, emotionally, and spiritually.

As we have grown, changed, and evolved as humans, the Universal is always guiding us. As creatures of complete free will, we can develop our potential and in this way expand the self-knowing of the numbers. They guide us, and, in turn, we continue to work on and develop them.

LETTERS AND NUMBERS

Each letter of the Latin alphabet (the alphabet we use when reading and writing the English language) has its own numerological value, based on its order. This system is very straightforward: A has the value of 1, B has the value of 2, and so forth, all the way down to Z, which has the value of 26 (which is converted into 8 by adding 2 and 6).

Number Values of the Alphabet

A	1	N	14 = 5
B	2	O	15 = 6
C	3	P	16 = 7
D	4	Q	17 = 8
E	5	R	18 = 9
F	6	S	19 = 10 = 1
G	7	T	20 = 2
H	8	U	21 = 3
I	9	V	22
J	10 = 1	W	23 = 5
K	11	X	24 = 6
L	12 = 3	Y	25 = 7
M	13 = 4	Z	26 = 8

10 to 1

You can clearly see that 10 becomes 1, but even though it is converted, it does not lose its 10 value. It takes the value of the 10—all the numbers combined—and becomes a special sort of 1. This special value is endowed with a vibratory combination of all the 10 qualities, though now in a singular form. So when 10 changes to 1, there is a vibratory expansion that occurs.

▼ ▼

THE PURE LETTERS

The alphabetical letters A through I correspond to the pure numbers 1 through 9, so those letters are also pure. Each letter's characteristics are identical to the number with which it corresponds. For the rest of the alphabet, the corresponding numbers are compound numbers that are converted to their pure roots. In numerology, the art of energy, this conversion process creates a greater complexity within the root number, but it also adds greater variety, a quality we recognize as the basis of humanity.

For instance, if a man's name is Bill (which begins with a B, second letter of the alphabet), he will have a firm vibration of 2, which signifies relationship. The more B's in a name (for instance, if his name were Bob), the more the quality of the pure 2 is carried. Now, let's say your name is Ursula. It begins with a U, a letter that correlates to 21, and you know that 2 + 1 = 3, so the interpretation might be that you are a relationship-oriented single person who loves fun, which is the true expression of balance.

Other examples: G is a 7, which as we have already seen creates the flow pattern of seeking and of stillness. P is also a 7—its corresponding number is 16, and 1 + 6 = 7—but in the case of Pamela and Paul, the combination of 1 and 6 brings to the 7 a flow line of the G singularity and comfort that are components of the G and 7 seeker.

▲ ▲

Each Path Is Different

Each letter becomes a pure root number, but the path it travels to get to the root—the flowing, for instance, made by the 2 and 4 to create the 6—is different. The magi understood this, and used the energy flow lines of various number combinations to redefine the pure number.

▼ ▼

The letter X, which is number 24 in the sequence of the alphabet, has the root number 6 (you add the 2 and 4 together). The 2 brings an interest in relatedness. The 4 invests X with the power to structure. When these join in flow lines with the 6, you have a person who is stable, enjoys relationships, and is a comfort to be with.

Numerical Values of Letters

A	1	Singular
B	2	Balancer
C	3	Creator
D	4	Structurer
E	5	Person of action
F	6	Comforter
G	7	Seeker
H	8	Stable power
I	9	Humanitarian
J	10 = 1	Justice
K	11	Spiritual contributor
L	12 = 3	Creative force for self and others
M	13 = 4	Strong, creative structure
N	14 = 5	Bringer of creation to action
O	15 = 6	Self-trusting adventurer
P	16 = 7	A force for creative analysis
Q	17 = 8	Powerful and autonomous
R	18 = 9	Struggle with use of power
S	19 = 10 = 1	Great spiritual vision
T	20 = 2	Necessity of making a choice
U	21 = 3	Receptive creativity
V	22	Transformation of mental ideas to physical manifestation
W	23 = 5	Defined and creative action
X	24 = 6	Standing strong and protecting
Y	25 = 7	Decision maker
Z	26 = 8	Great intuitive power

THE FLOW LINES OF LETTERS

You see flow lines everywhere. They are created through the incessant inter-action between form and space, both of which are necessary for enacting out-come. The letters' flow lines follow exactly the same laws as those of the numbers.

Remember, the first nine letters of the alphabet (from A to I) are pure. The rest of the letters, from J to Z, are compound letters. In them, the flow lines combine to create more and more variety and profusion. Their units of energy are ever growing, creating life as we know it.

FLOW-LINE STRUCTURE OF A.

This letter is a well-grounded symbol that stands on two legs. The top half is a pyramid pointing up. The bottom half is a container for the Earth's energy.

A pyramid is the most efficient way to draw universal energy to Earth. The base receives this energy and stabilizes it. The symbol is further grounded by the container made for Earth's energies in the lower half. The center is the horizontal line, which provides further grounding.

The letter A is singular, grounded, and contained. It represents one's own counsel, as well as those who are able to get intuitive knowledge and draw it into action.

FLOW-LINE STRUCTURE OF B

The letter B is made up of two same-sized semicircles that are perfectly balanced. They are connected by a vertical line on the left, which meets pre-cisely with the connection to the semicircles.

The semicircles form two same-sized energy containers. The upper one contains the spiritual and mental type of energy. The lower contains energy of the emotional and physical realms.

The letter B represents balance and inward stability. It is steady, the letter of a builder.

FLOW-LINE STRUCTURE OF C

The letter C forms a single line that extends into but does not complete a circle. It curves to its left, and the symbol has a rounded base and top.

It is a protected container, rounded, receptive, one that is mingling ener-gies within. It has a rocking, self-righting relationship to the ground.

This letter is durable, comforting, creative, and resilient.

FLOW-LINE STRUCTURE OF D

The letter D forms a large semicircle that curves to the right, which is coupled with a vertical line that precisely meets the tips of the semicircle.

Its strong vertical flow line anchoring a semicircle creates a contained energetic space.

This letter finds its own gateway by providing the gate for others. It is strong and comforting, structuring and grounding.

FLOW-LINE STRUCTURE OF E

The letter E is made up of four straight lines. Three are horizontal, and each one is half the length of the anchoring vertical straight line. The horizontal lines connect top, center, and bottom, creating two balanced, structured spaces on its right.

The flow line of E is a strong vertical grounding line on its right with three horizontal flow lines that direct the vertical, extending flows to the mental, emotional, and physical. Energies of the mental and emotional commingle in the upper space. The emotional and physical commingle in the lower space.

This letter represents great analytical skill and the ability to understand and structure. It is very stable when engaged with life, comprised in equal parts of the spiritual and mental, emotional and physical.

FLOW-LINE STRUCTURE OF F

The letter F is formed by three straight lines. One is a strong vertical line between heaven and Earth; the other two are horizontal lines, each one-half the length of the vertical line. One forms a top; the other meets the vertical at the middle. The vertical line forms the base.

The strong vertical flow line on its right draws down the mental energy from the top line and the emotional energy from the middle line. These join and ground on a single spot. The energies commingle in the structured upper area. The lower area makes a strong, singular connection to Earth.

This letter represents forceful beliefs and rigid or fixed opinions. It relies on mental clarity, but it may need support.

FLOW-LINE STRUCTURE OF G

The letter G forms an almost fully contained circle, with a rounded base and a horizontal line that is connected to the lower end of the incomplete circle.

The incomplete circle creates a container on the left, as it curves to the right and ends with a supporting line as a resting place for the energies it contains. The base is kept from the freedom of rocking by the internal platform of support.

This letter is a comforter, receiver, and strong supporter. It will take on burdens and stabilize itself through them.

FLOW-LINE STRUCTURE OF H

The letter H is formed by two strong vertical lines extending up and down on either side of a horizontal line, which creates a bridge that is the exact center point of the two vertical lines.

The two points of contact with the heavens flow directly into Earth. They are stabilized by the middle line, and they create two structured openings.

This letter is very strong. It represents those who walk with confidence, stay strong under outside pressure, and have powerful insights and vision.

FLOW-LINE STRUCTURE OF I

The letter I is formed by a central vertical line, topped and bottomed by two horizontal lines that are each one-third the length of the center line.

The upper horizontal line stabilizes and supports the spiritual energy that is drawn down by the vertical center line. The horizontal lines also reach out to the mental energies both to the right and to the left, drawing the mental in to support the spiritual energies. The base provides perfect balance for the symbol.

This letter is delicate but stable. It represents a private inner world, mental understanding of spiritual wisdom, and a clear adjustment of one's life in order to live what is felt intuitively.

FLOW-LINE STRUCTURE OF J

The letter J is formed by an upper horizontal line connecting to a central vertical line, which joins a semicircle on the bottom.

Its flow line extends both ways into the mental while it supports the spiritual. The strong central line flows into a semicircle at the base. This creates a rocking relationship to Earth, with some balance problems.

This letter represents weights and measures, spiritual insight, and looking for the balanced approach. Letter J can be self-absorbed because of balance issues, but it has the power to generate rebirth when balance occurs.

FLOW-LINE STRUCTURE OF K

The letter K is formed by a strong vertical line that reaches up and down, as well as by another line that is bent at the midpoint, creating a diagonal line to join the strong vertical.

The flow line of the vertical is directed to heaven and Earth, as is the single diagonal line meeting at midpoint. The internal space created is a V, open to receiving heaven and receiving Earth.

This letter is a self-directed spiritual teacher. It is spiritually uplifting and stable. Balanced between heaven and Earth, this letter is aware of both of them.

FLOW-LINE STRUCTURE OF L

The letter L is formed by a strong vertical line that joins a base horizontal line half its length.

The flow line pulls from the heavens and from the ground, and it directs the flow line out the left side.

This letter is a force to reckon with. It is filled with direct action. Often spiritually motivated, it drives the self as hard as it drives others.

Shape Shapes Vibration

In numerology, the shaping of each letter is critical. A well-shaped letter will provide the maximum vibration. (The same is true for numbers.) If you have messy handwriting, it might do you good to practice your letters—just like you used to do in grade school.

FLOW-LINE STRUCTURE OF M

The letter M is made up of two parallel, vertical lines joined by two diagonal lines meeting at their midpoint on the ground.

The energy of its flow line comes from its strong relationship to the Earth, which is seen in the bases of its upward-pointing triangles. However, this letter also manifests downward-pointing triangles that harness the energies from heaven.

This letter carries the qualities of very grounded femininity, earthy and nurturing. It is like a wise mother bear—M knows when to give a kiss and when to give a kick.

FLOW-LINE STRUCTURE OF N

The letter N is formed by three straight lines of the same length—two single verticals connected by a diagonal that intersects the top of its left vertical and the bottom of its right vertical.

N's flow lines ascend from the Earth to touch the heavens. The flow of the diagonal draws the force of heaven and Earth to touch points. The empty spaces are receptive triangles.

This letter is a seed sower, and it can bring the ability to increase.

FLOW-LINE STRUCTURE OF O

The letter O is a complete circle that can be started at any point. It has neither a beginning nor an end, and it contains within itself a fully enclosed empty space.

This letter represents vast sight. It is visionary and intuitive. It controls deep, quiet inner rhythms, and it contains great wisdom.

FLOW-LINE STRUCTURE OF P

The letter P is formed by a straight vertical line with a semicircle connecting on its right from midline to its upper point.

Its vertical line is supported by Earth. In its semicircle, P contains the space of heavens and emotions.

This letter is gracious and well meaning. It is a powerful builder and represents spiritual structuring.

FLOW-LINE STRUCTURE OF Q

The letter Q is a perfect, complete circle with a root extending below the line.

Its flow line is a circle balanced between heaven and Earth, with a root going down to the energies of the Earth. The Q circle forms a contained space for all the energies to mingle.

This letter is complete and individualistic. It is female in power, and it carries great authority.

FLOW-LINE STRUCTURE OF R

The letter R is formed by a straight vertical line with a semicircle on its upper right side and a diagonal that intersects where the lower semicircle joins the vertical and then goes straight to Earth.

Its flow-line energy feeds on the direct connection from heaven to Earth, and its semicircle contains a comingling of mental and spiritual energies. A lower leg of the R represents the energy that runs through the physical.

This letter represents self-acceptance and genuine contact with another. It comes to elevate karma.

FLOW-LINE STRUCTURE OF S

S is formed by two semicircles facing opposite directions—the upper semicircle opens to the right, and the lower semicircle opens to the left.

The curves of S join heaven and Earth and rise up much like a serpent to the heavens, ambling through the energy fields.

This letter represents mystical and intellectual wisdom, earthly charisma, the movement of life, and serpentine force.

FLOW-LINE STRUCTURE OF T

The letter T is formed by a vertical line that begins in Earth and ends at the top, where it is covered by an intersecting horizontal line. The horizontal line supports the heavenly energies with a mental analysis. Vertical draws this force to the Earth.

This letter is about seeing your options or being caught between two choices. It may be pinioned or surrendering.

FLOW-LINE STRUCTURE OF U

The letter U is formed by a single, flowing line that draws the heavens to the Earth.

Its flow line connects the spiritual to Earth with a rounded base, creating a space of great receptivity.

This letter is about receptive strength, warmth, and a promise that heaven knows the way, but Earth gives the tools to progress. In English, Q is always paired with U—great female empowerment.

FLOW-LINE STRUCTURE OF V

The letter V is formed by two diagonal lines that meet at the base. Its flow lines create a drawing-down from heaven and a seeding into Earth. V represents an image of arms reaching upward. It transforms ideas into physical reality, and it creates ideas and follows through as a builder. It is a majestic letter.

FLOW-LINE STRUCTURE OF W

The letter W is formed by four even diagonal lines that create three open-ended triangles. Two of the lines receive the heavens, grounding into two focused points to the Earth. The third, in the middle, provides a center and receives the Earth.

This letter is a blender of ideas, a mediator. It understands heaven's way and Earth's centeredness.

FLOW-LINE STRUCTURE OF X

The letter X is made up of two straight lines crossed at the midpoint. Its flow lines cross from right to left on a diagonal flow, receiving from Earth and heaven and centering it at the midpoint.

This letter is all about endurance and the balanced perspective. It is a letter about being courageous, here to benefit self and others.

FLOW-LINE STRUCTURE OF Y

The letter Y is formed by three straight lines intersecting at the midpoint, two on the upper half and one supporting on the lower half. Its energy flow joins at a midline center, where the upper flow joins into the mingled flow to Earth. This letter represents the decision maker. The letter Y is balanced and carries the wisdom from the spiritual.

FLOW-LINE STRUCTURE OF Z

The letter Z is made up of two horizontal lines connected by a diagonal line that crosses the center area. Its flow lines are well connected and supportive of heaven and Earth. Its cross line provides additional connection and strong support. This letter represents prophetic vision, good will, benevolence, and impact. It is intuitive in matters of human affairs.

▲▲▲▲▲▲▲▲▲▲▲▲▲▲▲▲▲▲▲▲▲▲▲▲▲▲▲▲

It's All a Pattern

Every aspect of your life is part of a grand pattern. As you begin to interpret these patterns, you gain a new dimension in your understanding of what it's possible to experience—hidden talents, special abilities, and areas of strength that could suggest important work or a life path you perhaps have not yet envisioned.

▼▼▼▼▼▼▼▼▼▼▼▼▼▼▼▼▼▼▼▼▼▼▼▼▼▼▼▼▼

Your Soul Essence Number

Numerological formulas are tools to help you expand your awareness of your most basic and reliable characteristics. Your deepest core characteristic represents your soul essence. An ancient numerology formula in this section will help you determine your soul essence and how to settle into it so that you can become the fullest expression of who you are and who you are meant to become.

You are the spark that illuminates your life. You carry within yourself all that is required to love your life in exactly the direction that is perfect for you and your learning. There is just this one little issue standing in your way, and it has to do with choice. In a very real sense, the life you have right now is the result of every choice and decision you have ever made. If you have areas of your life you want to change, change the way you make your decisions. Numerology can help with that.

▲▲▲▲▲▲▲▲▲▲▲▲▲▲▲▲▲▲▲▲▲▲▲▲▲▲▲▲

Commit to the Creator

Numerology teaches that you have been cast from the Creator as a spark of personal essence. You travel the universe learning about the nature of yourself as this spark, always learning through a variety of experiences that are available. You speed through time and space in a micro-millisecond of time that is your own space. Your personal quality is your most sacred commitment to the universe and the Creator. It is this constant elevation of your own qualities within the experience of life that is at the heart of the reason for life itself.

▼▼▼▼▼▼▼▼▼▼▼▼▼▼▼▼▼▼▼▼▼▼▼▼▼▼▼▼▼

Your soul essence is the centerpiece of your nature. Like the pebble falling into water that creates a ripple effect from the impact, you are similarly constructed, according to numerology. First, you bring your nature into your life. Your birth time and date become the entry point that sets the coordinates for your life journey. You have a preplanned life-lesson focus, and you immediately relate to this commitment. Next, your soul nature and life lesson coordinate with your birth year. After that comes the best manifestation of your talents. All of this is comforted and centered by your reconstructor of self-love. Finally, all of these qualities coordinate with your name. Then, from these concentric circles—which you can also understand as patterns of yourself—you interact with life.

YOUR SOUL ESSENCE IS THE CORE OF YOU

The first order of your life's business is to determine your soul essence vibration. This is your most important mission because until you have your own energy packaging together, it isn't really possible to bring harmony to your connections to life. In this harmony, you must also be able to have **synchronicity**, a good rhythm of learning and balancing support throughout the remainder of your life experience.

Here is the ancient formula:

1. Write out your full name (first, middle, and last) in capital letters. Shape your letters according to the flow-line patterns you have learned.
2. Write the correct root number above each vowel. Again, shape your numbers in the old numerological way. To refresh your memory, here are the numerical equivalents for each vowel:
   A = 1
   E = 5
   I = 9
   O = 15 = 6
   U = 21 = 3
3. Add up the vowel root numbers of your first name, middle name, and last name.
4. Finally, add up the final vowel root numbers for each name.

As you write out the letters of your name, remember that you are working with flow lines, which means you are working with energy. To get the essence of the flow line vitality, you need to make sure each step is done in keeping with the wise authority of the ancients. Letters must be written out with circles, semicircles, and straight lines.

The following is an example of how to calculate your soul essence number:

| 5 | | 1 | 5 | | | | 5+1+5 = 11 |
| E | L | L | A | E | | | |

| 5 | | | 9 | | 6 | 6 | | | 5+9+6+6 = 26 = 8 |
| E | L | I | N | W | O | O | D | |

$$11+8 = 19 = 10 = 1$$

It is very important that you use your true name as you calculate your soul essence number. If you are addressed differently by different people, please consider which name resonates with you most deeply.

Your Soul Essence Number

First name: _____   Total: _____

Middle name: _____   Total: _____

Last name: _____   Total: _____

Final total: _____

Soul essence root number: _____

The soul essence number that emerges from this formula can remind and confirm to you the nature of your deepest, most meaningful essence. This is what you came into this lifetime to express, in all the affairs of your life. It is the part of yourself that you long to know about and that you were made to share fully with others. To live life from this center core of yourself is to live from your soul.

NUMEROLOGY IS THE ART OF PLACEMENT

These carefully constructed placement charts set the coordinates for the energetic aspects of your numerological formula. This will help to increase your insight and intuition into what the units of combining energy are expressing. Don't make the mistake of assuming that these steps hold no value. Bad things aren't going to happen if you skip them, of course, but the best things won't happen either.

As you work on your numerology formulas, always remember to write out the letters and numbers in the simplified, numerological way, as you have seen them appear in this book. Moreover, remember that when you work with words, you write the numbers *over* the vowels and *under* the consonants.

LOOKING WITH AN ANCIENT EYE

But what does your soul essence number represent? You have two ways of finding out. First, you can consult the ancient masters of numerology, who have compiled this information over thousands of years. Second, you have the power of intuition to look inside yourself and find your own interpretations.

Numbers Are a Part of You

Numerology is common to all, but at the same time it can be very personal. Numbers are living energies, and they are everywhere, even as a part of you. That means that you have within you an exact understanding of what they are.

Meditate and look inside yourself to find the meanings of the numbers, and then see what the masters have left for us as their interpretations and experiences (as the following sections describe).

SOUL ESSENCE 1

This is the essence of one who is here to claim the qualities of learning and giving that are associated with singular contributions. Achievement, creation, invention, family, and friends are expressions of the 1's ability to achieve and create success. The 1 is loyal, a leader who is fair and given to spurts of amazing generosity. The 1 shows and inspires others by personally demonstrating what he or she is capable of doing as an individual.

Soul Essence 1

Symbol	Possible Behavior
Straight vertical line	Stands alone
Connected up and down	Draws from heaven and Earth alone
Narrow line	Keeps self very singular

The task of soul essence 1 is to see life as a self-reflector and not as a theater to perform in. In doing that, the balance of appreciating the equality of all things—including the 1—becomes the treasured drop of wisdom gained from the life.

SOUL ESSENCE 2

Soul essence 2 is filled with the capacity and desire for contact with others. This personality loves individuals, groups, communities, nations, and the world as a whole. The 2 essence is a tireless worker for others, who wants to create environments in which people thrive, in which the focus is usually comfort, security, peace, and harmony. The desire to create a better world promotes the ability of the 2 to be diplomatic, empathic, emotionally sensitive to the unsaid words of others. This in turn creates an astounding ability to welcome in all and then more: "Always room for one more."

Soul Essence 2

Symbol	Possible Behavior
Rounded top	Receptive
Straight horizontal line	Very steady
Large container	Lots of space for life and others

There is a natural humility that goes with the 2. This creates a quiet, sometimes obscure life and an amazing ability to find blessings in the small wonders of life. The only rigidity is in the support of others, which 2 will do with a quiet force few will withstand.

The learning is to gain the golden drop of wisdom through developing a commitment to a sense of purpose and direction that gives direct benefit to the 2.

SOUL ESSENCE 3

This soul essence is pure, light, and fun. This is an essence that loves to share and inspire joy and happiness. This tends to automatically draw friends and admirers by the droves. The 3 soul essence draws fun from everyone and everything. Like a happy puppy, the 3 goes through life with ears flapping and tail wagging, engaging with a pure joy of being alive.

The 3 essence doesn't recognize tragedy and loss as a reason for depression or self-doubt. It is not really true that the 3 essence is a specialist in escapist behaviors; instead, it is more that every situation has a silver lining, and it is this element that the 3 essence sees and relates to.

You will never find 3 essences holding onto any memories that make them dour. The victim view is simply not part of their character or how they approach life. This essence is the joy of living, and life is indeed a pleasure. The cup is not only always half-full, but that half is bubbling over the top.

Soul Essence 3

Symbol	Possible Behavior
Very rounded	Relaxed and flexible
Balanced, but looks like rocking comes often	Likes to move around and sample all life has to offer

The lesson that 3 essence can derive from life is to settle down, focus, concentrate, and enjoy life. That means enjoying not just the ripe fruit but the whole process—and that includes planting, tending, pruning, nurturing, and finally eating the fruits of life. This means learning to use patience as a tool for keeping interested in the process. The 3 essence has virtually no concentrated patience.

SOUL ESSENCE 4

The 4 essence is the pure soul of dependability, structure, loyalty, and trust. In other words, this essence is everything you would associate with a firm, solid expression of the best of values, morals, and traditions. Because of the amount of structure that is creating the space, you have a person who is very disciplined—for a cause.

This is a soul essence who upholds the most basic structures or morals of the culture. In the Western world's case, this would be partnership loyalty, family care, a respectable job, and true patriotism. This soul essence is traditional, not particularly inventive, but very loving. The 4 essence is invested in both needing and giving a consistent and constant support. The 4 soul essence is inclined to see others' needs before his or her own and is therefore capable of putting others first when making decisions.

Soul Essence 4

Symbol	Possible Behavior
A strong structure	Very structured person
Sharp angles	Likes things to be clear and direct
Base much smaller than the top	Receives much from heaven and takes the time to turn this bounty into action

The 4 soul essence will learn the value of always adding to and updating self-knowledge to avoid a limited point of view and holding onto the past. The 4 essence will also gain wisdom on having the scope of self-knowledge to withhold that which cannot be freely given.

SOUL ESSENCE 5

The 5 soul essence is the mental seeker and emotional explorer who is constantly on the move. This essence is restless and freedom oriented, the shaker-mover energy personified. Constant curiosity makes the 5 essence very adaptable to life but not often really changed by it. Something of a dilettante, this essence adds a special liveliness to any situation it finds itself in.

They are usually ready to move on to the next experience whenever the present one no longer holds the attention or interest of their vastly experiential nature. This natural way of expanding into the full panoply of life's banquet embraces most dearly the arts, music, great food, travel, and fine clothes and jewels. To this soul essence, all these things mean the good life that has been sought, embraced, and fulfilled.

Soul Essence 5

Symbol	Possible Behavior
Strong upper mental reach	Curious mental energies
Strong, structured emotional space	Emotions and drive to succeed are one
Very rounded, grounded base	Constantly on the move

The learning that the 5 essence will have as life naturally unfolds includes loyalty, consistency, fascination with the process, and a patient acceptance that everything opens, but only in its own time. You can't get a bush to bloom by telling it to.

SOUL ESSENCE 6

The 6 soul essence is the nurturer. It embodies a powerful essence of protective friendship, loyal love, a comfy home, and a deep, steady root that gives endless support to others. Deeply connected to physical and emotional rootedness, the 6 essence carries a deeply comforting, calming, and reassuring quality that speaks of life as a challenge at times but one that remains eminently trustable. The 6 essence demonstrates to others how to hold back the fear of life's unexpected twists and turns and believe in the power of comfort and sustaining love as an ever-present force to balance the impermanence of change.

Soul Essence 6

Symbol	Possible Behavior
Soft and rounded	Feminine and nurturing
Returns to itself	Keeps loved ones safe
Protected space	Protects

The 6 essence is inclined to work out of the home or in a very homey refuge, a protecting environment, counseling or conducting laws that protect. The 6 essence expresses all the qualities one associates with home in all aspects of life.

Everyone is greeted as a guest/friend and is given stable, loving, parental support. The 6 essence has a great natural compassion and empathy for others. The 6 essence will give tremendous love and support to others. That's because deep within, the 6 essence knows he or she is fully protected and nurtured by spirit. This deep acceptance of protection as a birthright brings comfort and acceptance to anyone in times of well-being, as well as in struggle and even in times of peril.

The lesson that 6 essences will draw from life is to be able to develop a flexible boundary between themselves and others. This boundary will enable them to have a more objective and firm, assertive response to people and life events.

SOUL ESSENCE 7

The 7 soul essence is the most enigmatic or least knowable of the numbers. This essence is always alone, with an involved and evolved relationship to his or her inner world of science, philosophy, and other pursuits of the intellect. It is this relationship that is the 7 soul essence's primary relationship. Because this inner world is the 7 soul essence, he or she is inclined to perform his or her life, becoming a living example of the scientist, the philosopher, or the doctor, instead of just being a human being.

The soul essence of 7 is so deeply engaged with the world possibilities conceived in the mental that it is easy to become the embodiment of them. Filled with wisdom, but too inner related to be easily skilled socially, the 7 essence can give to others vast, intrinsic, and valuable wisdom and be more aligned with the wisdom than with the people.

Soul Essence 7

Symbol	Possible Behavior
Strong mental line	Moved by intellectual inquiry
Diagonal line going down	Goes for the bottom line
Very defined	Loner

The 7 essence loves to examine from every angle. This essence analyzes everything and hates to be drawn into messy human stuff—fighting, dirty hand work, chaotic environments. With a talent for order, containing a deep and private well of self and an odd combination of spiritual and survival fears, the 7 essence can only be loved if the other person takes the time to know him or her.

The 7 essence will automatically be learning how to be alone and, at the same time, fully content and never lonely. Also, empathy and compassion for the challenge of true life events will create a more personal attitude with life in general. As the 7 essence becomes more comfortable with life, much of the fear and longing transforms to courage and the ability to find beauty in the wee moments of life.

SOUL ESSENCE 8

The 8 soul essence can be summed up very simply in these two words: expects success. Imbued with talents for organization and systems of any kind, and further blessed with an affinity for large affairs and events and the personal power to conceive, organize, and direct them, the 8 essence has the love and ability to achieve on a great scale.

The 8 essence will never ask another to work harder, give more, or strive more than he or she does. But others should watch out, because they are tireless workers, imbued with their visions, energized by their imaginations and projects, and filled with love when they are creating great things. This essence is a power source of hard work to create good.

Soul Essence 8

Symbol	Possible Behavior
Two complete, connected circles	Very complete power
Two circles connected in the center	Balanced
Rounded on all sides	Doesn't collapse under pressure

As life rolls along, the 8 essence will learn tolerance and the balanced hand of justice for those that are endowed with other, very different qualities. They will develop patience with the process, recognizing the goal can only be achieved when the process is well supported.

SOUL ESSENCE 9

The 9 soul essence is the expression of universal awareness and all that universal wisdom expresses. This becomes extraordinary generosity because the 9 essence always feels completely cared for by the universe. The 9 essence's great faith in universal abundance enables the 9 to express a very high order of love.

This has to do with sacrifice, but without victimization; sympathy, but without pity for another; understanding without arrogance; and service without treating the person served as a needy, lesser being.

Soul Essence 9

Symbol	Possible Behavior
Upper circle	A higher look at things
Straight line to Earth	Self-directed
Upper circle is complete	Complete universal wisdom

The 9 essence longs to have deep personal love, but this essence emanates such a deeply universal impersonal quality of love that the deep human love is often hard for the 9 essence to really achieve. The 9 essence, who is beautiful inside and out and beloved by most, is often moved to share his or her wisdom in the media to connect with the most people, not for his or her ego but to get the wisdom out.

As the 9 essence goes through life, there will be the inevitable lessons, and these generally have to do with clarity in regard to the abilities and nature of others. Emotional steadiness can become illusive as the 9 encounters earthly challenges. Like Jesus throwing over the money changers' tables in the temple, the 9 essence can struggle for emotional steadiness.

SOUL ESSENCE 11

The 11 essence is filled within. This essence carries a daily expression of what a spiritual teacher is. In the old definition of spiritual teacher, the teacher stood on the podium and lectured, encouraged, and enlightened the masses. This is the 11 of yesterday. The 11 essence still has this love of God before its love of humanity, but it tends to express ideals without being accessible as a human being. But the 11 essence is more and more evolving into a deeply human person who glows with amazing spiritual dimension in the blessed, ordinary muck and mire of human life. The 11 essence is a treasure of spiritual teaching and deeply personal human love that ignites the best in all it meets.

Soul Essence 11

Symbol	Possible Behavior
Two parallel lines	Balanced
Goes up and down endlessly	Wisdom from knowing the best and worst
A road space between two straight lines	Knowledge fills it up

As the 11 essence lives his or her life, more and more appreciation will develop for the amazing, even miraculous ways people lead their lives and how the glow of human love empowered by spiritual truths emerges somewhere in every situation.

SOUL ESSENCE 22

The 22 soul essence embodies the characteristics of all the other numbers, including the qualities of the 11 essence, combined. As a result, you have someone who understands the laws of the universe and knows that these laws are useful only if they are applied in harmony with nature's laws—a powerful, practical builder. He or she does not build for personal power, ego needs, experimentation, or from personal insecurities. The 22 essence builds to improve existence on the physical level so all else can grow and thrive. This essence is a true believer in the maxim that in order for human growth and potential to ignite, create, and be grand, the practical, physical aspects of life must be in place.

Soul Essence 22

Symbol	Possible Behavior
Two very firm bases	Very, very grounded
Fits together perfectly	Easily find compatible common ground with others
Two different types of containers	Retains much knowledge and wisdom regarding life

The soul essence, the center of your nature, then expands through other number patterns, each sculpting your energetic flow into life. The first area to have this influence is your touchdown moment, or the moment of your birth.

The Power of *Kronos* and *Kairos*

You may be surprised to find that there are two different but equal kinds of time: One is linear and the other is not. Each is imperative to your ability to live a good quality of life. The Greeks had names for these two movements of time. **Kronos** was time as you might commonly think of it, measured by clocks and calendars. **Kairos** was the opportune moment for something to happen in accordance with the timing of the universe (synchronicity). As a practitioner of numerology, it is important that you learn to balance your life using both measurements of time. Organize your life according to Kronos, but always be cognizant of the more powerful force of Kairos that can emerge at any time.

THE POWERS OF KAIROS TIME

The challenge you'll face as you dig more deeply into numerology is to learn to respond well to all the experiences Kairos brings your way while you live in tune to Kronos time. Kairos time is a master teacher. It is the voice of the universe, its guiding hand. There is clearly nothing in life that is as demanding or as imposing of its own will than Kairos time. It is what is meant by the old adage, "Time knows no master."

THE POLARITY OF KAIROS

Kairos guides you to openings and closings, beginnings and endings. It is always drawing you into experience that enhances learning, deepens spirituality, and shows that there is a force of life experience and timing that goes far beyond the human ability to guide, direct, or even understand. Kairos is the timing of great mystery that inspires love and fear. It is the movement of life guided by another force. While you can't control or guide Kairos, you can learn to live in harmony with it.

SIGNS OF MOVEMENT IN KAIROS TIME

When you experience harmony with Kairos time, you will notice that your timing is spot on. You are in the right place at the right time. You get the phone call when you *really* need it. The job opens at exactly the precise moment. You had almost given up, and then—there it was. You walk into a restaurant, and there is the love of your life. You're having health problems, and you overhear in a conversation just what you need to know to make the best decision. You're feeling glum, and as you walk across the street, you reach down, grab a flyer blowing across the street, and it advertises just the perfect seminar for you.

Each one of these experiences is a door opening in the movement of Kairos time. Each one gives you the nudge, guidance, or help you need to progress your life. It is also Kairos that brings unexpected loss and forces us to progress ourselves in the ways we often long to avoid.

KAIROS BRINGS OPPORTUNITY

You control the quality of the opportunity that Kairos brings to you. As much as you might hate to admit it, you have no control and virtually no influence over another person's life path and life choices (even if that person is your mate or child or parent), but you do have absolute control and even responsibility for how you interact with the opportunities that present themselves in your life.

ANOTHER WAY TO SEE KAIROS

The lessons that show up in your life are in Kairos time, meaning you can't control their timing. In fact, you are not able to control the timing of your life's big events, such as the moment of birth or death, when you fall in love, the moment you get the great job, resolve an old conflict, or face the challenge of an accident. Every one of these is controlled by the universe. Since Earth is a school, such timing necessarily is controlled by the Divine. Otherwise this place would be a mess, with everyone out of harmony with everything. And that would violate the profound harmony of the universe, one so beautiful and incomprehensible that it inspired the genius of Albert Einstein to refer to it as the mind of God.

Improve Your Response

Although you can't control outcome, you can completely control the quality with which you interact with the Kairos process. You can elevate the quality of your response to life's challenges and difficult lessons, thereby enhancing the quality of the entire situation. When you do this, know it is for your highest benefit.

When you follow the guidance revealed through the wisdom of your numbers, you shift into harmonious alignment with the movement of time. You arrive at the door of life prepared, relaxed, and ready to learn. As you continue to see your numbers as your guides, you will see synchronicity showing up more often. You will be in the right place at the right time. It might begin to feel as if life is being orchestrated just for you.

Your soul essence number shows you how to bring your every essence into syntony with Kairos time. When this occurs, you occupy the most soul-satisfying spot for you. You achieve soul alignment by beginning each day expressing the attitudes of your soul number. Doing so ensures that you feel better about your life.

LEARN FROM THE NUMBERS

Remember, the soul number emanates your attitude, but the life task (or life lesson) number helps you deal with your experiences. It is applied repeatedly to each challenge you have. You might see life lessons show up in the following ways (in the context of numerology):

- If you are a free spirit and you have a 4 lesson, the universe wants you to become more responsible and grounded with more substance in your experiences.
- If you are a serious guy and your life lesson is a 3, you get to have fun and learn to let life bring you pleasure.
- If you're a people person and your life task is a 1, you are here to promote yourself and learn a new type of self-reliance.

YOUR PERSONALITY MASKS

Your personality (revealed by the single digit number derived from adding the letters of your name) is how you impart yourself to the world. It is the pattern of behavior you are known by. Oddly enough, if allowed to develop and grow without wise guidance (as it almost always does), the pattern actually hides what you aren't good at. If you are a man with self-esteem issues, you will show the world someone very macho. If you have an intense inner anger, you might outwardly appear to be sweet. Or, if you are an arrogant person, you may show others a mask of shyness.

The list is endless.

GUIDE YOUR PERSONALITY WITH WISDOM

When you live from your authentic self, you won't create a wall to hide some aspect of yourself behind. Living from the inside out means living fully engaged with life; expressing the real you in the world brings you true happiness. To be able to position and reposition yourself in the framework of Kairos time, follow the numbers' guidelines in establishing or reestablishing a personality that allows you to be real, honest, and perfectly aligned to opportunity as it occurs. You might do this by adjusting the spelling of your name, dropping your middle name, or changing your name, for example.

The Key to Synchronicity

Kairos makes synchronicity possible. Synchronicity is the signature of the gods—being in the right place at exactly the right time. When Kairos opens that door to a new experience, you engage and have an experience that was completely unplanned but full of impact and meaning for you. To be in harmony with the movement of time is the ultimate goal of numerology.

NUMEROLOGY AND THE KARMIC WHEEL

The idea of karma has been interpreted differently by various people and cultures, but there are a few basics that everyone agrees on. The belief in karma is accompanied by belief in reincarnation, which assumes that this world is a school for learning that each soul, or energy, returns to in different forms for the purpose of self-development and self-evolution. The ancient magi taught that it's a very difficult school because each person is developing four areas of him- or herself—physical, emotional, mental, and spiritual.

If karma teaches you anything, it is that the same situation can elicit many different responses in you if you take the time to consciously respond. Most people react. And, they often react the same way to the same lesson. But think about it. When you know the lesson that is showing up in your life (because it's likely shown up before), you can choose a response and the sequence in which the response takes place that improves your quality according to your own standards. That is the goal.

Avoid Repeating Negative Behaviors

The ancient magi taught that behavior repetition is the most negative condition, to be avoided at all costs. When you resort to repeating the same behaviors in reaction to stressful or challenging situations, you deny yourself the opportunity for personal growth with new and fresh insight. If the pattern continues, your opportunities for self-knowledge stagnate, completely hooking you into an endless cycle of repetition and nongrowth. In other words, you become bound to destiny's karmic wheel.

Perhaps you are like others who occasionally (or more frequently) avoid taking personal responsibility for their actions. There are many reasons you might not face the consequence of your actions or choices head on. The most common evasive techniques are the following:

- **Self-righteous rage:** I smashed his car because he hit me first.
- **Self-absorption:** I wanted to listen to my friend, but I couldn't stop thinking about my life.
- **Self-protecting judgment:** Those jerks are auditing me. I don't deserve this.
- **The victim:** I am suffering so much over my pet's illness, I can't do anything.
- **The escape artist:** Oh well, it's all meant to be, so I am not going to really engage with any of it.

- **Denial:** This life event doesn't fit with what I believe life should bring me, so I am going to ignore it until it goes away.

These are common reactions to life's events. And they are reactions guaranteed to create repetitive reactions—unthinking, habitual, knee-jerk reactions to life—karma. They are tactics of avoidance so you do not have to be fully present and engaged. But actually, when you choose to engage and be fully present to what is transpiring, you never have to repeat that situation again. The soul cannot shine when you practice avoidance and disengagement. Instead, what comes forward is a personality characteristic (strengthened by each incident of avoidance) that takes itself *way too seriously*. The joyous response to the opportunity life has brought you is subsumed in your repetitive reaction to it.

The life lesson breaks up the repetition. You do something new, and that means you respond to the event with a new, fresh approach. First there is a fear about putting yourself out there in an unfamiliar way. Feel the fear, and do it anyway. Then comes the amazement that life is changing. You are rearranging your vibration to create a desired outcome. Over time, life feels somehow more vibrant and meaningful. Put a stop to repetitive behaviors and those around you are more inclined to do the same. It's called "shifting the paradigm." This is a different kind of karma repetition. This is freedom, and it is life's lesson.

REPETITIONS AND THE RHYTHMS OF LIFE

Consider the difference between habits of repetition and the rhythms of your life. Behavior repetition is a way of relating to every single situation as if it were the same situation or required the same old response. These are deeply entrenched psychological behaviors that stem from the past. We all have these habits, and they do the same for each one of us. They prevent growth, true joy, and spontaneity from occurring.

Rhythms are very personal and intimate aspects of our lives. Your rhythm in life is how you came into syntony with the symphony of life. Your rhythm is an internal sense of centeredness and groundedness that has nothing to do with the outer world. You find your rhythm alone. Your reconstructor of self-love helps, and doing things in private and at your own pace and timing helps. Your rhythms are the personal time you express as you move through the larger musical score of life.

TRANSCEND HABITUAL BEHAVIOR

If you are like most people, you tend not to think about your habits. You don't periodically review and reevaluate their impact on your life. But habits are so much a part of you that you live and hide within them. Bad habits, especially, indicate how much you have given up on your personal quest for growth and self-knowledge. The magi taught that learning is a step-by-step process. Knowledge of numerology can help you optimize timing, choices, and opportunities so you can recreate your life anew.

DEVELOP THE VIRTUE OF PATIENCE

The magi also taught that the challenges of life are easier met when you practice patience. In our modern world when karma comes knocking, before taking any action or responding in any way wait ten seconds. During that time decide whether or not the action you are about to take is a knee-jerk reaction, the right thing to do at the right time, or if no action is the best course. Patience, you'll soon find, is a great teacher and helpful ally.

Use Numerology to Unearth the Power of You

What would you do with your life if anything were possible? What dreams would you pursue? What wishes would you make come true? Your inner world is perhaps best represented in numerology by your soul number. This inner world information that is unique to you is found in your soul number. You'll recall from reading the preceding material that you arrive at your soul number or essence by adding up the numerical value of all the vowels in your birth name and then reducing them to a single digit. Or you can use an Internet calculator that takes your name and reduces it to your soul number for you. See *www.simplynumbers.com/html/interactive/sn_int_soul.asp*.

The rest of the world may not see the traits that your soul number reveals because of the masks you wear that block the energy or flow of your soul number through your life expression. The flow or lack of it is governed by the blockages you put in place. But when you remove the impediments to live from your authentic self, then the soul shines forth in its fullness. Then anything is possible.

GETTING PRACTICAL

Numerology is easy once you grasp basic information for working with and interpreting the symbolism of numbers and as you further illuminate the meaning using the light of your intuition. Whether you want to understand yourself better, recast your life in a new direction, or understand how your life and its lessons align with someone else's, crunch the numbers in the context of numerology. The numbers signifying your soul essence, personality, life task, and year vibration combine with your special talents and abilities to create you. The whole package of you includes the vibration (of your qualities) that you brought into this life expression. These were God's gifts to you. What you do with this package is your gift to the Divine.

You will come up against life lessons, but numerology can help you see clearly what you are to learn. By changing how you respond to these lessons, you are loosening the fetters of karma that bind you. You can even alter destiny's path—remember what you learned about changing your name. It's a radical shift, but for some people it's the right thing to do.

Or, you can compute a personal destiny year. Knowing your personal destiny year means you can optimize your response to the opportunities that become available to you during that year, as well as hone your understanding of the deeper value that the year holds for you. Your personal year is the sum of the following three numbers: the root number of the current year, the root number for your birth month, and the root number for your birth day. You don't have to be a numerological adept to gain insights into specific life areas or issues in your life. Sometimes a simple casting chart will produce amazing answers. Such is the power of this ancient art form.

Relationships

The first essential step to a good relationship is to know yourself. If you don't know yourself or if you don't have a concrete self-awareness, then a truly satisfying relationship is virtually impossible to create. The first relationship tool numerology offers is the tool for self-awareness.

Your soul essence number is your lucky-in-love number. You'll recall that it's the number you get when you add up the vowels in your birth name (if that's a compound number, add each digit together until you reduce it to a one-digit number).

Your soul essence number is your energetic coordinate to a happy love life. The soul is the essence of love. You'll recall, there are ten essence numbers—1 through 9, and 10, which includes everything and adjusts to a different type of 1—because Earth is a 10 vibration planet. You can compare your soul essence number with that of others for compatibility comparisons—to see how well you flow into each other.

Here are easily compatible soul essence numbers:

- **1 and 10:** Each understands the value and struggle of individuality, and each has a different perspective that lends a slightly different and helpful slant.
- **2 and 4:** Both are stabilizers and have an understanding of how stability feels and what the joys and challenges are. Both support and stabilize in different ways, but the gluing quality is the same.
- **3 and 5:** On the move, restless, and experiential, neither wants to slow the other down. The commitment is to now, to the experience, to the truth that emerges in the fast-moving, ever-changing panorama of life.
- **6 and 8:** Successful builders of family and substance, both expect to be successful and depend on outward success to confirm the soul's success. Both bring comfort and protection.
- **7 and 9:** These are the thinkers, analyzers, and the seekers of the culture, dedicated to the betterment of humanity and the discovery of truth through the disciplines of the mind.

Much of what happens between two people who have chemistry is electric, or numerological. That energy is there from the start, from that first moment, and it will always be there. What you can do is guide the flows, gently nudge the wonderful and mysterious connection into a rewarding, loving association. Love will show you yourself. Love will show you what you love to accept in yourself and what is heartrending to self-accept in your nature. It is the great teacher in life. Through the outpouring of this most basic truth of life, you either grow through your connections of love or wall away yourself, severing connections because the mirror love holds up is too challenging to bear.

You can also use numerology to find the personality number of your partners, friends, lovers, or business associates. Just remember, though, that number is the persona they show the world and isn't necessarily the "real them." The personality number is computed by adding only the consonants of the full birth name. See the following.

Sex

Your numerological destiny numbers can help you figure out if you and your lover are compatible, challenging, or a natural fit. To do the calculations, you'll have to first compute your destiny number and your partner's. After that, you can do a comparison of the numbers to see if your passions match up (likely the sex will be hot) or if one is hot and the other is cool (lukewarm sex if you don't take time with each other to understand the other's passionate needs). For example, the natural fit of a 1 is with another 1, 5, or 7. More challenging would be a number 1 with a 2, 4, or 6. A number 1 is compatible with a 3 or 9. A number 1 and number 8 could work well, too, for you both are energetic and know what you want.

Money

Numerology teaches that at the moment of birth you are imbued with the energy imprint that includes specific strengths and weaknesses, talents and defects, and even your set point for happiness (pessimist or optimist). These factors impact your ability to attract money into your life. One way numerology can help you become more prosperous is to learn how the energy of your destiny number (based on the numbers of your birth date, added together and reduced to a single digit) interacts with financial prosperity. Find your destiny of fate number (the numbers of your birth year + month + day added together and reduced to a single digit). Then add to that single digit your day number (the day of the month you were born, for example, 26 becomes 2 + 6 = 8, your day number) to arrive at a new number (reduced, if necessary to a single digit) to evaluate or enhance your money-making potential.

For example, a money number 1 is a money generator throughout a lifetime. Money number 2 tends to be overly generous so wealth is not reflected as much as giving money away. Money number 3 has a lucky aspect and attracts money but also quickly spends it. Money number 4 works diligently for money and saves. Money number 5 grows wealth so long as he or she is diligent, focused, and works hard. Money number 6 enjoys a stable financial picture and money is abundant. Money number 7 faces eccentricity and can swing from striking it rich to losing it all. Money number 8 can experience tremendous wealth but also great losses, possibly from overspending on a lavish lifestyle. Money number 9 attracts wealth without too much effort, yet often gives it away in philanthropic causes.

Health

Numerical correlations can be made between the day (of the month) when you were born and your quality of health. Numerology can also reveal the types of health issues you might face. For example, people who generally have good health are believed to be born on the following days: 1, 10, 19, and 28. They are number 1's. When a health issue arises, it will often be in the area of the heart or stomach. The number 2's born on 2, 11, 20, or 29 in a calendar month may face health issues pertaining to the chest and the organs of the chest. Number 3's born on 3, 12, 21, or 30 may have health issues relating to their legs and other limbs. Number 4's born on 4, 13, 22, and 31 days possibly will face health issues related to urinary tract, as well as respiratory, issues.

Number 5's are born on 5, 14, and 23 and can be affected by skin afflictions and problems with liver and bile ducts. Number 6's, born on 6, 15, and 24, can face health issues related to nose, throat, and lungs. Number 7's have birthdays on the 7, 16, and 25 and might possibly face potential health issues pertaining to circulation. The number 8's are born on 8, 17, and 26 and may have issues with their eyes, teeth, liver, and blood pressure. The number 9's have birthdays on 9, 18, or 27. Their health issues may involve fevers or kidney trouble.

Health is your greatest asset. Knowing where your body's weaknesses are located, based on numerology, means you can take special precautions, giving extra consideration to those areas during times when you might be especially stressed.

Work

Life path numbers point to the kind of work that might best fit your life expression. For example, if you are a number 1, you would excel as a self-employed person or someone involved in building or construction since you have traits of determination and leadership. As a number 2, you would do well in fields involving compassion such as counseling, teaching, or diplomacy. If you are expressing as a number 3, your life work is about creativity and social expression and you would make a great actor or artist. Number 4's are practical and diligent and make great accountants and lawyers. Number 5's have focus and discipline and would make wonderful teachers or librarians. If you are a number 6, you would do well in jobs where you serve others as a health provider or caregiver. Number 7's are analytical and wise and excel in religious vocations or scientific endeavors. Number 8's are extroverted and charismatic; they excel as politicians and business leaders. Number 9's, because they are so caring, make wonderful environmentalists, humanitarians, researchers, and political leaders.

For business and career questions, you can use numerology that keys in on numbers associated with your job or company name and numbers in the location (the numerical address and the letters converted to numbers for the street, for example). Numerological information for a company you want to start might include the date the business was conceived or your launch date, what name would ensure optimal success, building location or place where the business might be established, and other such relevant information.

Work can be related to your life path or life task numbers. The life-task number is arrived by totaling up the day, month, and year of your birth. Supportive numbers are those numbers that, with little effort, and usually with pleasure, can support another. This alignment of the numbers is particularly important with the life task. The life task is a commitment to learn something about which you have no idea of what to do or how to do it. It is your lesson. It is how you are progressing your soul's learning. It is the centerpiece of life, and it is hard. It is wonderful to have a relationship with another who has a life-task number that by its very nature gives often needed support to learn a hard lesson through real life experiences.

Summary

There is a secret power in numerology that has survived thousands of years. In ancient times, the seers used it to foretell events but also manipulated numbers to change outcomes and alter fate. You have learned how the ancients viewed numbers as imbued with energy; how they solved their problems through an understanding and manipulation of numbers. The nine pure numbers show up in the world around you every day, just as they did thousands of years ago. They are available to you as personal guideposts to indicate whether you are on or off your path of destiny. You've learned how to extract numbers from letters to find their numeric value in order to compute your soul essence number. The ancient Greek idea of Kronos, Kairos, and synchronicity are no longer abstract concepts but ideas that you can actually put to work in your life, today, right now.

Using numerology, you can size up a friend, family member, coworker, business associate, fellow student, or lover and right away figure out whether or not your relationship will be challenged or compatible. You know the right disciplines of study and career paths to follow, based on your soul essence. Your health will be a precious asset you will safeguard now that you know which areas might need special attention during your life.

Now it is up to you to harness the esoteric power of your special karmic and soul numbers to have the shimmering life, rich with meaningful symbolism, truly meant just for you.

Part Five

THE ENNEAGRAM

It is in our idleness, in our dreams, that the submerged truth sometimes comes to the top.

—Virginia Woolf, English author, essayist, and publisher

Your new life of power begins with a search for your authentic self, hidden behind the personality traits and characteristics that you show the world. Like most people, your personality formed early in life. You assumed certain behaviors as coping mechanisms for negative experiences. When you are stressed, coping mechanisms are essential to hide vulnerabilities that you don't want others to see. However, these behaviors and characteristics over time form the amalgam of your personality. But is it really you?

You are born with a true self that encompasses everything you possessed before your early childhood environment influenced your development. This true self is also known as your essence. It exists deep within you, behind the mask that conceals from others what you truly feel or fear. Masks change your perception of who you are. For example, a shy and lonely person becomes the class clown. The successful tycoon hides behind projects of enormity to hide his insecurities about one-on-one commitments. To be all you are truly meant to be is to unmask yourself, connect with the real you, and begin to live your life from the inside out, openly and authentically. You have a powerful tool to help you in the Enneagram.

Introduction: What Is the Enneagram?

The Enneagram of Personality is a typing system believed to have roots in Judeo-Christian and Sufi mysticism. Mystics, priests, psychologists, and social scientists have all utilized the Enneagram; however, in the hands of contemporary interpreters it has evolved into a powerful system for understanding human personality. When you understand who you are in the context of the Enneagram personality typing system, you can begin to peel back the mask to reveal the radiant and powerful being you truly are.

THE BASICS

The core of the Enneagram system is the interrelationships of nine basic personality types (also called **enneatypes**). Think of the enneatypes as representing nine different bundles, each containing habits or deeply ingrained ways of thinking, relating, and reacting. Each enneatype is represented as one point on a nine-pointed star enclosed in a circle—the Enneagram's symbol. The star's lines connect the position of each enneatype around the circle's circumference. These lines show the enneatypes' interrelationships and describe their tasks. Although you might recognize characteristics in all of the nine types that seem to resonate with you, one type will dominate. That stated, you are not simply a personality type number and label. The Enneagram compensates for that as well.

You will have a dominate personality type, a wing, and two direction indicators for how you advance toward growth or respond to stress. You can use the Enneagram's information about ego assets and limitations to become your best self, eschewing unhealthy or pathological traits that limit growth. Instead you'll be able to make conscious choices to attain the fullest and healthiest potential of all the types. In this way, you draw each type's power, as you need it to be balanced and fully functioning. You will, however, start from where you are, using your personality type as the point of departure on the path to self-realization.

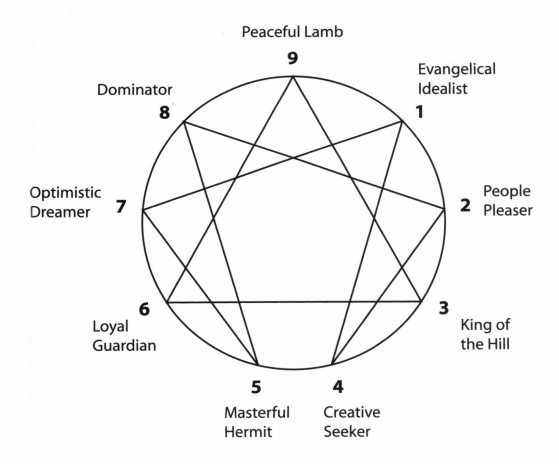

THE ENNEAGRAM PERSONALITY TEST

The complete Enneagram Personality Test is located in the appendix. The test has been designed to uncover your primary pattern and link it to your enneatype. It is important when taking this test, or any of the other Enneagram tests, to answer questions based on who you really feel you are rather than on whom you would like to be. For older people, take the test thinking of the way you were when you were twenty. It is also helpful to consider how you react under pressure.

If you take the test and don't feel as if the results are accurate, you may have misidentified your wing or you may not be seeing yourself clearly.

Immerse Yourself in the Enneagram

To get the most out of this system, Enneagram theorists and teachers encourage deeper study. Studying the system helps you more fully understand the nuances of personality. In addition, it facilitates a better understanding of yourself and others, helps you evolve, and enables you to live more fully as your best self.

Your Essence

Enneagram style is not who you are; it is what you habitually and consistently do. Your enneatype or personality is both dynamic and structured, like water flowing downhill from a stream. Understanding this dynamic flow of energy—or your patterned ways of behaving—helps you delineate ways that you can make changes in your life. Your essence is you, stripped of your ego. It's your authentic, fully integrated true self. Moving toward your essence doesn't eliminate your personality or ego, it merely frees you to make choices rather than succumb to fixated behavior. It expands your vision of yourself.

When you regress, you move further away from your true essence; when you progress, you move closer to your true essence. Your essence is more than the sum of everything in your psyche, of which your core personality is only a part. It's the point at which the restrictions imposed upon your core personality are truly liberated, allowing the other elements of your unencumbered true self to emerge. In other words, your core personality or enneatype contains methods of coping or adaptive responses that allow you to function in the world. Your ego boundaries within your core personality determine the degree of compulsion or rote response that defines your life. These behaviors are the fixations that shape your core personality. As you integrate, you free yourself from such fixations and increasingly learn to live from your essence.

THE PATHOLOGICAL DESIGNATION OF AN ENNEATYPE

The way you have learned to express yourself in the world and the way you communicate who you are to others is through your enneatype. The personality traits of your type become your most enduring way of perceiving, relating to, and thinking about the world and your place in it. A healthy person develops and sustains a flexible ego. An ego-driven personality functions, but it is often too reliant on reactionary impulses (behaviors) or too restrictive to express his or her true self. An unhealthy ego may become pathological—rigid, inflated, or deflated—and definitely does not serve its owner well.

Dynamics of the Enneagram

Most scholars believe that a combination of your genetics and your early childhood environment determines your core personality or type. They also believe that you retain your core personality throughout your life. The Enneagram provides a framework to help you understand the patterns you developed for seeing and organizing the world. These patterns are formed from the interaction between your genetic disposition and the early childhood environment you grew up in. Your parents or caretakers played a primary role in how you came to see and interact in the world. Everyone develops an ego that eventually obstructs their essence. The Enneagram helps you understand how your ego formed, how neighboring types influenced you, and in which direction—and how—you can progress to achieve wholeness and live your life with integrity emanating from your true self.

PROGRESSING TO WHOLENESS WITHIN YOUR TYPE

The Enneagram type numbers are not reflective of superiority in any way and are placed on the Enneagram circle according to the compilation of characteristics that formed each personality. No one progresses from one number to another, and, in fact, Enneagram theorists believe that your enneatype does not change. However, you can progress in your own development or develop patterns of behavior within your enneatype that reflect the healthier aspects of your personality.

Most theorists agree that there are three major gradients of behavior within each type, identified in Jungian terms here as follows:

- **Self-actualized:** highly functioning personality
- **Ego-driven:** normally functioning personality
- **Pathological:** highly dysfunctional personality

In other words, depending on what is occurring in your present life and how you are coping with any challenges, you are capable of progressing upward or regressing backward within your individual type.

FUNCTIONING WITHIN FAMILY

Your ego or Enneagram style is not the same as your essence or true self. The essence you were born with gets suppressed, denied, or even lost by your efforts to respond to or cope with your childhood circumstances. You form an ego that allows you to function within your familial and larger world. If your family is healthy and nurturing, you are likely to form a healthy, functioning personality; however, if your family is dysfunctional and destructive, you are likely to form a pathological personality (filled with defense mechanisms and maladaptive behaviors) that will eventually veil your essence. If everything goes exceptionally well, you may develop a self-actualized personality that encompasses the full spectrum of your conscious and unconscious psyche; it expresses and reflects your true essence. Unfortunately, many people will have to deal with all sorts of denial, personality distortions, and behavior malfunctions to unveil their essence.

ADDING NUANCE WITH A WING

Every enneatype has a wing—one of the types on either side of it that provides subtle, or not so subtle, nuances to its personality. In other words, your personality consists of one enneatype and a mixture of your enneatype with one of the two types adjacent to it on the circumference of the Enneagram. For example, Ones have either a Nine wing or Two wing; Fours have either a Three wing or Five wing; Sevens have either a Six wing or Eight wing.

POSITIONING OF YOUR WING MATCHES YOUR ENNEATYPE

The wing both complements your basic personality and encompasses important and sometimes contradictory elements within your personality. It illustrates and defines another side to your personality that will increase your own and everyone else's ability to understand the totality of your personality. Like the positioning of each type on the Enneagram, the wings have also been positioned according to the same Enneagram concepts that define how your personality was formed. As such, they will be congruent with your core enneatype.

Steady on Your Wings

Your wing remains constant. Even when you are stressed, the wing is always with you and is neither released nor clutched to your side. When stressed, you typically—consciously or unconsciously—lean toward your stress point when it comes to behavior shifts.

WINGS CAN BE HEAVY, MODERATE, OR LIGHT

Wings determine your secondary fears and desires, as well as the motivations that drive you and the traits or behaviors you develop to form your personality. The proportion of primary (core personality) and secondary (wing) influences can differ significantly. If your wing constructs a large portion of your personality, it's called a heavy wing. If the wing is present but your personality is heavily influenced by the core personality, you have a moderate wing.

If your core personality completely dominates the secondary personality to the point that it is almost imperceptible, you have a light wing. In each case, the core enneatype always dominates the overall personality.

A PERSONALITY FOUR ELEMENTS COMPRISES

As you progress through life, you are either moving toward your security point (growing, expanding) or regressing toward your stress point (deteriorating and contracting). The points (for personal growth or pathology) are determined by connecting enneatypes. All were intentionally aligned by their placement on the circle. These points explain behavior fluctuations, as well as emerging or reactive characteristics that are unexpectedly revealed or purposefully mined as you grow into a mature adult. Basically, you consciously or unconsciously adopt positive or negative behaviors or characteristics from two other enneatypes—as determined by your security point and your stress point—that can become part of your overall personality. Thus, your overall personality typology consists of four aspects:

- Your core personality or enneatype
- Your wing
- Your security point
- Your stress point

The Goal of Self-Actualization

The pinnacle of self-actualization is an inspiring yet elusive goal that implores humans to reach the ultimate state of being—joyfully whole and detached from worldly concerns. The process of actualization is ongoing. Humans are always in a state of flux, spiraling upward or downward in their quest for transformation. However, striving to become your best self is a worthy pursuit.

OPENING YOURSELF TO SELF-ACTUALIZATION

Your progression toward fully integrated wholeness likely will involve a conscious decision to seek growth and development. You may decide it's time to seek ways to let go of restrictive behaviors and open up to your full potential.

You may experience the sort of grace that occurs when everything in your life is going exceptionally well and you simply blossom. Or you may opt to set the process in motion by purposefully addressing issues that you know have held you back.

NOTICING CLUES THAT YOU ARE PROGRESSING

Potent clues for a progression toward self-actualization can be found in your security point, as indicated by your placement on the Enneagram, or in the high side of your stress point. For example, a Nine seeking to progress toward self-actualization can choose to adopt behaviors consistent with a self-actualized Three or a self-actualizing Six; a progressing Five can opt to act like a self-actualizing Eight or a self-actualizing Seven. The positive qualities inherent in the progression toward self-actualization will help you fully see the limitations created by remaining fixated in your type and will give you an inkling of the behaviors, attitudes, beliefs, and actions that will help expand your personality toward your true self, or essence.

It's a Marathon, Not a Sprint
You don't leap from being healthy to being psychotic, or vice versa. Achieving these behavioral states is the result of a progressive movement either toward health or a steady, regressive deterioration into pathology.

REACHING THE ULTIMATE GOAL

Your ultimate goal is to become a fully integrated, self-actualized personality. At this ultimate stage, you will unveil your essence and open yourself to spirit; you will have broken free of ego limitations and reconnected to the source of life. You will know yourself, and you will know others. You will have faith in yourself, the Divine, and others—at this stage, you will be in touch with yourself and the universe. Now let's turn to the enneatypes themselves and their characteristics.

The Enneatypes

The following list reveals the nine enneatypes with a number and a descriptive label. These labels are not meant in any way to be demeaning but rather descriptive—to quickly encapsulate the complex picture of each personality. In the section that follows this list, a comprehensive description is given, with positive and negative aspects of the personalities.

- **Type One**—Evangelical Idealist
- **Type Two**—People Pleaser
- **Type Three**—King of the Hill
- **Type Four**—Creative Seeker
- **Type Five**—Masterful Hermit
- **Type Six**—Loyal Guardian
- **Type Seven**—Optimistic Dreamer
- **Type Eight**—Dominator
- **Type Nine**—Peaceful Lamb

TYPE ONE

Prominent Enneagram scholars and authors Don Riso and Russ Hudson dubbed the One personality the Reformer. Helen Palmer and David Daniels, also well-respected Enneagram scholars and authors, preferred the Perfectionist. A One personality has also been called the Critic and the Good Person. This book uses the term "Evangelical Idealist" because it covers more thoroughly the central concern of the One personality, which is to internalize, live by, and promote moral principles. Ones are typically passionate defenders of what they perceive as the one, good, true, right way to live. Whether it's a religious precept or a philosophical ideology, Ones have a cause to trumpet. Their ideology or theology usually has rigid rules that Ones feel compelled to follow and that they vigorously desire others to follow as well. They are always aiming to be the best person they can be, which leads to an obsession with perfection. Ones can be overly critical, harshly judgmental, and punishing to themselves and others.

Ones are usually principled, disciplined, self-controlled types who keep society on its toes and the trains running on time. They want, above all, to do the right thing and live by a set of capital *R* rules. Ones take their responsibilities very seriously and generally think long and hard before they speak or act. If they breach their own rules, they tend to punish themselves. Pathological Ones are often self-righteous, intolerant, and cruel. Self-actualized Ones can be wise mentors, realistic advocates for worthwhile causes, dedicated public servants, healthy and effective coaches and teachers, and inspiring truth tellers.

The Ups and Downs of Ones

Ones can be objective, balanced, moral, conscientious, repressive, critical, controlling, and perfectionist. They lie awake at night terrified that they are not sufficient and that they will be rightfully blamed for whatever goes wrong. They hide their tendency to feel like they are the only ones even trying to do things right. They harbor a nasty streak of resentment toward others and feel so compelled to be right at all costs that it frequently costs them their relationships and any real chance for a joyful life.

A few famous people are commonly identified with the One enneatype, including Ralph Nader, William Bennett, Martha Stewart, Hillary Clinton, Michael Medved, Jack Kevorkian, Confucius, Greta Van Susteren, and fictional characters such as Jack Webb's character in *Dragnet* and Dana Carvey's Church Lady from *Saturday Night Live*.

TYPE TWO

Riso and Hudson chose as their type Two label the Helper, while Palmer and Daniels preferred the Giver. This type has also been called the Caretaker and the Loving Person. I selected "People Pleaser" because Twos are typically inclined to sacrifice their own desires for the sake of their family, coworkers, or society. Twos are the lovers of the Enneagram, those people who love you so much they'll do anything for you, even if they just met you. Twos need you to love them to feel secure in the world, so all their giving has massive strings attached.

While Twos can certainly be compassionate and empathetic, they are often helpful to a fault. On the plus side, Twos are the concerned, nurturing, warm-hearted types for whom service is the most noble—and natural—calling, which means they play very important roles in society.

Twos are very relationship focused, which means they tend to put personal connections first in their lives. Twos need to love and to be loved, which means they often have a hard time saying no. They sense your needs almost before you know you have them, and it drives them crazy that you can't do the same for them.

When they aren't emotionally healthy, Twos will use emotional manipulation in attempts to win your love. At their worst, they become flagrant self-serving martyrs and emotional vampires willing to suck you dry to get their emotional fix. However, when they are operating at peak capacity, Twos are genuinely altruistic caregivers—frequently doctors, nurses, and counselors. Their honest concern for others leads them to make the world a more loving place.

Why You Need Twos

Common adjectives used to describe Twos include selfless, loving, empathetic, helpful, giving, codependent, possessive, manipulative, and prideful. They seek to hide the fact that they really don't feel worthy of love. Underneath that, however, they don't want you to know that they are pretty sure that you need them and cannot live without them. They struggle with a false sense of pride and shoot themselves in the foot by emotionally manipulating others at the expense of developing honest relationships—with themselves or anyone else.

As an insight into Two behavior, some famous Twos include Barbara Bush, Mia Farrow, Desmond Tutu, Tammy Faye Bakker, Kathie Lee Gifford, Princess Diana, Monica Lewinsky, Florence Nightingale, Mother Teresa, Bill Cosby, and fictional characters such as the children's icon Mr. Rogers, Mary Poppins, and Counselor Troi from *Star Trek: The Next Generation*.

TYPE THREE

Riso and Hudson labeled a Three personality as the Achiever. Palmer and Daniels preferred the Performer. Others have dubbed this type the Succeeder and the Effective Person. This book calls this personality type "King of the Hill" because Threes will claw their way to the top of their chosen professions; in fact, they feel compelled to clamor over anyone who gets in their way to achieving maximum success. They have a deep-seated need to be seen as the top dog—prestigious, powerful, rich, and highly enviable.

Energetic, focused, and often driven, Threes are also the Enneagram's chameleons. They will mold themselves to be whatever is going to get them what they want or whatever will earn them the most money, get the girl or guy who will make them look the best, or rise to the top of a social group, be it the country club crowd or the local chapter of the Teamsters. Threes focus on work and material success and often identify so strongly with their accomplishments that they feel that they are what they do. They want to do very well and look good while doing it, so they are attracted to high-profile jobs and lavish lifestyles. They are often drawn to politics, Hollywood, or other high-status professions.

Charisma Versus Deceit

Threes can be ambitious, accomplished, competitive, goal-oriented, charismatic, opportunistic, conniving, and false. Their secret fear is that there really is nothing under the mask they present to society. They struggle with being deceitful and selling themselves short when they make career, social status, money, and a manufactured image more important than their friends, family, and, ultimately, their own true selves.

Pathological Threes can become cold-hearted, devious opportunists willing to do whatever it takes to succeed. But at their best—when they are balanced—Threes are gracious, self-assured, highly accomplished, and admirable people who embody American cultural values.

Some famous people who embody Three energy include David Bowie, Dick Clark, David Copperfield, Tom Cruise, Michael Jordan, Elvis Presley,

Sumner Redstone, Oprah Winfrey, Tiger Woods, O. J. Simpson, and fictional characters Jay Gatsby from *The Great Gatsby*, Scarlett O'Hara (*Gone with the Wind*), and Shakespeare's Macbeth.

TYPE FOUR

Riso and Hudson chose the Individualist for type Four. Palmer and Daniels selected the Romantic. Others have called this type the Artist and the Original Person. In this book, type Four is dubbed the "Creative Seeker," primarily because Fours are typically creative, artistic personalities who spend their lives seeking the real identity they suppressed as children. Fours are also constantly searching for ways to express their deepest feelings, particularly the bittersweet melancholy they secretly cherish.

Sensitive, idealistic, and creative, Fours are the Enneagram's artists—if not literally then temperamentally. They seek the solutions to all of their problems within their own feelings and tend to be introspective types, drawn to both beauty and tragedy and the expression of beauty and tragedy through art. They possess a refined sense of the aesthetic and can be demanding and uncompromising about their personal vision of a project or pursuit. They are also easily wounded by criticism. Not surprisingly, they are drawn to the arts, but any creative endeavor has its appeal.

A pathological Four turns her darkest feelings inward and is in danger of becoming highly self-destructive—even alarmingly masochistic. Unhealthy Fours may spend copious amounts of time wallowing in their self-created sense of hopelessness and acting as if they hated themselves. However, when the Four has a balanced personality, he is able to use his inner turmoil to face the world squarely and then contribute his creativity by completing beautiful art with an original point of view.

Famous personalities that reflect the Four enneatype include Diane Arbus, Charles Baudelaire, Leonard Cohen, Marlon Brando, Kurt Cobain, Eric Clapton, Judy Garland, Johnny Depp, Bob Dylan, Jack Kerouac, Billie Holiday, John Malkovich, Edgar Allan Poe, Anne Rice, Vincent van Gogh, and fictional characters such as Blanche DuBois and Hamlet.

How Special Is a Four?

Fours are artistic, expressive, discerning, unique, melancholy, self-absorbed, withdrawn, and elitist. Their secret fear is that they really aren't special after all, and they seek to hide their contempt for anyone who has less discerning sensibilities. Despite their elitist attitude, they struggle with envy, mostly in desiring things or people that are not interested in them or that gave up on them long ago.

TYPE FIVE

Riso and Hudson labeled type Five the Investigator. Palmer and Daniels preferred the Observer. Others have dubbed this type the Thinker and the Wise Person. In this book, type Five is the "Masterful Hermit," because Fives love their solitude and they love to obtain a masterful knowledge of whatever most interests them. Fives retreat from the world in order to understand the world; and when healthy, they are not tragic hermits but self-contained and self-sustained people who enjoy their own company.

Curious, insightful, and highly analytical, Fives are often viewed as the Enneagram's brainiacs. While it's true that some become eccentric and increasingly secretive, they can also be introverted yet very attractive and desirable people. Fives possess a questing intelligence and are happiest when they are gathering knowledge. They usually develop a highly specialized and well-developed skill, often in technical areas. They are detail oriented and preferential to libraries, research, and delving deeply into the subjects that interest them. They tend to keep others at arm's length, and they can be arrogant about their pet theories.

Pathological Fives do, unfortunately, tend to lose their grip on reality, alienate their friends, and devolve into a swarm of fears and extreme eccentricities. Fives use their mastery, knowledge, and incredible perceptiveness to make discoveries in science, improve processes in a range of industries and disciplines, and share profound insights that change the world.

The Withholding Five

Fives are typically wise, farsighted, knowledgeable, perceptive, intense, disconnected, eccentric, secretive, and stingy. They are secretly afraid that others will literally engulf them, as in swallow them whole. They don't want you to know that they're smarter than you and are probably the only ones who really know what's really going on. They are greedy in the sense of withholding themselves and not sharing their energy, and they can become so self-absorbed that they retreat too far from the fold.

Famous Five personalities include Bill Gates, Thomas Edison, Albert Einstein, George Stephanopoulos, Agatha Christie, Steve Wozniak, Georgia O'Keeffe, Phil Spector, Thelonious Monk, and fictional characters such as Ebenezer Scrooge and Sherlock Holmes.

TYPE SIX

Riso and Hudson labeled a Six the Loyalist. Palmer and Daniels call this type the Trooper. Others label a Six the Team Player. In this book, the term "Loyal Guardian" is used for Sixes because they are typically the most loyal type in the Enneagram and because they guard themselves against fear by either finding something they can believe in or by fighting against something they perceive as dangerous. Sixes can serve an important role as guardians of our societal values, but it's important to note that Sixes flip from being phobic to counterphobic—ardently avoiding what they fear by doing something radical to prove they aren't afraid.

Once a Six challenges authority and determines the best course of action, she dedicates her life to following the rules and holding others to equally high standards. However, if she feels betrayed, she will attack the person, organization, or government that she believes failed her.

Sixes often deal with a fear of being in the world by either finding something or someone who makes them feel part of something larger than themselves that they can truly believe in, or by finding something or someone to rebel against. More than anything, Sixes want to feel secure, safe, and fully supported. Whichever route they take, they investigate and challenge new ventures until they know what they are dealing with. They can be endearing, lovable people, but they can also send very mixed signals.

When Sixes lose their sense of security and fall apart, they can become hysterical, violent fanatics who see conspiracies everywhere. However, when they are stable and evolved, Sixes find the courage that is within them, which frees them to trust others, help build communities, and share their inherently positive, cooperative spirit.

Sixes and Insecurity

Sixes have been described as loyal, cooperative, engaging, likable, obedient, and alternately contradictory, evasive, cowardly, and paranoid. Sixes are terrified that they will lose the support and guidance of others, but most of their relationships are little more than Band-Aids for their own insecurities, which leave them feeling separate and resentful. They are the type most susceptible to fear, and they get in danger when their self-doubt and reactive impulses cause them to test others' commitments to them, which often destroys the relational security they crave.

Famous people who embody Six energy include Woody Allen, Warren Beatty, Richard Nixon, Penny Marshall, George Carlin, Ted Turner, Suzanne Somers, Jon Stewart, Spike Lee, J. Edgar Hoover, Andy Rooney, and fictional characters George Costanza from *Seinfeld*, Kate in *The Taming of the Shrew*, and Ahab in *Moby Dick*.

TYPE SEVEN

Riso and Hudson named type Seven the Enthusiast; Palmer and Daniels preferred the Epicure. Others used the Materialist and the Joyful Person. This book uses the "Optimistic Dreamer" label for Sevens because they are the ultimate optimists, forever dreaming of a bright future and busy having a good time while awaiting it. Sevens typically possess marvelous, almost magical, energy and synergy that propel them and everyone around them toward enthusiastic adventure. Of course, Sevens have a host of nagging fears that ultimately drive them, but they cover them well, embodying the idea that a distracted mind is a happy one.

Sevens are often energetic, versatile, magnetic, and, by all appearances, perpetually happy. They are the Enneagram's renaissance people—talented and accomplished in many disparate fields and constantly reinventing themselves and their environments. They are generally adventurous, impulsive pleasure seekers with a boundless zest for life, but they often struggle with commitments and would rather move on to something new than complete something that now bores them. They've got quicksilver minds and are often restless and hyperactive. In truth, they use frenetic activity and the thrill of adventure to mask anxieties. A lot of comedians who harbor an unseen dark side are Sevens.

When their defenses fail them, Sevens become manic, impatient, hedonistic, and willing to run over anyone who gets in the way of their next plan. When healthy, Sevens are productive, deeply grateful, unfailingly generous people who fully assimilate their experiences and bring a deep and special joy to the world.

Scatterbrained Sevens

Sevens can range from enthusiastic, optimistic, multitalented, versatile, playful, and generous to hyperactive, scattered, impulsive, and irresponsible. They worry about others weighing them down or depriving them of eternal happiness. They don't want anyone—even themselves—to realize that their relentless search for the silver lining in every cloud is a fear-driven response to avoid pain at all costs. They can go overboard with gluttony, are excessive in everything they do, and disintegrate when hyperactivity and escapist optimism keep them separated from true intimacy and discovering their real potential.

Famous personalities that provide a glimpse into Sevens include Katie Couric, George Clooney, John F. Kennedy, Sr., Michael Caine, Robin Williams, Ray Bradbury, Magic Johnson, Regis Philbin, Richard Branson, Sarah Ferguson, Tom Robbins, and fictional characters Peter Pan and Isadora Wing of the novel *Fear of Flying*.

TYPE EIGHT

Riso and Hudson labeled type Eight the Challenger. Palmer and Daniels selected the Boss, and others refer to this type as the Leader and the Powerful Person. In this book, the label for Eights is the "Dominator," for fairly clear reasons—their whole thing in life is to win every battle and dominate when it comes to money and power. Eights typically want to rule the world and will gleefully squash anyone who challenges them or blocks their way to the top. They usually have a massive lust for life that only the acquisition of power can fulfill.

Strong, decisive, and bracingly self-confident, Eights are often seen as the Enneagram's thousand-pound gorillas. They can be fiercely independent and honest, but they are energized by confrontation. They believe in going after what they want and often take on leadership roles at work and in social groups. They will protect their friends and are even capable of being surprisingly sensitive. When career driven, Eights' work provides a means to gain control over their lives and destinies; they can become workaholics and power mongers.

When pathological, Eights can become hard-hearted, lashing out at any attempt to control them, recklessly overestimating their own power, and mowing down anything and anyone who gets in their way. But when they are balanced, whole human beings, Eights use their strength and courage to champion worthwhile causes for the right reasons—to benefit society—rather than to reflect or fortify their own ambitions. Healthy Eights find the strength that lies just beneath the surface when they trust others enough to allow themselves to be vulnerable.

▲▲▲▲▲▲▲▲▲▲▲▲▲▲▲▲▲▲▲▲▲▲▲▲▲▲▲▲▲

Biggest Dog in the Yard

Eights are powerful, protective, determined, confident, and forceful, but also defiant, intimidating, destructive, and sadistic. They don't want anyone to know that they are really afraid of being dominated by others. They do everything to prevent you from knowing that their boastfulness and bullying are a shield for weakness. Their lustfulness—for life, for power—is way over the top, and their downfall happens when their compulsive need to be strong and in control cuts off their ability to empathize.

▼▼▼▼▼▼▼▼▼▼▼▼▼▼▼▼▼▼▼▼▼▼▼▼▼▼▼▼▼

Famous people who represent Eight energy include Humphrey Bogart, Lucille Ball, Napoleon Bonaparte, Fidel Castro, Alan Dershowitz, Indira Gandhi, Charles Barkley, John Gotti, Dennis Miller, Rush Limbaugh, Johnny Cash, Barbara Walters, Geronimo, the late Texas governor Ann Richards, and fictional characters Zorba the Greek and Petruchio in *The Taming of the Shrew*.

TYPE NINE

Riso and Hudson labeled Nines the Peacemaker. Palmer and Daniels preferred the Mediator, and others have selected the Preservationist and the Peaceful Person. This book named this type the "Peaceful Lamb" because Nines often spend their lives avoiding conflict at all costs and love being the sweethearts of the Enneagram. Nines cannot envision a world absent of peace and harmony and thus consider it their mission to impose it. Nines are willing to sacrifice everything for the sake of peace in the family, peace in the community, peace in the church, peace everywhere.

Nines are undeniably agreeable, peaceful, and extremely wary of conflict, making them equivalent to Zen masters in the Enneagram. Nines who have evolved to the highest rungs of their personality spectrum are truly spiritual leaders who practice divine detachment. They love, but they also release and allow everything and everyone to evolve according to their divine design.

The average, ego-driven Nine, however, practices detachment as a way to avoid anything that will create anxiety. They will repress anger and deny feelings for eons, even when their loved ones are literally feeling frozen out by unspoken resentment emanating from the peaceful Nine. Nines can make great diplomats and mediators, but their indecisiveness, neutrality, and foot dragging can also drive their family or coworkers nuts.

At their best, Nines are flexible, modest, and realistically optimistic, but Nines surrender their sense of self for the sake of relationship and can eventually become disconnected from their own lives. They essentially live their unfocused lives lost in a dense fog.

Pathological Nines are capable of actually harming the ones they profess to love so much through emotional neglect and passive-aggressive striking back. Nines can be deadly but silent. If they are balanced, however, Nines experience an emotional awakening and focus the right amount of attention on themselves and their loved ones. When in top form, Nines have a palpable, confident serenity that makes them incredibly effective communicators, calming mediators, and fully connected partners.

▲▲▲▲▲▲▲▲▲▲▲▲▲▲▲▲▲▲▲▲▲▲▲▲▲▲

Nines Hiding Behind Closed Shutters

Nines are modest, trusting, easygoing, self-effacing, and patient, but also complacent, accommodating, repressed, passive-aggressive, apathetic, and numb. They cower in fear that if they rock the boat, everyone won't love them anymore. They try to hide the fact that their nothing-bothers-me exterior covers a core of anger and resentment, but it leaks out in stinky, silent, unexpected ways. They are lazy in the sense that they don't invest the energy required to reveal their true feelings, express their real desires, or take responsibility for their own spiritual growth.

▼▼▼▼▼▼▼▼▼▼▼▼▼▼▼▼▼▼▼▼▼▼▼▼▼▼

Nines get into trouble when their habit of ignoring problems and dissociating to avoid conflicts allows neglected troubles in work and in relationships to fester, become serious, and present a real danger to themselves and others.

Famous Nines include Ronald Reagan, Fran Leibowitz, Tony Bennett, Bill Clinton, Clint Eastwood, Jimmy Stewart, Walter Cronkite, Jerry Seinfeld, Grace Kelly, Sandra Bullock, Patty Hearst, the Dalai Lama, and fictional characters Dorothy in *The Wizard of Oz*, the bumbling detective Columbo, and Edith Bunker of *All in the Family*.

Wing Subtypes

One of the enneatypes on either side of your core personality type (on the circle) becomes the wing that provides complexity and dimension to your personality. For example, say you are a One. You will have either a Nine or a Two wing. A Four will have either a Three or a Five wing. Sevens have either a Six or Eight wing; and so on. Understanding the concept of wings and how they function helps explain how personalities can vary widely within each core personality typology. For example, a Six with a Five wing will be intrinsically different from a Six with a Seven wing.

Wings determine your secondary fears and desires, the motivations that drive you, and the traits or behaviors you develop to form your personality. The proportion of primary and secondary influences can differ significantly. If your wing influences a large portion of your personality, it's frequently called a "heavy" wing. If the wing is present but your core personality still takes center stage, you have a "moderate" wing. If your core fixation completely dominates your secondary personality to the point that it is almost imperceptible, you have a "light" wing. In each case, the core personality dominates the overall personality. For example, a Seven with a light Eight wing will exhibit mostly Seven behaviors, while a Seven with a heavy Eight wing will show strong Eight characteristics in addition to typical Seven behavior; a Seven with a moderate Eight would be somewhere in between.

TWOS WITH A ONE WING

Ones internalize a set of moral principles, and they usually behave somewhere in between genuinely loving evangelical idealists and judgmental, critical, perfectionist tyrants. Twos are people pleasers who fluctuate between being true altruists and manipulators who use their ability to determine what someone wants so they can win love. Ones are usually convinced they know the one, true, right way; Twos are usually too reliant on others for self-validation. So how do these two combine?

One energy often lends a sense of moral purpose that helps ego-driven or pathological Twos with a One wing lean toward altruism, as opposed to being so focused on getting their immediate needs met that they ingratiate themselves to a few people whose favors they want.

When it works well, One wing energy brings a cool rationale or a desire for a moral purpose that serves to temper Twos' cloying emotional warmth. They may even circumvent their own needs to adopt important social issues or campaigns.

Unfortunately, in reality, most ego-driven Twos with a One wing live with conflicting impulses—to remain dispassionate and rigidly idealistic (judgmental perfectionist)—or to feel sympathy for others and act with kindness (loving altruist). Even when they do feel compassion, the One wing often makes Twos quick on the draw with moral and personal judgments against their loved ones, as well as themselves.

At their worst, Twos with a One wing can be controlling, manipulative, self-righteous, self-destructive, and rigid. Believing they know best, they feel justified in manipulating or attempting to control their loved ones. And they often refuse to believe that they are wrong about anything and will vehemently deny aggressive feelings.

TWOS WITH A THREE WING

Because they are in the same feeling, or relationship triad, Twos with a Three wing are more compatible than Twos with a One wing, who are in different triads. In this case, both enneatypes in the triad are focused on relationships and have an uncanny ability to observe and interpret other people's emotions. When they are self-actualized, both personalities relate very well to other people. Twos still gauge other people's emotions to create relationships, but the Three wing makes them more confident, charming, and outgoing. They simply are more attractive and more approachable than your average Two.

Rather than being so focused on being seen as lovable, the Three wing often makes Twos focus on being seen as successful. Both types are always highly aware of what others think about them, but the Three wing wants social status and will show off to impress others, often to the point of casually dropping names regardless of whether they even know the person being mentioned. This Two wants you to admire him and will create a persona if necessary. Reasonably functioning Twos with a Three wing have enough martyr energy left to control ego inflation, but they often go from feeling guilty when they breach moral standards to being terrified that they will be humiliated or lose social status if they make any public missteps.

Who's a Two with a Three Wing?

Twos with a Three wing often project a charming, poised, confident, and friendly persona that can harbor unbridled ambition to be at the top of their field. The musical galaxy provides examples in the form of Luciano Pavarotti, Barry Manilow, Tommy Tune, Sammy Davis Jr., and John Denver. These successful performers epitomized showmanship combined with a distinctive, friendly, and engaging personality.

When pathological Twos have a Three wing, the combination can be deadly—to themselves or to someone they once claimed to love. If the Three's energy led to the development of a persona that they then feel compelled to maintain, any perceived betrayal or threat of being exposed may make these Twos hostile and aggressive. They can also be all too willing to sink to the lowest depths to get what they want from others. If they feel vulnerable, ongoing frustration may lead to disintegration in the form of pathological obsession, jealousy, and violence.

THREES WITH A TWO WING

When a Two wing endows a Three personality with genuine warmth and empathy, a Three frequently becomes a genuinely attractive, sociable, charming, and likable person. Rather than having to manufacture these traits to maintain an image, they have integrated these traits. Such individuals may have Threes' animated, energetic, and entertaining qualities, but these are usually tempered by a realization that other people are important, that it's good to focus on these other people occasionally, and that others also deserve to have their needs and desires met.

When a Two wing reinforces negative Three behavior, you get people who crave attention and recognition so vigorously that it's hard for them to maintain their cool when others don't sufficiently appreciate everything they do. They are often openly hostile when someone dares to expose their flaws. They need you to love them and to admire their fabulousness; if you don't, they hate you for it.

THREES WITH A FOUR WING

Threes are all about public persona, climbing over whoever gets in their way to becoming king of the hill, master of their game, superstar to the max, or whatever makes them rich. Fours are all about introspection, depth, and finding their true self so they can finally be proved unique and special. Fours are infatuated with their own feelings, particularly melancholy; Threes would rather think about what they feel and manufacture upbeat feelings than brood. Fours are about intensity; Threes are about surface. Threes tend to be extroverted; Fours tend to be introverted.

Thus, a Three with a Four wing endures internal skirmishes on a regular basis, which can manifest in manic-depressive swings. They can't help being image conscious or feeling compelled to work hard to achieve exceptional recognition, but their Four wing tends to make them more subdued and much more in touch with their real emotions. Rather than caring what others think of their accomplishments, they are more concerned about what they feel about their accomplishments.

When it works really well, a Four wing helps a Three value her inner life and present her real, as opposed to a false, self. These Threes still want to excel at what they do, but unlike Threes with a Two wing, they do so quietly because they want to do something meaningful that nourishes them far more than they want to do something solely to impress through money or status.

Who's a Three with a Four Wing?

According to *The Enneagram Movie and Video Guide*, Threes with a Four wing who possess a sensitive artistic sensibility combined with a more introspective, cool, calm, and collected personality include Richard Gere, who embraces Eastern religions; former President Jimmy Carter, who founded Habitat for Humanity; intellectually inclined talk show host Dick Cavett; and author Truman Capote.

Negative Four energy may cause Threes to swing from a tendency to over-indulge in misguided self-reflection and end up doubting themselves at every turn, to arrogantly believing that they are smarter than their critics and brandishing their superiority. Fours' energy sometimes makes Threes vulnerable to emotional instability and low-grade depression.

FOURS WITH A THREE WING

Fours with a Three wing actually fare a little better than Threes with a Four wing. In this case, a Three wing energizes lethargic Fours. All that pent-up creativity gets a boot when it links up with real-life financial goals. Three energy also helps brooding Fours come out of their introspective shell and at least want to feel good about themselves. These Fours are definitely more energetic and often more sophisticated in their tastes—they may even want a high-profile job or luxurious digs to show off.

When they surrender the more typical lack of self-esteem, Fours with a Three wing are able to set concrete goals and transition quickly into Three-type action. A healthy dose of Three motivates them to go beyond dreaming and actually produce works of art that reflect well upon themselves and their desired, self-created image.

Because they can be keenly intuitive, highly creative, dynamic, talented, and ambitious, many Fours with a Three wing look more like Sevens, particularly if they also have a lusty sense of humor and a sparkling dash of pizzazz. But Fours with a Three wing are more in touch with their feelings and willing to weave their emotional context into their creative work than most Sevens.

Even though Threes' extroversion tames Fours' tendency to mope or succumb to melancholy, they may swing from one extreme to another. They may behave like the life of the party and then go home feeling very much alone and lonely, or they may be melodramatic and flamboyant one minute and quiet and secretive the next.

FOURS WITH A FIVE WING

A Five wing often adds intellectual muscle to Fours' feeling-intensive, hypersensitive modus operandi, bringing complexity and depth to their lives and to their creativity. The blending of a piercing intellect with emotional intensity helps them become confident in their individualistic skin and more capable of utilizing their insights in productive ways. They burn with creative fervor and often produce successful works of art. They also try to think their way out of their emotional doldrums.

On the other hand, Fours with a Five wing may become more conservative, self-contained, subdued, private, and analytical. When they take on more of the analytical bent of Five energy, they are often drawn to solitary professions such as a researcher, using their intellect to be a scientist, or using their fascination with feelings as a psychologist or therapist.

Who's a Four with a Five Wing?

Many Fours with a Five wing are geniuses in their creative field. According to *The Enneagram Movie and Video Guide*, prime examples include Diane Arbus, Marlon Brando, Eric Clapton, Kurt Cobain, Bob Dylan, Sylvia Plath, Arthur Rimbaud, Edgar Allan Poe, and Virginia Woolf. All combined exceptional intelligence with an artistic soul, which resulted in original works of art that captured the world's attention. Unfortunately, many of them fell prey to a Four's susceptibility to a deeply pathological depression that led to suicide.

On the negative side, Fours with a Five wing can become even more introspective and solitary. Sometimes Five energy leads to quirky or idiosyncratic behavior, or a feeling of being so different they feel alienated. This could result in further social withdrawal and longer periods of isolation that, unfortunately, bolster Fours' proclivity for unproductive brooding or feeling sorry for themselves. Fours with a heavy Five wing who spend too much time alone can get lost in nonproductive rumination, depression, and morbidity.

FIVES WITH A FOUR WING

A Four wing brings emotional subtext to a typically cool, calm, and collected Five. Without question, they are more sensitive, empathetic, and emotionally supportive. A heavy Four wing means the Fives have easier access to their emotions, which assists them in being either more humanistic and focused on the emotional welfare of others or more self-absorbed and focused on how they feel about what's happening in their own lives.

▲▲▲▲▲▲▲▲▲▲▲▲▲▲▲▲▲▲▲▲▲▲▲▲▲▲▲▲

Who's a Five with a Four Wing?

According to *The Enneagram Movie and Video Guide*, examples of Fives with a Four wing include Tim Burton, David Byrne, Agatha Christie, T. S. Eliot, Albert Einstein, Gary Larson, George Lucas, David Lynch, and Georgia O'Keeffe.

▼▼▼▼▼▼▼▼▼▼▼▼▼▼▼▼▼▼▼▼▼▼▼▼▼▼▼▼

Fives' creativity is also bolstered by having a Four wing. They probably won't be as melodramatic, brooding, or focused on the emotional intensity of their work as Fours, but these Fives may use intellectual constructs to create works of art, such as writing imaginative philosophy, mathematics books, or inventive science fiction novels. They might be very attracted to the Enneagram, for instance, where the cool rationale of psychological concepts as they relate to personality formation incorporates spirituality and intuition.

FIVES WITH A SIX WING

Although Fives remain their detached, intellectual, loner selves, a heavy Six wing could make them feel more dependent on other people and perhaps create a burgeoning urge, or at least an occasional desire, to mix with people. It may bring improved people skills, or at least a slight opening up, even if it's only to ask Sixes' typical probing questions.

However, Sixes' tendency to flip from phobic to counterphobic behavior may make Fives more fearful; they are still more likely to move forward, albeit with skepticism and caution. However, once they form alliances or friendships, Six wings help reticent Fives form trustworthy relationships, and once they've bonded, they are more loyal.

▲▲▲▲▲▲▲▲▲▲▲▲▲▲▲▲▲▲▲▲▲▲▲▲▲▲

Who's a Five with a Six Wing?

Robin Williams's portrayal of Oliver Sacks in *Awakenings* showed a typical Five with a Six wing behavior. He was a quirky, idiosyncratic doctor who was socially awkward. His Six wing led him to have a questioning mind, and a little counterphobic Six behavior occurred when he went against his profession's conventional wisdom and tried a radical treatment on patients everyone else had written off.

▼▼▼▼▼▼▼▼▼▼▼▼▼▼▼▼▼▼▼▼▼▼▼▼▼▼

Fives with Six wings may have even stronger analytical skills and be attracted to scientific or mathematical professions, but a negative Six wing can bring fear to the table and cloud the Five's normal ability to think clearly.

SIXES WITH A FIVE WING

Sixes with a Five Wing are more shy, cautious, and withdrawn, which others often mistake as being cold and standoffish. It's really just that Fives have a tendency to need private space, opportunities to observe before engaging, and a need to seek solitude until they can wrap their minds around whatever is bothering them. Like Fives, these Sixes are simply more introverted, intellectual, and attracted to solitary activities such as research or informational gathering. Fives' love of being alone to process and contemplate can benefit phobic Sixes' need for outside approval. Although it could lead to paranoia, most Sixes with Five wings remain loners because they simply like to protect their privacy, acquire knowledge to distinguish and separate themselves, and even shield themselves from too much outside interference.

Who's a Six with a Five Wing?

According to *The Enneagram Movie and Video Guide*, examples of Sixes with a Five wing include Warren Beatty, Gene Hackman, J. Edgar Hoover, Spike Lee, Richard Nixon, Janet Reno, and Brian Wilson. Movie roles that portray Sixes with a Five wing include Martin Landau in *Crimes and Misdemeanors*, Sam Neill in *The Piano*, and Anthony Perkins in *Psycho*.

A Five wing helps Sixes perfect a smooth exterior that hides a percolating intelligence and a lot more depth than you would imagine. Negative Five wings can amplify Sixes' phobias or counterphobias, particularly when Sixes spend too much time alone brooding over past hurts. When mixed with paralyzing Six fear, some start believing that danger lies everywhere and may become increasingly antisocial and paranoid.

SIXES WITH A SEVEN WING

A Six with a Seven wing seems almost the complete opposite of a Six with a Five wing. These Sixes are ready to party. Seven's energy makes them playful, spontaneous, adventurous, and far more impulsive than your classic fearful Six. These Sixes hold a few more positive thoughts about the world and trust themselves and others enough to take an occasional risk. If they're not careful, however, Seven's energy can lead a Six to ruin—overindulgence in alcohol, drugs, or casual sex is not uncommon among this set.

Who's a Six with a Seven Wing?

According to *The Enneagram Movie and Video Guide*, examples of Sixes with a Seven wing include Kim Basinger, Rodney Dangerfield, Judy Davis, Ellen DeGeneres, Carrie Fisher, Diane Keaton, Richard Lewis, Julia Roberts, Susan Sarandon, and Jon Stewart. Movie roles that captured the Six with Seven wing personality include Woody Allen in anything, Billy Crystal in *City Slickers*, Bill Murray in *What About Bob?*, and Meg Ryan in *When Harry Met Sally*.

Like Sevens, Sixes with a Seven wing attempt to control their underlying fear with frenetic activity, sometimes reaching manic phases. Many become comedians who write clever jokes and tell funny stories about their foibles to cover their underlying depression.

Negative Seven wing influences create internal confusion that manifests in mood swings, amplified fears, nervous jitters, and blaming others. It's as if Seven's energy makes these Sixes covet fame and fortune, but they still lack the confidence to really go for it.

SEVENS WITH A SIX WING

Sevens with a Six wing are a little bit more down-to-earth and interested in sitting still long enough to forge relationships. They care whether you like them or not, and once they've committed to a relationship are more likely to be loyal, faithful, and stick with it through thick and thin. And lucky you, because they are often warm, gracious, and sweet.

Sevens with a Six wing are also light on their feet and full of charm. They seem sweet, vulnerable, and somewhat silly, but it's obvious a clever mind runs the show. They also have charming senses of humor and entertain many with their infinitely endearing stories. A lot of comedians are also Sevens with a Six wing, but they tend to be the ones without a heavy dark side hidden under their jocular persona. Their natural gluttony can be for the desire for information instead of appetite.

Who's a Seven with a Six Wing?

According to *The Enneagram Movie and Video Guide*, examples of Sevens with a Six wing include Dave Barry, Jackie Chan, Chevy Chase, Goldie Hawn, Magic Johnson, Eddie Murphy, Brad Pitt, Martin Short, Lily Tomlin, and Robin Williams. Movie roles that portray Sevens with a Six wing include Ruth Gordon in *Harold and Maude*, Audrey Hepburn in *Breakfast at Tiffany's*, Sidney Poitier in *Lilies of the Field*, and George Clooney in *One Fine Day*.

If they are pathological, Sevens with a Six wing can be interminably sensitive, weepy, fearful, and clinging. It's as if they become easily unglued and spin off in divergent destructive cycles: latching on to negative partners and then abruptly breaking things off, sleeping around very indiscriminately, or drinking or eating too much and then starving themselves. Some develop a proclivity for really mean humor, the kind you see in some cartoonists.

SEVENS WITH AN EIGHT WING

Sevens with an Eight wing can be marvelously exuberant, cheerful, and friendly. Additionally, they can be assertive, competitive, bold, confrontational, and aggressive. When a lust for intensity and gluttony combine, Sevens with an Eight wing are often prone to chemical addiction. Sevens with an Eight wing mask their fear by meeting it head on. Luckily, they're not intent on mowing you down like Eights, but they can still make your heart quiver if they're directing anger toward you.

Sevens with an Eight wing care more about having a good time than amassing power, but they do like accumulating nice things to spice up their lives. And one needs money to buy fancy clothes, cars, houses, so Sevens with an Eight wing are ambitious and hardworking. It's just that they have another side—a playful side.

Who's a Seven with an Eight Wing?

According to *The Enneagram Movie and Video Guide*, examples of Sevens with an Eight wing include Michael Caine, George Clooney, Francis Ford Coppola, Cary Grant, Tom Hanks, Jack Nicholson, and Barbra Streisand. Movie roles that depict Sevens with an Eight wing include Jeff Bridges in *Tucker*, Ray Liotta in *Good Fellows*, Jack Nicholson in *Batman*, and Roy Schneider in *All That Jazz*.

Sevens' joie de vivre combined with an Eight's powerful focus makes them multitalented, dynamic, inventive, and fascinating. They can be visionary, full of bright ideas and the energy to bring them to fruition.

If they're pathological, however, they are frequently narcissistic and demanding. The world revolves around them and their immediate needs, which they expect to be fulfilled immediately.

EIGHTS WITH A SEVEN WING

These Eights take on the tendency of Sevens to see a positive outcome. They blend their usual realism with a sentimental idealism. Seven's energy tames the lion in Eights and helps them learn to sublimate at least some of their more aggressive feelings.

As Eights they are still business oriented, but a Seven wing makes them energetic, quicker on the draw, and more entrepreneurial or visionary. A Seven wing also helps them be more sociable, often to the point of going overboard at parties.

Who's an Eight with a Seven Wing?

According to *The Enneagram Movie and Video Guide*, examples of Eights with a Seven wing include Lucille Ball, Richard Burton, Sean Connery, Rush Limbaugh, Ann Richards, Grace Slick, and Donald Trump. Movie roles that depict Eights with a Seven wing include Matt Damon in *Good Will Hunting*, Michael Douglas in *Wall Street*, James Earl Jones in *The Great White Hope*, and Christine Lahti in *Leaving Normal*.

Pathological Eights with Seven wings are highly susceptible to the diseases of excess—alcoholism, drug addiction, shopping addictions. When their anger becomes distorted, they are capable of vicious behavior.

EIGHTS WITH A NINE WING

When Eights have a Nine wing they are more in tune with others, which helps them gain a more expansive, all-encompassing view of life. Nines' desire for equanimity tones down the Eights' lust for power, helping them achieve a more balanced personality. They are more relaxed, more inclusive, and even somewhat introverted. Their energy quiets down, creating opportunities for them to be mild-mannered and receptive; they even take other people's views under consideration occasionally.

Who's an Eight with a Nine Wing?

According to *The Enneagram Movie and Video Guide*, examples of Eights with a Nine wing include Johnny Cash, Fidel Castro, Michael Douglas, John Huston, Evel Knievel, Mao Tse-tung, Golda Meir, Robert Mitchum, and Queen Latifah. Movie roles that depict Eights with a Nine wing include Humphrey Bogart in *Casablanca*, Russell Crowe in *L.A. Confidential*, Judd Hirsch in *Ordinary People*, and Jack Palance in *City Slickers*.

Unfortunately, all that Eight anger doesn't totally disappear. If provoked, the dormant anger that was lying just under the surface spews out, wounding people who don't deserve it. A pathological Eight with a Nine wing can become desensitized, cruel, and chronically abusive.

NINES WITH AN EIGHT WING

A healthy Nine with an Eight wing exudes a palpable, albeit quiet, charismatic confidence. They look and feel comfortable in their own skins—a little too good—and are usually very good at maximizing the sort of king-of-the-jungle command they personify. They almost always get what they want—as if it were their destiny to have it all along.

Unfortunately, under the auspices of Eights' aggressive tendencies, Nines' can lose their congenial disposition and become narrow-minded and willful. If they are pathological, at some point their anger will surface—abruptly and out of proportion. They may be so desensitized that they don't notice the damage they've just inflicted, and they often feel sufficiently justified in going for their opponent's throat.

On the positive side, they have a touch of Eights' energy, which helps most Nines be more confident, assertive, outgoing, and capable of actual rebellion. However, they are more typically torn between needing peace and quiet and wanting to grab whatever they want, or displaying an urge to merge and wanting to push people away.

NINES WITH A ONE WING

Self-actualized Nines with a One wing have improved focus. They can actually get their ducks in a row, prioritize, and get things done in a timely manner. Positive One energy also helps Nines set firm boundaries based on crystallized views of what is right and what is wrong. They develop their own values instead of blindly accepting what those around them think or feel. Their strong sense of moral imperatives may spur them to tackle social issues or develop missionary zeal for worthwhile causes.

However, pathological Nines with a One wing may wield their values as weapons, becoming hypercritical, condescending, and judgmental. Worst of all, they usually treat themselves equally bad. When things fall apart, they may latch onto a zealot and walk around blindly following the wrong path as if they were under a bad spell.

ONES WITH A NINE WING

When Ones with strong moral codes have a Nine wing that brings a certain discomfort with actual reality, they often become a bit too cool, calm, and collected and are emotionally disconnected. Self-actualized Ones with a Nine wing know and value the benefits of remaining emotionally detached in terms of being principled, rational, logical, and fair, particularly in the pursuit of ideals. Most ego-driven Ones with a Nine wing tend to simply detach or become apathetic.

▲▲▲▲▲▲▲▲▲▲▲▲▲▲▲▲▲▲▲▲▲▲▲▲▲▲▲▲▲

Who's a One with a Nine Wing?

Examples of Ones with a Nine wing who became gifted speakers and well-respected—perhaps surprisingly passionate—champions of social, political, or environmental causes because they primarily retain a cool, detached, rational air include Al Gore, Carl Sagan, Ralph Nader, Sandra Day O'Connor, and Margaret Thatcher.

▼▼▼▼▼▼▼▼▼▼▼▼▼▼▼▼▼▼▼▼▼▼▼▼▼▼▼▼▼

In fact, many ego-driven Ones with a Nine wing can be brilliant thinkers, but they tend to compartmentalize their brains and suppress their hearts, creating disparate behaviors that swing from utmost discipline to laziness, diehard passion (about ideals) to indifference. Their anger, however, reverts to a Nine's more typical passivity, as in primarily covert, and is more often expressed through sharp retorts or bitingly sarcastic comments.

When a heavy Nine wing brings negativity, Ones hide behind emotionally stark black-and-white thinking, no longer pretend to care about other people, and often cope by projecting their dark emotions onto others and then railing against them. They are especially prone to ignore personal and relationship components of the world.

ONES WITH A TWO WING

Unlike Ones with a Nine wing, who can be emotionally bland, Nines with a Two wing have to cope with pesky warm and fuzzy feelings toward people that butt right up against their usual cool rationale.

Self-actualized Ones with a Two wing extend their moral codes to embrace love of their fellow man and actually stop to consider the very human emotional impact their behavior may have on others. They can be rational and objective as well as warm and empathetic at the same time. In contrast to Ones with a Nine wing, who embrace and fight for ideals, Ones with a Two wing embrace and fight for people. Most Ones with a Two wing meld their ideas about what is right and wrong with a desire to help their fellow humans.

▲▲▲▲▲▲▲▲▲▲▲▲▲▲▲▲▲▲▲▲▲▲▲▲▲▲▲▲

Who's a One with a Two Wing?

Examples of fiery, action-oriented Ones with a Two wing who take on contentious social values and wage political campaigns—because they are as passionate about people as they are about the ideals or principles involved—include Jane Fonda, Mario Cuomo, Bill Moyers, Vanessa Redgrave, Jerry Brown, and Joan Baez.

▼▼▼▼▼▼▼▼▼▼▼▼▼▼▼▼▼▼▼▼▼▼▼▼▼▼▼▼

This new interest in people leads many ego-driven Ones with a Nine wing to flip from a desire to control themselves to a desire to control those around them. Unlike Ones with a Nine wing, who focus on ideals, dysfunctional Ones with a Two wing focus on how they can force people to adhere to their moral codes. As such, they often appear smug, overconfident, and narrowly defined. If someone questions their moral or behavioral authority, they may fly off the handle. Judge Judy would be a lively example of this.

When Ones with a Two wing are pathological, they can be condescending and intolerant, wielding anger and guilt like a sword. They become intractable in the face of criticism and eventually become increasingly self-righteous and hypocritical, yet are blind to their own faults.

Your Instincts and Your Enneagram Type

Humans are born with three primary instincts for survival—physical, emotional, and intellectual. As people develop, they tend to favor one instinct over another—choosing their heads, or hearts, or guts—to observe, interpret, react to, and interact with their inner selves and the outer world. The instinct that suits you most has a major effect on the formation of your personality or Enneagram type. Understanding how your primary instinct affects your type will help you understand your underlying motives and ways of perceiving and operating in the world.

UNDERSTANDING YOUR PROCESSING MECHANISMS

In response to your early childhood experience you learn to process information through your sensitivity to feelings and emotions, your physical or gut instincts that tell you whether you're in a good or bad situation, or through what you see and think using your intellect or brain. Intuition seems to play a role in all three triads in the sense that all the enneatypes have access to their intuition, but they may receive it through their feelings, physical reactions, or thoughts. Enneagram scholars believe that placement on the Enneagram circle reflects which primary instinct you use to navigate through life. The following types are placed into corresponding instinctual modes:

1. Heart or emotional instinct: types Two, Three, and Four
2. Head or intellectual instinct: types Five, Six, and Seven
3. Gut or physical instinct: types Eight, Nine, and One

What this means is that Twos, Threes, and Fours are in tune with their emotions and are keenly sensitive to other people's moods or emotions. They tend to focus on personal relationships and intimacy and will listen to their hearts when it comes to sizing up other people or making decisions about their lives.

Fives, Sixes, and Sevens are more in tune with their mental or intellectual processes, which means they rely on rationality and reason to interpret their worlds and interact with others. More than the other six types, they like to process information through their mental intellect.

Eights, Nines, and Ones are more in tune with their physical self or gut instinct when it comes to sizing up people or making decisions about their lives. Since they are acutely aware of their physical bodies, they are more focused on physical survival than the types who rely on other primary instincts.

Gurdjieff's Intellectual Center

George Ivanovitch Gurdjieff, an influential twentieth-century spiritual teacher, theorized that all humans have a "higher emotional" and a "higher intellectual" center, but most people cannot access their higher selves because their lower selves (personality or ego constructs as determined by how you have learned to use or misuse your thinking, feeling, or physical centers) distract with their constant chatter, habitual behavior, and functionary defenses. According to Gurdjieff, in order to evolve, you have to unscramble your ego and quiet your mind.

THE TRIAD GROUPS

The triads within the Enneagram model include the heart group (those who feel and display emotions more readily than other types; Twos, Threes, and Fours are in this category); the head group (the cool, logical, objective types who rely on intellect to guide them; Fives, Sixes, and Sevens are in this category); and the gut group (those who rely on their gut reaction and intuitive response to others; Eights, Nines, and Ones fall into this category).

Use the Enneagram to Unearth the Power of You

Sophisticated enough with its highly nuanced complexities to have received scientific validation and yet easy to understand and use, The Enneagram is an effective self-empowerment tool. With it, you can transform negative and self-defeating behaviors into positive, transformative ones that enhance your life.

Through the process of self-discovery, you can claim the power to reveal the authentic you to the world and save enduring and meaningful relationships.

GETTING PRACTICAL

Use the Enneagram Personality System to first understand yourself. Then, why not encourage your friends and others to take the test. Knowing the personality type of your friends, lovers, family members, bosses, and business associates can be a secret gift, giving you insights into why they are exhibiting certain types of behaviors in specific situations. Never again will you have to ask, "Where did that behavior come from?" Now, you'll know.

Relationships

The Enneagram increasingly has become a popular tool for enhancing, managing, and even repairing romantic relationships. It is even used by modern-day matchmakers. The Enneagram can be a powerful indicator in your quest to find a compatible mate. The system can help you learn about the quirks, needs, and expectations that hinder your relationship, as well as the hidden needs of your partner and ways to fulfill those needs.

It's tempting to think about relationship compatibility in terms of *type* compatibility—as in he's a Three and she's a One, and that has disaster written all over it, or they're both Fives so they should get along fine. None of the leading Enneagram teachers believes that any two people are more or less likely to be compatible solely based on enneatypes. The beauty of the Enneagram is that it can help you see underlying motivations, expectations, fears, and misconceptions (your own and those of others). It may well help you finally understand life from someone else's point of view.

TWOS, THREES, AND FOURS IN RELATIONSHIPS

Twos need to feel important, loved, appreciated, and needed; they need others to validate their feelings and make them feel special. Their egocentric desire to be loved makes them willing to do whatever it takes to prove that others need and love them. They eagerly sacrifice themselves believing the recipient of their love will grow to love them. Twos let their needy hearts rule over their heads. They fear and deny their own aggressive tendencies, which leads to repression and resentment. Twos project their neediness onto others.

Threes possess superb skill at reading cues and tailoring their communication to succeed at winning you over. They are the smooth operators, glib talkers, the deal closers. While great relationships may elude them, they will put a lot of effort into looking like they are doing all the right things.

Fours feel emotion intensely and like it that way. It's almost as if they have an aversion to shallowness. Light-hearted relationships and one-night stands are not for them. Their relationships tend to be intense, even transformative, and not only for them but for their friends, partners, and business associates as well.

FIVES, SIXES, AND SEVENS

Fives require safe and trustworthy relationships, understandable and reasonable expectations, and social propriety. They need plenty of private time and space and are happiest when they can progress in relationships at their own pace.

The personalities of Sixes are filled with paradox. They display characteristics of being equally weak and strong, shy and outgoing, and they flip-flop from one ego state to another. They spend their lives rebelling against authority or surrendering to it. In relationships, they need someone or something to believe in, and once they find that person, business, philosophy, cause, government, or theology, they devote themselves to it.

Sevens love life, people, parties, and everything wonderful that life and relationships with others bring. There's no looking back and no reliving unhappy experiences. Sevens just want to be happy, and they'll have a fascinating life—even if it only happens in their daydreams.

EIGHTS, NINES, AND ONES

Eights find conflict energizing, so if you are seeking a nice, quiet relationship, you might want to steer clear of an Eight. Don't hide information or keep secrets from Eights; they don't like it.

Nines may passively agree with you, hiding their own desires. They are great listeners and excel at going with the flow. This is both their gift and their curse since it inherently means agreeing with others to the detriment of their own wishes.

Ones can easily feel overwhelmed by the responsibility they take on in a relationship. They never want to make the wrong choice and agonize over the possible right one. They can often be self-critical and also self-righteous. Their work ethic is strong and their passion for right over might is equally strong. You'll always know where you stand with Ones as they are guided by logic and high principles.

Sex and Intimacy

According to Jung, libido is not connected to your sex drive alone, but instead refers to your overall psychic energy or what gives your personality juice. The opposite of what turns you on would be what turns you off.

INTIMACY WITH TWOS, THREES, AND FOURS

Unhealthy Twos can be powerful seducers or seductresses, but you will owe them unconditional love in return. Additionally, boundaries are problematic for Twos, as Twos seek balance between the polarities of intimacy and distance. Without realizing it, Twos unwittingly set up situations in which they can be exploited. When it happens, they are surprised, angry, and retaliate, feeling justified at being used or abused. For example, think of Glenn Close's character, a pathological Two, in the movie *Fatal Attraction*. Threes are self-focused in the arena of sex and seduction. Threes like looking the part of the seductive lover—the makeup, clothes, hair, nails, perfume—whatever they believe the idealized lover looks like within the context of the culture. Thus, Threes have a healthy self-image of their seductive prowess and will eagerly share themselves and their knowledge in bed with a partner. Fours love the inner idealized experience of love perhaps more than the actual lover and lovemaking. Intensity junkies, these people can live on opposite coasts and love with wild abandonment when they finally are together in one bed. Separation only serves to intensify the experience in the imagination of the Four who is apart from the lover; however, with the lover around a lot, the Four can become disillusioned and critical.

INTIMACY WITH FIVES, SIXES, AND SEVENS

Fives want emotional one-on-one intimacy and like the potency of great sex as a well-kept secret (remember they live in their heads). If your Five ever seems a bit parsimonious about emotional intimacy and sex, it's because he believes that his battery pack for the emotional energy needed for sensational sex has a limited life and he has fears about being the sexual titan you maybe think he is (fears of being inadequate). But what life there is in his battery budget will be spent on you since he won't waste it if you are not the one for him.

Sixes are constant worriers, second-guessing themselves and their decisions, and they frequently seem ambivalent. This is not necessarily a good thing when it comes to sex. But rest assured that when Sixes find someone to believe in, they devote themselves to that person with unfailing loyalty. Sevens love new experiences and beginnings as long as these experiences are intense. Sevens engage in magical thinking (creating solely through the process of imagining). The poetry of Walt Whitman gives a clue as to how powerful the imagination of a dreamy Seven can be. They have an appetite for the spice of life—variety. They might swear undying love to you tonight, but tomorrow is a new night . . . maybe a new lover. They won't lie about it to you either because they are so honest.

INTIMACY WITH EIGHTS, NINES, AND ONES

Eights will freely admit to being driven by lust—lust for life, lust for money, lust for culinary excellence, lust for yachts, lust for luxury cars, lust for sexual fulfillment. To Eights, life is an adventure begging to be lived, and restraint is the kiss of death. Power and domination for Eights go together like hand and glove. But lust isn't the same as love. Remember that when an Eight is lusting after you.

Nines can lose themselves in relationships where their lovers' needs take precedence over theirs. Although easily satisfied, Nines will do what is necessary just to get along when things aren't working quite the way they would like.

Hot sex or not, Nines will go along with what their partners want. But if they coast too long, sublimating (and not voicing) their needs and desires, they will feel disappointment. And then, while they are going along with the flow, they might just drift away from their partners and into someone else's arms.

Ones are concerned about what is morally right, and so they might not engage in sex that seems to them morally wrong or deviant. They might not be the most adventurous partners in bed. Their moral fixation can have them repressing their own sensuality because of where those feelings of passion might lead (for example, vice or sin).

Money

Each of the nine enneatypes, not surprisingly, has differing views about finances; however, like any relationship, an enneatype's relationship with money will depend on whether or not the type is healthy or pathological, whether money speaks to his security issues or not.

TWOS, THREES, AND FOURS AND FINANCES

Twos are extremely giving of themselves. They will wear themselves out for others, seemingly without needing reciprocation. But that is a false image. They have enormous expectations about pay-offs, being paid back, being paid what they think they are worth.

Threes are generally ten times more focused on money and success than family. Their relationship with money tends to be driven. There is never enough, so they have to keep making more. Fours have a deep need for both—they need someone (family) to nurture and a decent wage to ensure their own survival and that of their loved ones. To this end, they will work tirelessly to earn money.

FIVES, SIXES, AND SEVENS AND FINANCES

Fives can be miserly with money and affection, as they may suffer from a deeply ingrained fear of never having enough (Howard Hughes is an example of an ego-driven Five). Fives fear the lack of money, so they work hard, make more, and hoard what they have.

Sixes, because they are natural pessimists, believe money that is here today will be gone tomorrow. Their paranoia may drive them to become possessive; however, a self-actualized Six will see money as a way of achieving life goals.

For Sevens, money can be made from their larger-than-life dreams. They will work as hard as necessary to acquire their wealth.

EIGHTS, NINES, AND ONES AND FINANCES

Eights are naturally business-oriented and they lust for money. With it, they enjoy power, privilege, and domination. Nines, when they have money, tend to give it away because they want love and acceptance; they are often inclined to be humanitarian and philanthropic. Ones are highly self-controlled, have a strong sense of purpose, and will strongly strive to overcome adversity. That means that they will often become workaholics not because they need money for survival but because giving their all to their work or calling is the right thing to do.

Health

Since the Enneagram Personality system deals with behaviors related to emotional and psychological wellness or pathology, it follows that if someone is healthy and balanced in those areas, physical health will probably mirror that; however, if unhealthy levels of anger or resentment are present, physical health can be negatively impacted as well.

TWOS, THREES, AND FOURS AND GOOD HEALTH

Twos are the selfless lovers and givers who need you to need them. But because these caregivers and nurturers tend to give so much they can experience physical and emotional exhaustion. They need to learn balance, caring as much for themselves as for others.

Threes are energetic, charismatic, and sexy, receiving plenty of validation from the world that they are attractive and accomplished. Threes can confuse the happiness and well-being they derive from external sources with inner happiness. Their internal emotional conflict can literally make them sick.

Emotional expression is easy for Fours, but when stressed they can become moody, melancholy, and depressed. Those feelings can lead to self-indulgences that can lead to health concerns.

FIVES, SIXES, AND SEVENS AND GOOD HEALTH

Self-actualized Fives have the fabulous qualities of being mentally acute, resourceful, inventive, and competent. But they tend to worry too much. They need to focus on ways to deal with stress and worry to feel peaceful. Sixes are often plagued with anxiety and phobia and could benefit from yoga to deal with stress release. Pleasure-seeking Sevens can be so occupied with the pursuit of sensual pleasure that they don't consider the risks to their bodies. Also, they are often prone to addictions.

EIGHTS, NINES, AND ONES AND GOOD HEALTH

Eights act out aggressive behaviors, often to cover deep-seated anxieties. They can be forceful and exacting in their efforts to control their environments and others. That tendency applies to their health. Given to being blunt and direct, they appreciate those qualities in others, especially those in the health profession. An Eight will demand to know the truth about his or her health issue and then will want to face it head on. Eights have strong physical energy and a powerful lusty appetite for the good things in life. Health issues are often triggered by their overindulgences.

Ego-driven Nines suppress anger and avoid anything that creates anxiety, but that doesn't mean that they protect their good health. Repressed anger and denial of emotion can eventually show up in the body as disease. They try to hide their inner anger and resentment, but it leaks out in stinky, silent, unexpected ways. Nines would benefit from some emotional release therapy to stay well.

Ones like things to be smooth running and that goes for their bodies. These individuals are action oriented. Because they can be workaholics, they get plenty accomplished, but it may be to the detriment of their health and well-being. Their bodies hold tension and sometimes their inability to achieve perfection can result in depression.

Work

Each enneatype's personality traits, innate drive, and passion for what they do necessarily affect their work ethic and performance. When the job they are doing meshes well with their talents and abilities, the result is good but when that is not the case, the work suffers.

TWOS, THREES, AND FOURS AT WORK

Self-actualizing Twos have the ability to channel their feelings into creative projects and expand their intuitive understanding of themselves and others. Ego-driven Twos see themselves as exemplary bosses, who only want what is best for you (but often it is what is best for them). Threes are the Enneagram's business types. They make excellent sales people. If you ask them to do something, rest assured they will not only do it, but do it well. These are the people who will work doggedly and determinedly until they reach the pinnacles of success. They thrive on goal setting and accomplishing. Think Oprah Winfrey and Arnold Schwarzenegger. Healthy Fours have an emotional richness that finds expression in creative works—whether in business projects or personal hobbies and pursuits. Unhealthy Fours can be whiny to coworkers and friends and harbor a false sense of entitlement (believing they legitimately deserved that raise or promotion to project manager).

FIVES, SIXES, AND SEVENS AT WORK

The Fives are the researchers, writers, scientists, thinkers in think tanks, and futurists. They thrive on independent thinking and excel at work that utilizes their intellectual prowess and idealistic notions. They are excellent communicators, efficient project coordinators, and are headstrong yet effective leaders who embrace progress. Think Albert Einstein and the Buddha. Healthy Sixes have charm, tact, patience, and the willingness to endure drudgery if need be. They can keep a business, a bureaucratic agency, or a political machine like the White House smooth running and efficient. Think George H. W. Bush and Richard Nixon. Sixes are among the best problem solvers in the world. Sixes pay close attention to what's going on, have X-ray vision when it comes to anticipating everything that can go wrong, and will protect themselves by fixing problems if they can. They make excellent middle managers.

EIGHTS, NINES, AND ONES AT WORK

Eights are powerful, honest, and loyal to a fault. They are natural defenders and protectors. Your business will be safe with them, unless they are unhealthy eights and then their natural leadership power becomes more like that of a general in the war room, only it's the boardroom.

Nines get along with nearly everyone—they are peaceful, solid, and assertive. They are peacemakers so the personnel in your office, lab, or department will get along with a Nine in charge (unless she's an unhealthy Nine who has subjugated her assertiveness and ends up doing the bidding of others). Nines' work practice is often like the tortoise in the race with the hare—slow (getting started) but steady wins the race and gets the job done.

Healthy Ones seek to improve things based on what they believe is their clear vision and balanced judgments. However, as they become unhealthy, they tend to see things, people, and situations in terms of a narrow, moralistic view. Then they are given to criticize and judge.

Summary

In this section, you've learned about the power inherent in the Enneagram Personality Type system. You have discovered the nine enneatypes, the wing subtypes, and the dynamics of the system. You've gained insights into the primary instincts as they relate to the enneatypes. You've learned how the Enneagram can deepen your awareness about how you move into certain patterns of behavior when stressed or other behaviors when you are growing or self-actualizing. Your highest good, you now know, lies in deep self-knowledge. Further study of the Enneagram can help you achieve the all-important harmonious balance of your characteristics and behavior tendencies as you transform into a fully self-actualized person, completely individuated, integrated, and whole.

Building upon the knowledge you've acquired so far can transform how you live your life every day. In every moment, there is the power to change how you respond to stress, how you choose friends and lovers, how you set goals and reach for your dreams, how you see yourself. Living authentically from your true self means you are able to reach into infinite potential and manifest your best life now using the secret power of You.

Part Six

CONCLUSION: PUTTING IT ALL TOGETHER

A Brighter Future

Your potential future may be written in the stars, revealed in your hands, seen through the symbolism of the cards in a Tarot spread, calculated through your life path number, or suggested in your enneatype, but you have free will—which gives you options. You can hope that good things will come. You can wait and see. Or, you can choose to create a bright and beautiful vision for your life using what you have learned through the ancient arcane arts. Why not put your passion and vision to work and trust the process.

TEACHING OTHERS

There are more avenues today than ever for sharing your knowledge with others. People say that if you want to learn something really well, talk about it, write about it, and teach it. Whether the ancient art that you connect most powerfully with is astrology, Tarot, palmistry, numerology, or the Enneagram, consider sharing your knowledge by teaching others. Write articles, columns, or blog. Lead a webinar, conduct a live or web workshop, or teach a class. You don't have to be the world's leading expert; you simply have to have passion for your subject and the desire to share it. Consider how it might even lead you to the life work you are best suited to do.

TRANSFORM YOUR THINKING, TRANSFORM YOUR LIFE

If you change nothing, nothing will change. But if you change one thing, one thought, one action, a shift occurs. Psychologists are fond of saying that it only takes one person to shift a paradigm. When you put that saying into practice in your life, you immediately see its power. You begin to shift your life's energy through positive thought and intent. Everything starts in the power of thought. When yoked to the force of your will, it becomes possible for you to manifest anything your heart truly desires. Creation happens through thought, intention, and action since each applies energy around you that coalesces in infinite potential to draw the object, circumstances, or people to you. All are forms of energy.

AWAKENING THE ENERGY CENTERS

According to some metaphysical schools of thought, your subtle (ethereal body) has seven centers (chakras) that extend in a line from your tailbone (lowest) to the crown of your head (highest) along your spinal column. Each of these centers has an energy vibration associated with physical, emotional, and psychological well-being. When these energy centers are awakened, the power associated with the center is also activated. For example, when the centers associated with the heart, throat, eye (third eye at the point between your brows), and crown are enlivened, you can hear, smell, see, and know (in the strongest intuitive sense) what you cannot hear, see, smell, and know simply by using the senses of your physical body.

Yoga and meditative practices greatly aid in awakening these energy centers. It is through these centers that you perceive the subtle world of spirit. Ultimately, your goal is to know your true self in its most subtle essence—you as a spiritual being having a life experience in an earthly body.

The Power of You

Most people don't realize *they* are the prize of their own lives. Harvard psychologist Daniel Gilbert asserted that Americans think they want to be rich and thin. Gilbert noted that beyond earning enough for the basic necessities in life, extra money doesn't add much to the pursuit of happiness. The conclusion you can draw: many people don't know what truly makes them happy; worse, they don't know that they don't know.

Your happiness comes from within . . . always—never from other people. You have a set point, some believe for happiness. It's a good bet that you are happier when you are emotionally, physically, psychologically, and spiritually balanced. External and internal factors can knock you off balance, so when you clear out the mental clutter and negative chatter, let go of psychological dead weight, and open the way for new energy to come in, it does. Also, by visualizing brilliant white light or sunbeams bathing your body, your mental/emotional energy shifts. Experience that light as restorative and curative, its energy as love permeating everything in the cosmos. Light is cleansing, invigorating, and empowering. You have the power within you to visualize it. Energy follows thought. Thought arises from emotion. From a place of peace (in harmonious alignment with the authentic You), you create your world, your life, your happiness. That is the secret power of You.

THE
ENNEAGRAM
SELF-TEST

Why This Test Works

Clarence Thomson, MA, is the author of *Parables and the Enneagram* and coauthor of *Out of the Box: Coaching with the Enneagram* and *Enneagram Applications*. Thomson has been teaching the Enneagram internationally for over fifteen years and was a featured speaker at three international Enneagram conferences. He has two master's degrees: one in theology and one in social communications, from the University of Ottawa and Université de St. Paul.

Thomson developed a test to identify enneatypes, which he offers free on his website: *www.enneagramcentral.com*. For the past five years, Thomson estimates that he has received more than 5,000 hits a month, and his feedback is that 90 percent of those who take the test feel as if the test definitely nailed their enneatype.

The only fairly consistent complaints come from Nines, who report that they don't tend to recognize themselves using his test when other tests have revealed them to be a Nine. Also Sixes and Fours occasionally report that they showed up as a Nine. According to Thomson, "Nines don't recognize themselves in daily life; it's one of their primary issues. When Sixes are stressed, they feel overwhelmed and feel like Nines; and Fours, already a withdrawn type, confuse their melancholy with Nine's sense of hopelessness."

Thomson based his test on psychologist Karen Horney's book, *Our Inner Conflicts*. According to Thomson, it is Horney's theory that people generally react to life challenges in one of three consistent, neurotic patterns:

- Moving against others
- Moving toward others
- Moving away from others

Thomson connected these psychological patterns to the following enneatypes:

- Types Three, Seven, and Eight are more egoistic and tend to react to life in an active and aggressive way—they move against others.
- Types One, Two, and Six are more subject to their own internalized superego and tend to play by the rules—they compliantly move toward others.

- Types Four, Five, and Nine all tend to cope with life or strife by withdrawing from life—they move away from others.

The test has been designed to uncover your primary pattern and link it to the appropriate enneatype. It is important when taking this test, or any of the other Enneagram tests, to answer based on who you really feel you are rather than on whom you would like to be. For older people, take the test thinking of the way you were when you were twenty. It is also helpful to consider how you react under pressure.

If you take the test and don't feel as if the results are accurate, you may have identified your wing or you may not be seeing yourself clearly. You could ask a few people who really know you well to take the test and choose what they think is true about you, and then compare the results. But please keep in mind that these tests aren't totally accurate by themselves. Nor are you totally bound by the parameters of one enneatype. You not only have fluctuating behavior within each enneatype, but you have an influential wing, as well as a security point and a stress point.

If you don't feel like the test has pegged you, it may be helpful to read the descriptions of each enneatype in Part 5 until you begin to see patterns of behavior. You can also find Enneagram seminars in many major cities throughout the world.

If you still aren't fairly sure you've identified your enneatype, you may have identified your wing, in which case you're close! Take heart; the more you study the Enneagram, the more you will figure out which type you are.

Enneagram Questionnaire Part One

Part One consists of three groups of twenty questions each. Answer each question by checking the box next to the response that best describes your personality. It might make your response clearer if you think of *Seldom* as false, *Sometimes* as maybe, and *Often* as true. Please remember that the results depend on you—the better you depict your true feelings the more accurate the outcome!

GROUP A1

1. I seem to know what should be done in most situations.
   - ☐ Seldom
   - ☒ Sometimes
   - ☐ Often

2. I find it easy to make moral decisions.
   - ☐ Seldom
   - ☐ Sometimes
   - ☒ Often

3. Compromise is wrong when making moral decisions.
   - ☐ Seldom
   - ☒ Sometimes
   - ☐ Often

4. I am good at getting along with people.
   - ☐ Seldom
   - ☐ Sometimes
   - ☒ Often

5. I am a natural facilitator.
   - ☐ Seldom
   - ☒ Sometimes
   - ☐ Often

6. I work well within systems.
   - ☐ Seldom
   - ☒ Sometimes
   - ☐ Often

7. I have some trouble with a lot of "shoulds" in my life.
   - ☐ Seldom
   - ☐ Sometimes
   - ☒ Often

8. What I should do is often more important than what I may feel.
    - ☐ Seldom
    - ☒ Sometimes
    - ☐ Often

9. Life is difficult.
    - ☐ Seldom
    - ☒ Sometimes
    - ☐ Often

10. Authority is important to me. We need to pay more attention to it than we usually do.
    - ☒ Seldom
    - ☐ Sometimes
    - ☐ Often

11. I have a keen sense of what people need.
    - ☐ Seldom
    - ☐ Sometimes
    - ☒ Often

12. I love to hear people's life stories.
    - ☐ Seldom
    - ☐ Sometimes
    - ☒ Often

13. Whom I'm with is more important than where we go.
    - ☐ Seldom
    - ☐ Sometimes
    - ☒ Often

14. I am good at making people feel special.
    - ☐ Seldom
    - ☐ Sometimes
    - ☒ Often

15. Sometimes I feel I do more for others than I do for myself.
    ☐ Seldom
    ☒ Sometimes
    ☐ Often

16. Sometimes I play the devil's advocate.
    ☐ Seldom
    ☐ Sometimes
    ☒ Often

17. Friends can always count on me.
    ☐ Seldom
    ☐ Sometimes
    ☒ Often

18. I stick with a job until it is finished.
    ☐ Seldom
    ☒ Sometimes
    ☐ Often

19. People need to earn my trust.
    ☐ Seldom
    ☒ Sometimes
    ☐ Often

20. I like the motto, "Be prepared."
    ☒ Seldom
    ☐ Sometimes
    ☐ Often

SCORING

Each selection has a value: Seldom (False) = 0, Sometimes (Maybe) = 1, and Often (True) = 2. Add up your scores and fill in the following to find your total for this group of twenty questions.

_2_	Seldom	× 0	=	_0_
_9_	Sometimes	× 1	=	_9_
_9_	Often	× 2	=	_18_

GROUP A1 TOTAL:　　　　　　　　_27_

GROUP A2

1. I hate conflict.
   - ☐ Seldom
   - ☒ Sometimes
   - ☐ Often

2. At a social gathering I usually wait for someone to choose me to talk to.
   - ☐ Seldom
   - ☐ Sometimes
   - ☒ Often

3. I like to have more information than most before I act.
   - ☐ Seldom
   - ☒ Sometimes
   - ☐ Often

4. My emotions seem more intense than others.
   - ☐ Seldom
   - ☐ Sometimes
   - ☒ Often

5. I have a hard time making decisions. I procrastinate.
   - ☐ Seldom
   - ☒ Sometimes
   - ☐ Often

6. I love to watch things at a distance. I am a natural observer.
   - ☐ Seldom
   - ☐ Sometimes
   - ☒ Often

7. I don't mind being a little different from the crowd.
   - ☐ Seldom
   - ☐ Sometimes
   - ☒ Often

8. I'm more sensitive than most people and I suffer because of it.
   - ☐ Seldom
   - ☒ Sometimes
   - ☐ Often

9. Solitude is important for me.
   - ☐ Seldom
   - ☒ Sometimes
   - ☐ Often

10. I can get by on less than most people can.
    - ☐ Seldom
    - ☐ Sometimes
    - ☒ Often

11. I can see all sides of every situation.
    - ☐ Seldom
    - ☒ Sometimes
    - ☒ Often

12. I am modest. I find it hard to self-promote.
    - ☐ Seldom
    - ☒ Sometimes
    - ☐ Often

13. I'm more patient than many of my friends.
    - ☐ Seldom
    - ☐ Sometimes
    - ☒ Often

14. People tell me their troubles.
    - ☐ Seldom
    - ☐ Sometimes
    - ☒ Often

15. I love bookstores and libraries.
    ☐ Seldom
    ☒ Sometimes
    ☐ Often

16. Others' needs seem more important than my own.
    ☒ Seldom
    ☐ Sometimes
    ☐ Often

17. I think my subjective opinions are often more important than surveys.
    ☐ Seldom
    ☐ Sometimes
    ☒ Often

18. Aesthetic development is crucial for a full life.
    ☐ Seldom
    ☒ Sometimes
    ☐ Often

19. I love privacy.
    ☐ Seldom
    ☒ Sometimes
    ☐ Often

20. Sometimes I have the feeling I am somehow defective.
    ☒ Seldom
    ☐ Sometimes
    ☐ Often

SCORING

Each selection has a value: Seldom (False) = 0, Sometimes (Maybe) = 1, and Often (True) = 2. Add up your scores and fill in the following to find your total for this group of twenty questions.

_2_	Seldom	×	0	=	_0_
_9_	Sometimes	×	1	=	_9_
_9_	Often	×	2	=	_18_

GROUP A2 TOTAL: _27_

GROUP A3

1. I like to put a little pressure on people to see what they're made of.
   - ☒ Seldom
   - ☐ Sometimes
   - ☐ Often

2. There's always room at the top—for me.
   - ☒ Seldom
   - ☐ Sometimes
   - ☐ Often

3. I like the phrase, "Just do it."
   - ☐ Seldom
   - ☒ Sometimes
   - ☐ Often

4. I'm a natural leader.
   - ☐ Seldom
   - ☒ Sometimes
   - ☐ Often

5. Sometimes I tend to step on some toes to get things done.
   - ☒ Seldom
   - ☐ Sometimes
   - ☐ Often

6. At a social gathering, I usually choose with whom I will talk.
   - ☐ Seldom
   - ☒ Sometimes
   - ☐ Often

7. I'm a natural optimist.
   - ☐ Seldom
   - ☐ Sometimes
   - ☒ Often

8. I tend to like a lot of variety in my life.
   - ☐ Seldom
   - ☐ Sometimes
   - ☒ Often

9. Given a choice between excitement and peace, I often choose excitement.
   - ☐ Seldom
   - ☒ Sometimes
   - ☐ Often

10. I have a low boredom threshold—I make things happen.
    - ☐ Seldom
    - ☒ Sometimes
    - ☐ Often

11. I have a lot of energy.
    - ☐ Seldom
    - ☒ Sometimes
    - ☐ Often

12. I enjoy work. Sometimes I can turn it into fun.
    - ☒ Seldom
    - ☐ Sometimes
    - ☐ Often

13. I thrive on competition.
    - ☒ Seldom
    - ☐ Sometimes
    - ☐ Often

14. I really know how to celebrate.
    - ☐ Seldom
    - ☐ Sometimes
    - ☒ Often

15. I tell it like it is. I don't pussyfoot around.
    - ☐ Seldom
    - ☐ Sometimes
    - ☒ Often

16. Justice is important to me. Sometimes so is revenge.
    - ☐ Seldom
    - ☐ Sometimes
    - ☒ Often

17. I am a natural champion of the underdog.
    - ☐ Seldom
    - ☐ Sometimes
    - ☒ Often

18. My least favorite word is *wimp*.
    - ☒ Seldom
    - ☐ Sometimes
    - ☐ Often

19. I get a lot done, more than most people, and I like to be recognized for that.
    - ☐ Seldom
    - ☒ Sometimes
    - ☐ Often

20. Clothes don't make the person, but one's image is important to me.
    - ☐ Seldom
    - ☒ Sometimes
    - ☐ Often

SCORING

Each selection has a value: Seldom (False) = 0, Sometimes (Maybe) = 1, and Often (True) = 2. Add up your scores and fill in the following to find your total for this group of twenty questions.

_6_	Seldom	×	0	=	_0_
_8_	Sometimes	×	1	=	_8_
_6_	Often	×	2	=	_12_

GROUP A3 TOTAL:　　　　　　　　　　　_20_

Part One Scoring

Compare your scores from all three groups. If your highest score was in Group A1, go to Part Two, Group B1 on page 308. If Group A2 shows your highest score, proceed to Part Two, Group B2 on page 317. And finally, if you scored highest on Group A3, go to Part Two, Group B3 page 326.

Enneagram Questionnaire Part Two

This part of the questionnaire consists of three groups, each consisting of three subgroups of sixteen questions each. You will answer questions in only one group, which is determined by your answers to Part 1. Answer each question by checking the box next to the response that best describes your personality. Again, be honest—your accurate score depends on it!

Answer the questions in Groups B1.1, B1.2, and B1.3 if your highest score in Part 1 was in Group A1.

GROUP B1.1

1. I have a knack for knowing the right way to do things.
   - ☐ Seldom
   - ☒ Sometimes
   - ☐ Often

2. I don't like compromise.
   - ☐ Seldom
   - ☒ Sometimes
   - ☐ Often

3. "There is always room for improvement" is my motto.
   - ☒ Seldom
   - ☐ Sometimes
   - ☐ Often

4. Quality is more important than quantity—always.
   - ☐ Seldom
   - ☐ Sometimes
   - ☒ Often

5. We should all develop our full potential.
   - ☐ Seldom
   - ☐ Sometimes
   - ☒ Often

6. Life is difficult; we have to do our best.
   - ☐ Seldom
   - ☐ Sometimes
   - ☒ Often

7. "God is in the details." People should know how the system works.
   - ☒ Seldom
   - ☐ Sometimes
   - ☐ Often

8. I have a strong tendency to compare what is real with what would be perfect.
   - ☒ Seldom
   - ☐ Sometimes
   - ☐ Often

9. I have a tendency to evaluate things closely.
   - ☐ Seldom
   - ☐ Sometimes
   - ☒ Often

10. I think it is important to do good work in everything I do.
   - ☐ Seldom
   - ☒ Sometimes
   - ☐ Often

11. I have high standards for myself and for others, too.
   - ☒ Seldom
   - ☐ Sometimes
   - ☐ Often

12. I can get irritated when people don't meet or even have standards.
   - ☐ Seldom
   - ☒ Sometimes
   - ☐ Often

13. People need some kind of moral compass.
    - ☐ Seldom
    - ☐ Sometimes
    - ☒ Often

14. Sometimes I am clearer about what I ought to do than what I really want to do.
    - ☒ Seldom
    - ☐ Sometimes
    - ☐ Often

15. I have a strong sense of social responsibility and social order.
    - ☐ Seldom
    - ☒ Sometimes
    - ☐ Often

16. I always try to do my best, and the world would be a better place if everyone did their best.
    - ☒ Seldom
    - ☐ Sometimes
    - ☐ Often

SCORING

Each selection has a value: Seldom (False) = 0, Sometimes (Maybe) = 1, and Often (True) = 2. Add up your scores and fill in the following to find your total for this group of sixteen questions.

6	Seldom	×	0	=	0
5	Sometimes	×	1	=	5
5	Often	×	2	=	10

GROUP B1.1 TOTAL: 15

GROUP B1.2

1. I have a knack for knowing and meeting other people's needs.
   - ☐ Seldom
   - ☐ Sometimes
   - ☒ Often

2. I have a lot of fantastic friends.
   - ☐ Seldom
   - ☐ Sometimes
   - ☒ Often

3. I am modest and I help others get the spotlight.
   - ☐ Seldom
   - ☒ Sometimes
   - ☐ Often

4. I am naturally a nurturing person.
   - ☐ Seldom
   - ☐ Sometimes
   - ☒ Often

5. I'm good at giving people the perfect gift.
   - ☐ Seldom
   - ☒ Sometimes
   - ☐ Often

6. Love is the most important thing in the world.
   - ☐ Seldom
   - ☐ Sometimes
   - ☒ Often

7. I love to tell people their good points to encourage them.
   - ☐ Seldom
   - ☐ Sometimes
   - ☒ Often

8. I pride myself on being a people person.
   - ☐ Seldom
   - ☐ Sometimes
   - ☒ Often

9. I have this ability to see what people really need, sometimes even before they do themselves.
   - ☐ Seldom
   - ☒ Sometimes
   - ☐ Often

10. If I can, I try to meet those needs. I think it is important to be modest, so I don't flaunt my own needs.
    - ☐ Seldom
    - ☒ Sometimes
    - ☐ Often

11. I think relationships are the most important thing in the world and I have a lot of them.
    - ☐ Seldom
    - ☒ Sometimes
    - ☐ Often

12. People just naturally come to me, especially to share in times of stress or sorrow.
    - ☐ Seldom
    - ☐ Sometimes
    - ☒ Often

13. I am a good listener.
    - ☐ Seldom
    - ☐ Sometimes
    - ☒ Often

14. I think we get ahead in this world by helping others get what they want.
    - [ ] Seldom
    - [x] Sometimes
    - [ ] Often

15. I don't need much recognition, but I do get warm feelings when I am appreciated.
    - [ ] Seldom
    - [ ] Sometimes
    - [x] Often

16. I try so hard.
    - [ ] Seldom
    - [x] Sometimes
    - [ ] Often

SCORING

Each selection has a value: Seldom (False) = 0, Sometimes (Maybe) = 1, and Often (True) = 2. Add up your scores and fill in the following to find your total for this group of sixteen questions.

_0_	Seldom	×	0	=	_____
_7_	Sometimes	×	1	=	_7_
_9_	Often	×	2	=	_18_

GROUP B1.2 TOTAL: _25_

GROUP B1.3

1. I like to be the devil's advocate. It flushes out the whole truth.
   - ☐ Seldom
   - ☒ Sometimes
   - ☐ Often

2. People need to earn my trust.
   - ☐ Seldom
   - ☒ Sometimes
   - ☐ Often

3. I love family and community traditions. I do my share.
   - ☐ Seldom
   - ☐ Sometimes
   - ☒ Often

4. I'm good at community functions.
   - ☐ Seldom
   - ☒ Sometimes
   - ☐ Often

5. I'm my own worst enemy.
   - ☐ Seldom
   - ☒ Sometimes
   - ☐ Often

6. I don't trust authority figures, even though I know they are important.
   - ☐ Seldom
   - ☒ Sometimes
   - ☐ Often

7. I like jobs that have clearly assigned tasks. I'll do them well.
   - ☐ Seldom
   - ☒ Sometimes
   - ☐ Often

8. I'm a loyal friend.
   - ☐ Seldom
   - ☐ Sometimes
   - ☒ Often

9. My few trusted friends are really important to me.
   - ☐ Seldom
   - ☐ Sometimes
   - ☒ Often

10. It's important to have friends you can trust, because you can't trust a lot of so-called authorities.
    - ☐ Seldom
    - ☐ Sometimes
    - ☒ Often

11. The government, the media, and the medical profession—they all tell just their side of the story.
    - ☐ Seldom
    - ☐ Sometimes
    - ☒ Often

12. Sometimes I have trouble making up my mind.
    - ☐ Seldom
    - ☒ Sometimes
    - ☐ Often

13. It seems that any decision I make will bring trouble down on me.
    - ☒ Seldom
    - ☐ Sometimes
    - ☐ Often

14. I think I just worry too much.
    - ☒ Seldom
    - ☐ Sometimes
    - ☐ Often

15. You have to worry because you can't trust just anyone.
    ☒ Seldom
    ☐ Sometimes
    ☐ Often

16. Sometimes I go ahead and do what I worry most about, just to get rid of the tension.
    ☒ Seldom
    ☐ Sometimes
    ☐ Often

SCORING

Each selection has a value: Seldom (False) = 0, Sometimes (Maybe) = 1, and Often (True) = 2. Add up your scores and fill in the following to find your total for this group of sixteen questions.

_4_	Seldom	×	0	=	_0_
_7_	Sometimes	×	1	=	_7_
_5_	Often	×	2	=	_10_

GROUP B1.3 TOTAL: _17_

Answer the questions in Groups B2.1, B2.2, and B2.3 if your highest score in Part 1 was in Group A2.

GROUP B2.1

1. I love drama. Life is dramatic when lived fully.
   - ☒ Seldom
   - ☐ Sometimes
   - ☐ Often

2. It is important for me to be authentic.
   - ☐ Seldom
   - ☐ Sometimes
   - ☒ Often

3. Taste in matters of art, music, clothes, and manners is important.
   - ☐ Seldom
   - ☒ Sometimes
   - ☐ Often

4. I don't mind standing out in the crowd.
   - ☐ Seldom
   - ☒ Sometimes
   - ☐ Often

5. Sometimes I have to share my melancholy feelings.
   - ☐ Seldom
   - ☐ Sometimes
   - ☒ Often

6. I love being original. Creativity is important to me.
   - ☐ Seldom
   - ☐ Sometimes
   - ☒ Often

7. I think my emotions are more intense than most people's.
    ☐ Seldom
    ☒ Sometimes
    ☐ Often

8. I am more sensitive than most people. I experience more pain than most.
    ☒ Seldom
    ☐ Sometimes
    ☐ Often

9. The pain may be worth it, though; I enjoy beauty so much.
    ☒ Seldom
    ☐ Sometimes
    ☐ Often

10. It seems to me that a lot of people just skim over life.
    ☐ Seldom
    ☒ Sometimes
    ☐ Often

11. I can see beauty where others can't; this often sets me apart.
    ☐ Seldom
    ☒ Sometimes
    ☐ Often

12. I feel sort of different from ordinary people.
    ☐ Seldom
    ☐ Sometimes
    ☒ Often

13. My tastes seem more refined. I place a higher value on artistic sensitivity.
    ☐ Seldom
    ☒ Sometimes
    ☐ Often

14. I often have trouble in relationships because of my sensitivity.
    - ☐ Seldom
    - ☒ Sometimes
    - ☐ Often

15. Relationships start out fine, but then little things go wrong.
    - ☐ Seldom
    - ☒ Sometimes
    - ☐ Often

16. It seems like I can never have the perfect relationship I'm searching for.
    - ☒ Seldom
    - ☐ Sometimes
    - ☐ Often

SCORING

Each selection has a value: Seldom (False) = 0, Sometimes (Maybe) = 1, and Often (True) = 2. Add up your scores and fill in the following to find your total for this group of sixteen questions.

_4_ Seldom	×	0	=	_0_
_8_ Sometimes	×	1	=	_8_
_4_ Often	×	2	=	___

GROUP B2.1 TOTAL: _16_

GROUP B2.2

1. I need my privacy. I relish solitude.
   - ☐ Seldom
   - ☒ Sometimes
   - ☐ Often

2. Sometimes it feels like I'm invisible.
   - ☐ Seldom
   - ☒ Sometimes
   - ☐ Often

3. I like lots of information before I act.
   - ☐ Seldom
   - ☒ Sometimes
   - ☐ Often

4. I can get by on less than most people can.
   - ☐ Seldom
   - ☐ Sometimes
   - ☒ Often

5. I'm more logical about life than most.
   - ☒ Seldom
   - ☐ Sometimes
   - ☐ Often

6. I'd make a good reporter. I like to watch what's going on.
   - ☐ Seldom
   - ☐ Sometimes
   - ☒ Often

7. I really like to share information.
   - ☐ Seldom
   - ☐ Sometimes
   - ☒ Often

8. Descartes had it right: "I think, therefore I am."
   - ☒ Seldom
   - ☐ Sometimes
   - ☐ Often

9. What I think is important to me.
   - ☐ Seldom
   - ☐ Sometimes
   - ☒ Often

10. I need more privacy than others—time alone to think clearly about life.
    - ☒ Seldom
    - ☐ Sometimes
    - ☐ Often

11. I'm a keen observer of life.
    - ☐ Seldom
    - ☐ Sometimes
    - ☒ Often

12. I understand what is really going on.
    - ☐ Seldom
    - ☒ Sometimes
    - ☐ Often

13. I think I'd rather watch than participate in a lot of things.
    - ☒ Seldom
    - ☐ Sometimes
    - ☐ Often

14. When I'm alone I think more clearly and objectively than most people.
    - ☒ Seldom
    - ☐ Sometimes
    - ☐ Often

15. I don't get emotional when I make my judgments and decisions.
   - ☒ Seldom
   - ☐ Sometimes
   - ☐ Often

16. I like to plan things before they happen and then replay them in my mind.
   - ☒ Seldom
   - ☐ Sometimes
   - ☐ Often

SCORING

Each selection has a value: Seldom (False) = 0, Sometimes (Maybe) = 1, and Often (True) = 2. Add up your scores and fill in the following to find your total for this group of sixteen questions.

_7_ Seldom	×	0	=	_0_
_4_ Sometimes	×	1	=	_4_
_5_ Often	×	2	=	_10_

GROUP B2.2 TOTAL: _14_

GROUP B2.3

1. I can see all sides of a question.
   - ☐ Seldom
   - ☒ Sometimes
   - ☐ Often

2. I have some trouble asserting what I want.
   - ☐ Seldom
   - ☐ Sometimes
   - ☒ Often

3. I don't decide my priorities very easily.
   - ☒ Seldom
   - ☐ Sometimes
   - ☐ Often

4. I don't mind routine.
   - ☐ Seldom
   - ☒ Sometimes
   - ☐ Often

5. I hate conflict.
   - ☐ Seldom
   - ☒ Sometimes
   - ☐ Often

6. I have a little trouble with procrastination.
   - ☐ Seldom
   - ☐ Sometimes
   - ☒ Often

7. I'm a natural peacemaker and negotiator.
   - ☐ Seldom
   - ☒ Sometimes
   - ☐ Often

8. I'm sort of laid-back and mellow.
   - ☐ Seldom
   - ☒ Sometimes
   - ☐ Often

9. I understand others' points of view. I don't push mine if theirs are good.
   - ☐ Seldom
   - ☐ Sometimes
   - ☒ Often

10. I have some trouble taking initiative; I prefer to work with others.
    - ☐ Seldom
    - ☒ Sometimes
    - ☐ Often

11. Sometimes I don't pay enough attention to what I want myself.
    - ☒ Seldom
    - ☐ Sometimes
    - ☐ Often

12. I start out with good intentions, then end up doing something else.
    - ☐ Seldom
    - ☒ Sometimes
    - ☐ Often

13. I don't get angry much, and even when I do, I don't show it.
    - ☐ Seldom
    - ☐ Sometimes
    - ☒ Often

14. Occasionally I get a kind of sneaky revenge.
    - ☐ Seldom
    - ☒ Sometimes
    - ☐ Often

15. People really like me because of my pleasant personality.
    - ☐ Seldom
    - ☑ Sometimes
    - ☐ Often

16. I'm not threatening or pushy but I still get things done.
    - ☐ Seldom
    - ☐ Sometimes
    - ☒ Often

SCORING

Each selection has a value: Seldom (False) = 0, Sometimes (Maybe) = 1, and Often (True) = 2. Add up your scores and fill in the following to find your total for this group of sixteen questions.

_2_ Seldom	×	0	=	_0_
_9_ Sometimes	×	1	=	_9_
_5_ Often	×	2	=	_10_

GROUP B2.3 TOTAL: _19_

Answer the questions in Groups B3.1, B3.2, and B3.3 if your highest score in Part 1 was in Group A3.

GROUP B3.1

1. I love to succeed. I hate to fail. I don't fail much.
   - ☒ Seldom
   - ☐ Sometimes
   - ☐ Often

2. Clothes don't make the person, but they might make the sale.
   - ☐ Seldom
   - ☒ Sometimes
   - ☐ Often

3. I hate to waste time. I'm efficient.
   - ☐ Seldom
   - ☒ Sometimes
   - ☐ Often

4. Most people can't keep up with me. I accomplish a lot.
   - ☒ Seldom
   - ☐ Sometimes
   - ☐ Often

5. I believe in having goals and really working for them.
   - ☒ Seldom
   - ☐ Sometimes
   - ☐ Often

6. I like recognition for my hard work. Money is good, too.
   - ☐ Seldom
   - ☐ Sometimes
   - ☒ Often

7. Sometimes I have to set my emotions aside and get the job done.
   - ☐ Seldom
   - ☐ Sometimes
   - ☒ Often

8. I like the Army slogan, "Be all you can be."
   - ☐ Seldom
   - ☒ Sometimes
   - ☐ Often

9. I think it is important to succeed at what you try to do.
   - ☐ Seldom
   - ☒ Sometimes
   - ☐ Often

10. I work hard, I play by the rules (unless they're unfair), and I love to compete.
    - ☐ Seldom
    - ☒ Sometimes
    - ☐ Often

11. I think competition brings out the best in us and I love to be number one.
    - ☒ Seldom
    - ☐ Sometimes
    - ☐ Often

12. I'm a positive, upbeat person with lots of energy.
    - ☐ Seldom
    - ☒ Sometimes
    - ☐ Often

13. I may work a little too hard at times, but a little stress doesn't hurt anyone.
    - ☒ Seldom
    - ☐ Sometimes
    - ☐ Often

14. Success doesn't always come cheap, and you have to be willing to pay the price.
☒ Seldom
☐ Sometimes
☐ Often

15. I don't make the rules of life, but I do make the most of them.
☒ Seldom
☐ Sometimes
☐ Often

16. I can make a system work.
☒ Seldom
☐ Sometimes
☐ Often

SCORING

Each selection has a value: Seldom (False) = 0, Sometimes (Maybe) = 1, and Often (True) = 2. Add up your scores and fill in the following to find your total for this group of sixteen questions.

8	Seldom	×	0	=	0
6	Sometimes	×	1	=	6
2	Often	×	2	=	4

GROUP B3.1 TOTAL: 10

GROUP B3.2

1. I'm a natural storyteller. Polish improves truth.
   - ☐ Seldom
   - ☒ Sometimes
   - ☐ Often

2. I'm really resilient. I bounce back quickly.
   - ☒ Seldom
   - ☐ Sometimes
   - ☐ Often

3. I have a teensy problem with addictions: sweets, alcohol, drugs, or even new ideas. I like excitement and variety.
   - ☐ Seldom
   - ☒ Sometimes
   - ☐ Often

4. I can turn work into fun.
   - ☐ Seldom
   - ☒ Sometimes
   - ☐ Often

5. I'm better at starting things than finishing them.
   - ☐ Seldom
   - ☐ Sometimes
   - ☒ Often

6. Few have as much energy and enthusiasm as I do.
   - ☒ Seldom
   - ☐ Sometimes
   - ☐ Often

7. Humor is central in my life.
    - ☐ Seldom
    - ☐ Sometimes
    - ☒ Often

8. Most people aren't as happy as I am.
    - ☒ Seldom
    - ☐ Sometimes
    - ☐ Often

9. If you look at things right, you know they're going to work out.
    - ☒ Seldom
    - ☐ Sometimes
    - ☐ Often

10. People shouldn't dwell on the negative.
    - ☐ Seldom
    - ☒ Sometimes
    - ☐ Often

11. I always have lots of things to do that I like. Why do people sit around and complain?
    - ☒ Seldom
    - ☐ Sometimes
    - ☐ Often

12. Oh sure, I have troubles, too, but I can usually think of a way to live life to the fullest.
    - ☒ Seldom
    - ☐ Sometimes
    - ☐ Often

13. If something doesn't work, then stop doing it. Do something else; be creative.
    ☐ Seldom
    ☒ Sometimes
    ☐ Often

14. I appreciate the newness of things.
    ☐ Seldom
    ☐ Sometimes
    ☒ Often

15. I love to start new projects if the old ones get boring.
    ☐ Seldom
    ☒ Sometimes
    ☐ Often

16. I can't stand boredom. People who are bored or boring should do something about it.
    ☐ Seldom
    ☒ Sometimes
    ☐ Often

SCORING

Each selection has a value: Seldom (False) = 0, Sometimes (Maybe) = 1, and Often (True) = 2. Add up your scores and fill in the following to find your total for this group of sixteen questions.

_6_ Seldom	×	0	=	_0_
_7_ Sometimes	×	1	=	_7_
_3_ Often	×	2	=	_6_

GROUP B3.2 TOTAL: _13_

GROUP B3.3

1. Life is a war. I'm glad I'm strong.
   - ☒ Seldom
   - ☐ Sometimes
   - ☐ Often

2. I put a little pressure on people to see how they respond.
   - ☒ Seldom
   - ☐ Sometimes
   - ☐ Often

3. I tell it like it is. I don't pussyfoot around.
   - ☐ Seldom
   - ☐ Sometimes
   - ☒ Often

4. I like to use my power to get things done.
   - ☒ Seldom
   - ☐ Sometimes
   - ☐ Often

5. I'm a natural leader.
   - ☐ Seldom
   - ☒ Sometimes
   - ☐ Often

6. Sometimes I offend people without meaning to.
   - ☐ Seldom
   - ☒ Sometimes
   - ☐ Often

7. My least favorite word is *wimp*.
   - ☒ Seldom
   - ☐ Sometimes
   - ☐ Often

8. The shortest distance between two points is a straight line. I like that.
   - ☐ Seldom
   - ☐ Sometimes
   - ☒ Often

9. People should be straight, honest, and clear—no mealy-mouthed excuses.
   - ☐ Seldom
   - ☐ Sometimes
   - ☒ Often

10. Just do it.
    - ☒ Seldom
    - ☐ Sometimes
    - ☐ Often

11. Sometimes you just have to take matters into your own hands to get things done.
    - ☐ Seldom
    - ☒ Sometimes
    - ☐ Often

12. There's a lot of injustice. People of integrity just have to straighten things out.
    - ☒ Seldom
    - ☐ Sometimes
    - ☐ Often

13. I like action, results, and a clear understanding of what needs to be done—then I do it!
    - ☐ Seldom
    - ☒ Sometimes
    - ☐ Often

14. I don't mind a good fight to set things right, either.
    - ☑ Seldom
    - ☐ Sometimes
    - ☐ Often

15. I don't back down when I know I'm right.
    - ☐ Seldom
    - ☐ Sometimes
    - ☒ Often

16. People know they can count on me, no matter what.
    - ☐ Seldom
    - ☑ Sometimes
    - ☐ Often

SCORING

Each selection has a value: Seldom (False) = 0, Sometimes (Maybe) = 1, and Often (True) = 2. Add up your scores and fill in the following to find your total for this group of sixteen questions.

7	Seldom	×	0	=	0
5	Sometimes	×	1	=	5
4	Often	×	2	=	~~10~~ 8

GROUP B3.3 TOTAL: 13

Part Two Scoring

Fill in your Part Two scores below. Remember that you should have only three scores for this part of the test. Match your highest score to one of the nine enneatypes listed below.

Group	Score	Enneatype
B1.1	15	One: Evangelical Idealist
B1.2	25	Two: People Pleaser
B1.3	17	Three: King of the Hill
B2.1	14	Four: Creative Seeker
B2.2	14	Five: Masterful Hermit
B2.3	19	Six: Loyal Guardian
B3.1		Seven: Optimistic Dreamer
B3.2		Eight: Dominator
B3.3		Nine: Peaceful Lamb

ONE: EVANGELICAL IDEALIST

I have a strong tendency to compare what is real with what would be perfect. I have a tendency to evaluate things closely. I think it is important to do good work in everything I do. I have high standards for myself and for others, too. I can get irritated when people don't meet or even have standards. People need some kind of moral compass. Sometimes I am clearer about what I ought to do than what I really want to do. I have a strong sense of social responsibility and social order. I always try to do my best, and the world would be a better place if everyone did their best.

TWO: PEOPLE PLEASER

I pride myself on being a people person. I have this ability to see what people really need, sometimes even before they do themselves. If I can, I try to meet those needs. I think it is important to be modest, so I don't flaunt my own needs. I think relationships are the most important thing in the world and I have a lot of them. People just naturally come to me, especially to share in times of stress or sorrow. I am a good listener. I think we get ahead in this world by helping others get what they want. I don't need much recognition, but I do get warm feelings when I am appreciated. I try so hard.

THREE: KING OF THE HILL

I like the Army slogan, "Be all you can be." I think it is important to succeed at what you try to do. I work hard, I play by the rules, usually (unless they're unfair), and I love to compete. I think competition brings out the best in us and I love to be number one. I'm a positive, upbeat person with lots of energy. I make things happen and I don't mind if others recognize that. I may work a little too hard at times because it is hard to make life work on all fronts, but a little stress doesn't hurt anyone. Success doesn't always come cheap and you have to be willing to pay the price. I don't make the rules of life, but I make the most of them. I can make a system work.

FOUR: CREATIVE SEEKER

I am more sensitive than most people are, which is why I probably experience more pain than most. It seems to me that a lot of people just skim over life. The pain may be worth it, though; I enjoy beauty so much. It seems I can see beauty where others can't. This often sets me apart from others. I feel sort of different from ordinary people. My tastes seem more refined and I place a higher value on artistic sensitivity than many of my friends. I often have trouble in relationships because of my sensitivity. They start out fine, but then little things go wrong. It seems like I can never have the perfect relationship I'm always looking for.

FIVE: MASTERFUL HERMIT

Descartes had it right: "I think, therefore I am." What I think is important to me. I may require more privacy than others, but a person needs some time alone to think clearly about life. I'm a keen observer of life. I understand what is really going on. I think I'd sooner watch than participate in a lot of things. When I'm alone, I think more clearly and objectively than most people. I don't get so emotional when I make my judgments and decisions. I like to plan things before they happen and then replay them in my mind. Then I know what I really think and feel about what happened.

SIX: LOYAL GUARDIAN

I'm a loyal friend and my few trusted friends are really important to me. It's important to have friends you can trust, because you can't trust a lot of so-called authorities. The government, the media, and the medical profession—they all tell their side of the story and you have to listen with an inner ear to get the real message. Sometimes I have trouble making up my mind. It seems that any decision I make will bring trouble down on me. I think I just worry too much, but you do have to worry because you can't trust just anyone. Sometimes I just go ahead and do what I worry most about, just to get rid of the tension.

SEVEN: OPTIMISTIC DREAMER

Most people aren't as happy as I am. If you look at things right, you know they're going to work out all right. People shouldn't dwell on the negative. I always have lots of things to do that I like, and I don't see why so many people sit around and complain. Oh sure, I have troubles, too, but I can usually think of a way to live life to the fullest anyway. If something doesn't work, then stop doing it. Do something else; be creative. I have a little problem with some of my appetites but nothing to worry about. I appreciate the newness of things. I love to start new projects if the old ones get boring. I can't stand boredom. People who are bored or boring should do something about it.

EIGHT: DOMINATOR

The shortest distance between two points is a straight line. I like that. Straight, honest, clear, no mealy-mouthed excuses—just do it. John Wayne was right. Sometimes you just have to take matters into your own hands to get things done. There's a lot of injustice in the world and people of integrity just have to straighten things out. I like action and results. I like a clear understanding of what needs to be done and then I do it! I don't mind a good fight to set things right, either. I don't back down when I know I'm right. People know they can count on me, no matter what.

NINE: PEACEFUL LAMB

I'm sort of laid-back and mellow. I'm modest and can understand others' points of view. I don't push mine if theirs are good; I'll go along. I don't like conflict; I'd sooner get along and work together with people. I have some trouble taking initiative. I'd just as soon work with others. Sometimes I don't pay enough attention to what I want myself. I get distracted easily. I start out with good intentions, but then I end up doing something else. I don't get angry much, and even when I do, I don't show it. I might do a slow burn once in a while and occasionally I get a kind of sneaky revenge. People really like me because of my pleasant personality. I'm not threatening or pushy, but I still get things done.

GLOSSARY

While not all the following terms appear in the main text of this book, they're included here to help you in your further reading on these subjects.

affirmations

Positive statements that are repeated to impress and reinforce a particular belief.

air hand

The air hand features a square-shaped palm with long, slender fingers; it is known as the artistic hand.

Apollo finger

The third (or ring) finger. In palmistry, this finger represents creative spirit and a sense of inner balance.

Apollo line

This line ends on the mount just below the Apollo finger and shows the degree of inner satisfaction through creativity.

Apollo mount

A mount or raised muscular area under the third or Apollo finger. This mount is said to predict the potential for fame and personal wealth through creativity.

arch

Representing the more practical and material nature of the individual, arches are small, raised line patterns that occur on fingerprints. They can be either subtle or quite pronounced.

ashram

A spiritual hermitage or place where religious ascetics or hermits live.

AUM (also Om)

In Hinduism, regarded as the sound that is a complete expression of the Divine in that it encompasses Brahma (the Creator), Vishnu (Preserver), and Shiva (the Destroyer); also the primordial sound of vibratory creation.

bar

A short line (or series of lines) that appears to cut through a major line, symbolically creating an obstacle for the individual in a particular area of his or her life.

bow of intuition

One of the many secondary patterns that can occur on the percussion just beneath the Mercury or fourth finger. This marking is quite apparent on psychics and other highly intuitive people.

bracelets

Also known as "rascettes," these are the lines located across the wrists. According to Eastern palmistry, three or more rascettes indicate a long life.

break

Any interruption in the flow or direction of lines, indicating change that happens against our will.

chain

A series of links or islands that appear in patterns on the palm, usually along one of the three major lines.

chakras

The seven wheels of energy that lie in the subtle body along the spine from the tailbone to the crown of the head. These chakras from the lowest (tailbone) to the highest are *muladhara, svadhisthana, manipura, anahata, vishuddha, ajna,* and *sahasrara.*

chiromancy

The study of the lines of the palms. For many years, this was the way palms were read with the reader only looking at the lines and not taking shape, size, and consistency of the hand into account.

conical shape

The shape of the hand that is best seen when the fingers are all held together and the hand is cone-shaped.

Creator

One of many monikers for God; others include Divine Intelligence, Holy One, Divine Mind, Powers That Be, the Universe, Source, Infinite Potential, and the Nameless Formless One, among others; the aspect of the omnipotent, omniscient, and omnipresent God behind all that is and is not known.

cross

Crosses are obstacle lines that occur anywhere on the palm or fingertips; their crisscrossed patterns signify opposition.

destiny line
See **fate line**.

dominant hand

The hand you use more often for writing, eating, and performing tactile actions.

earth hand

A square hand with small, short fingers, it represents a practical, down-to-earth nature.

emotion

The mood created by positive or negative feelings in the body in response to internal or external stimulus.

Enneagram of Personality

A system of typology for understanding the human personality that outlines nine personality types or enneatypes.

enneatypes

The nine personalities identified within the Enneagram Personality system.

fate line

The major line that spans the vertical length of the palm, indicating your destined path in life. It can also pertain to career.

fire hand

Rectangular hand with short, spatulate-shaped fingers that represent an active, energetic personality.

girdle of Venus

A special marking that can occur between the Saturn and Apollo fingers. Anxious, hypersensitive people tend to have this mark.

grille

Also known in palmistry as anxiety marks, these mixed line patterns (consisting of both horizontal and vertical lines in a grid-like pattern) are quite common.

guru

A spiritual teacher.

head line

One of the three major lines in palm reading, this line extends horizontally under the four finger mounts and represents a person's intellectual abilities.

heart line

Located under the head line, this major line speaks to the individual's emotional state and sense of giving.

island

When a line on the hand splits in one place but then reconnects nearby, this is known as an island on the palm. Islands typically mean that the individual suffers from a marked lack of energy or vitality.

Jupiter finger

The first finger, pertaining to leadership ability and business sense.

Jupiter mount

Located just beneath the Jupiter or first finger, this mount represents the person's sense of inner strength and ownership.

kabbalah (also Cabala, Qabalah)

The practices and texts of Jewish mystical teachings that were developed by rabbis from the seventh to the eighteenth centuries. Initiates interpreted sacred Scripture through insights that allowed them to foretell the future. Kabbalah reached its zenith, perhaps, in the medieval period to the Renaissance.

Kairos

From the ancient Greek, meaning the right or opportune moment for something special to occur.

karma

The Hindu philosophy of retribution. The current life of an individual is attributed to his or her past thoughts, words, or actions; the consequence of past actions, good, bad, or neutral.

Karma Yoga

The yoga of action and service with non-attachment to the results of the efforts made; also selfless service where one dedicates one's actions to God as the Doer and through such service one surrenders his ego to directly experience the Divine.

Kronos (also Chronos)

The personification of time in Greek mythology. Time as measured sequentially, chronologically as opposed to Kairos.

life line
This major line on the palm curves near the thumb, downward toward the wrist. It signifies a person's health, vitality, and quality of life.

loop
Circular patterns that can be found either on the palms or on fingerprints.

Lower Mars mount
Found just above the Luna or Moon mount, this mount shows honesty, integrity, and general endurance.

Luna mount
The mount or raised muscular area on the outer palm of the hand that deals with matters of imagination, intuition, and creativity.

magi
Plural of magus, or ancient magicians and seers who could interpret the stars and influence fate.

major lines
The three primary lines of the hand, including the head, heart, and life lines; can also include the fate line.

Mars line
This line on the palm is found along the life line and is considered to be protective in nature.

maya
Cosmic delusion.

meditation
Interiorizing one's attention and focus of thought upon an aspect of the Divine.

Mercury finger
The fourth or little finger representing communication in the broad sense and temper in a limited sense.

Mercury line
One of the secondary lines occurring on the palm; indicates whether the individual has strong business skill or good health.

Mercury mount
The mount or fleshy pad located just underneath the fourth or Mercury finger that deals with health, commerce, and travel.

mixed hand
A rare hand type that incorporates many different shapes and characteristics that defy easy categorization.

moon
A crescent-shaped marking, usually white, on the surface of the fingernail.

Neptune mount
This mount, rarely mentioned in palmistry, is located between the Luna or Moon mount and the Venus mount. A thickly padded Neptune mount indicates charisma.

numerology

The esoteric study of numbers and their associated meanings and symbolism.

palmar ridges

The raised portions of the palm and their corresponding patterns.

palmistry

The ancient intuitive art of studying the hands to determine personality, health, and potential in life.

passive hand

The hand you use less often for major tasks; the opposite of the dominant hand.

patterns

Designs that occur naturally on the surface of the fingertips and palms.

peacock's eye

A whorl pattern that is encircled or contained within a loop pattern on the fingertips or palm. This is a protective sign, but often belongs to those with physical disabilities.

percussion

The outer edge of the hand, away from the thumb side of the hand. The shape of your percussion demonstrates whether or not you have a creative or practical personality.

phalanges

The individual sections of each finger, from joint to joint.

plain of Mars

The valley of the palm, surrounded by all of the raised mounts.

pointed hand

The shape that forms a point when the fingers are held together and the hand is examined in a flat, open-handed position. Pointed hands are often called psychic hands, since many intuitive types have this hand shape.

prana

In yoga, one of five vital breaths.

pranayama

Conscious breathing techniques undertaken to facilitate union of the soul with the Spirit.

psychic energy

A mental energy that can be detected and utilized in certain psychological activities.

Pythagoras

Greek philosopher considered by many to be the Father of Numerology.

rascette

The bracelet or lines of the wrist.

Ring of Apollo

This rather uncommon, curved line wraps around the Apollo finger near the mount of Apollo and denotes impaired creativity.

Ring of Saturn

Often called the pessimist's mark, this ring-like line can be located just under the Saturn finger (above the Saturn mount).

Ring of Solomon

Just as the biblical leader Solomon was known for his wisdom, so it is with those whose hands sport a ringlike line around their Jupiter finger.

sādhu

In Hinduism, a good or holy man (*sādhvī*, holy woman) who has renounced ordinary life to live a life of meditation, renunciation, and detachment as a wandering ascetic in the pursuit of final liberation from the endless cycle of birth and death.

samadhi

The state that is attained in meditation when the meditator withdraws his mind from the physical world and the senses, turns within, and becomes one with the object of meditation, God.

Saturn finger

The second (middle) finger. A long Saturn finger signifies a potential for depression.

Saturn mount

The mount located just under the Saturn finger. If this mount is noticeably raised, it can mean the person suffers from chronic depression.

Saturn line

The line that runs from the wrist to the Saturn finger dividing the palm into half. It is also known as the fate line.

secondary line

Any line that appears alongside or near the major lines of the hand.

self

Divine essence or soul of a person, different from the egoic Self.

simian line

This line occurs at the merging point of two major lines, head and heart, and points to deep emotions or a physical affliction that leads to greater introspection.

spatulate

A rectangular shape that takes on the characterization of a spatula; can pertain to either finger or hand shape.

spiritual eye

The eye of intuition located in the subtle body at the point between the eyebrows known as the *ajna* chakra; the doorway through which ones' consciousness must pass to achieve merging with the divine consciousness.

square mark

If this special marking appears on the palm, it offers the individual protection in the area associated with the nearest major line.

square shape

Hands and/or fingers that appear square in shape.

star

This unique marking can appear on any palm line or mount and can be a predictor of surprise, either happy or sad, depending on indications from other nearby lines.

synchronicity

The meaningful coincidence of two or more similar events that do not share the same cause, but occur within an indeterminate period of time.

Tarot

Cards used for divination; fortune-telling cards that originated during medieval times.

transformational thinking

Radical new ways of thinking that create a shift in consciousness.

travel line

Located near the bottom of the percussion of the hand, these lines indicate the type and length of travel or journeys in life.

triangle

A very lucky sign if it appears on the palm; indicates success beyond one's wildest dreams, along with the wisdom to handle it effectively.

universal laws

Various forces at work in the universe that conform to given behaviors under specific circumstances, but not, however, necessarily recognized by orthodox science as provable.

Upper Mars mount

Fleshy pad found between the Jupiter mount and the thumb; indicates whether a person is courageous (positive) or aggressive (negative).

Venus mount

A very popular mount in palmistry, located beneath the thumb; it indicates a person's sexual stamina and capacity for romance.

Via lascivia

This line, which can appear at the base of the percussion (near travel lines), is sometimes called the allergy line, since it can mean sensitivity to chemicals or airborne particles.

visualization

The act of intentionally creating images in the mind by using the imagination.

water hand

This hand type features a slender hand with long, pointed fingers. People with water hands are sensitive and sometimes secretive.

whorls

These secondary patterns, which can appear on both fingertips and palms, signify a closed mind, or a person who is not open to new thoughts or ideas.

yoga

From the Sanskrit root *yuj*, meaning "union," yoga means the union of the individual soul with the Divine Spirit; also, methods by which this union is achieved. Several methods of yoga include Bhakti Yoga, Hatha Yoga, Karma Yoga, Laya Yoga, Mantra Yoga, Jnana Yoga, and Raja (or "royal") Yoga.

yogi
One who practices yoga.

Yukteswar
Swami Sri Yukteswar Giri (1855–1936), known Incarnation of Wisdom, guru of Paramahansa Yogananda, disciple of Lahiri Mahasaya, and author of *The Holy Science*, comparing Hindu and Christian scriptures.

zones
Specific divisions of the hand often broken down into quadrants.

Index

Affirmations, 131–32, 136, 138
Air hands, 152, 153
Apollo (creativity) line, 145, 146
Apollo (ring) finger, 177–78, 181
Apollo mount, 172
Aquarius, 12, 23, 26, 29, 36, 40, 47–50, 51, 52, 56, 59, 62, 65, 109–10, 133
Aries, 12, 16–17, 18, 20, 25–26, 36, 41, 49, 51, 53, 57, 60, 63, 83, 133
Artemis, 91
Ashram, 154
Astrological signs. *See also specific signs*
    about: overview of, 11
    cusps, 11, 16–18
    delineated, 20–24
    health and, 60–62
    intercepted sign, 16–17
    money and, 57–59
    planets occupied by, 19–24
    relationships and. *See* Astrology, relationships, love and
    sex and, 52–57
    Sun signs, 20–24
    symbols, 12
    work questions and, 62–65
Astrology. *See also* Birth charts
    about: overview and definition, 9–10, 65
    aspects and symbols, 13
    basics, 10–11
    conjunction defined, 13
    energies (negative and positive), 10
    free will and, 11
    intuition, observation and, 11
    opposition defined, 13
    relationship questions and. *See* Astrology, relationships, love and
    sextile defined, 13
    square defined, 13
    symbols used in, 12–13
    Tarot and. *See* Astrology, Tarot and
    Trine defined, 13
Astrology, relationships, love and, 24–52
    about: overview of, 24–25; sex and, 52–57
    Aquarius, 47–50

Aries, 25–26
Cancer, 33–34
Capricorn, 45–47
Gemini, 30–33
Leo, 35–36
Libra, 39–41
Pisces, 50–52
Sagittarius, 44–45
Scorpio, 41–44
Taurus, 27–29
Virgo, 36–39
Astrology, Tarot and
    about: horoscope spread, 139–41; overview of, 74; Significators, 132–34
    Chariot, 89–90
    Death, 101–2
    Devil, 105–6
    Emperor, 83
    Empress, 81
    Fool, 76
    Hanged Man, 99–100
    Hermit, 93–94
    Hierophant, 85
    High Priestess, 79–80
    Judgment, 115–16
    Justice, 98
    Lovers, 87
    Magician, 78
    Moon, 111–12
    Star, 109–10
    Strength, 91–92
    Sun, 113–14
    Temperance, 103
    Tower, 107–8
    Wheel of Fortune, 96
    World, 117

Birth charts
    about: overview of, 14
    AS, DS, MC, IC, Eq, Vtx defined, 13
    aspects and symbols, 13
    example, illustrated, 15
    houses and house cusps, 10–11, 16–18
    planets and their symbols, 12

signs and their symbols, 12
    symbols used in, 13
    term definitions, 13
Bracelets (rascettes), 179–82

Cancer, 12, 21, 33–34, 38, 41, 47, 54, 58, 61, 63, 74, 89–90, 96, 133
Capricorn, 12, 23, 32, 34, 36, 45–47, 52, 53, 56, 59, 62, 64–65, 117, 133
Chakras, 125, 291
The Chariot, 88–90
Chiromancy, 182
Color, Tarot symbolism, 73
Conical (artistic) hands, 152
Creator, 147, 215
Cups, 118, 120–21, 133

Death, Tarot cards, 100–102
Destiny line. *See* Saturn (fate/destiny) line
Devil, 103–6

Earth hands, 153, 155, 184
Emotions, planets ruling, 18
The Emperor, 81–83
The Empress, 80–81
Enneagram Personality Test
    about: enneatypes and their characteristics, 335–38; overview of, 244; scoring summary, 335; why it works, 294–95
    Group A1, 296–99
    Group A2, 300–303
    Group A3, 304–7
    Group B1.1, 308–10
    Group B1.2, 311–13
    Group B1.3, 314–16
    Group B2.1, 317–19
    Group B2.2, 320–22
    Group B2.3, 323–25
    Group B3.1, 326–28
    Group B3.2, 329–31
    Group B3.3, 332–34
Enneagrams
    about: overview and definition, 241–42, 288
    basics, 242–43

dynamics of, 245
health questions and, 285–86
money questions and, 284–85
processing mechanisms and, 278–79
relationship questions and, 280–82
self-actualization and, 248–49
sex/intimacy questions and, 282–84
triad groups, 279
unearthing power of you, 279–88
work questions and, 286–88
your essence and, 244–45
Enneatypes (personality types). *See also* Enneatype wings
about: overview of, 242–43; practical applications for each number, 280–88; summary of types, 250; understanding processing mechanisms, 278–79; your instincts and, 278
defined, 242
diagram, 243
four aspects of, 248
functioning within family, 246
pathological designation of, 245
progressing to wholeness, 246
Type One, 250–51, 282, 284, 285, 286, 288, 335
Type Two, 251–53, 280–81, 282, 284, 285, 287, 335–36
Type Three, 253–54, 281, 282, 284, 285, 287, 336
Type Four, 254–55, 281, 282–83, 284, 285, 287, 336
Type Five, 255–56, 281, 283, 284, 286, 287, 336–37
Type Six, 256–57, 281, 283, 286, 287, 337
Type Seven, 257–58, 281, 283, 285, 286, 287, 337
Type Eight, 259–60, 281, 283, 285, 286, 287–88, 337–38
Type Nine, 260–61, 282, 283–84, 285, 286, 288, 338
Enneatype wings
about, 247; heavy, moderate, or light, 247–48; positioning of, 247; wing subtypes overview, 261–62

Ones with a Two wing, 277
Ones with a Nine wing, 276
Twos with a One wing, 262–63
Twos with a Three wing, 263–64
Threes with a Two wing, 264–65
Threes with a Four wing, 265–66
Fours with a Three wing, 266–67
Fours with a Five wing, 267–68
Fives with a Four wing, 268
Fives with a Six wing, 268–69
Sixes with a Five wing, 269–70
Sixes with a Seven wing, 270–71
Sevens with a Six wing, 271–72
Sevens with an Eight wing, 272–73
Eights with a Seven wing, 273
Eights with a Nine wing, 273–74
Nines with a One wing, 275–76
Nines with an Eight wing, 274–75

Fate line. *See* Saturn (fate/destiny) line
Finger mounts, 170–73
Apollo mount (third finger), 172
Jupiter mount, 171, 182, 185
Mercury mount (fourth finger), 172–73, 182, 187
planets associated with, 171
Saturn mount, 171–72, 176, 182
Fingers (palmistry and)
Apollo (ring) finger, 177–78, 181
fingertip indicators, 178
Jupiter (index) finger, 177, 178, 184, 185, 187
Mercury (pinky) finger, 178, 185, 187
Saturn (middle) finger, 171, 177, 178
thumbs and, 178–79
Fire hands, 153, 154
Flow lines
of 0 through 11 and 22, 198–203
completion potentials, 204
energies of, 198
gender of, 199
as guides, 205
of letters, 208–15
power of, 198
The Fool, 75–76

Gemini, 12, 20–21, 24, 26, 29, 30–33, 38, 40, 45, 49, 51, 52, 53–54, 57, 60, 63, 87, 94, 133
Glossary, 339–46
Gurdjieff, George Ivanovitch, 279

Hands (palm readings and). *See also* Finger mounts; Fingers (palmistry and); Palmistry; *other Palm references*
assessing your hand, 150–61
color/consistency, 151
element associations, 153. *See also specific elements*
fourth (pinky) finger analysis, 152
general characteristics, 150–52
hair on, 151
knuckles and angles, 156
movement, 151
percussion area, 161
size, 151
texture, 151
thickness, 151
zones of, 161
Hand shapes, 152–55
about: evaluating, 152
conical (artistic) hands, 152
mixed hands, 155
pointed (psychic) hands, 153
spatulate (action-oriented) hands, 154
square (practical) hands, 154–55
The Hanged Man, 98–100, 139
Head line, 145, 174
Health questions
astrology for, 60–62
enneagrams for, 285–86
numerology for, 237
palmistry for, 185–86
Tarot spreads for, 138–41
Heart line, 145, 175–76
The Hermit, 92–94
The Hierophant, 83–85
The High Priestess, 78–80

Intuition, developing, 11, 129–30, 196

Judgment (Tarot), 114–16
Jupiter
    energy quality, 10
    major influences of, 18, 19
    sign ruled by. *See* Sagittarius
    symbol for, 12
    Wheel of Fortune and, 96
Jupiter finger, 177, 178, 184, 185, 187
Jupiter mount, 171, 182, 185
Justice (Tarot), 97–98

Karma, 18–19, 97, 105, 115, 213,
    230–32, 233
Knuckles and angles, 156

Leo, 12, 21, 34, 35–36, 43, 45, 47, 50,
    51, 54, 58, 61, 63–64, 91–92, 133
Letters
    flow lines of, 208–15
    number examples, 206–7
    number values, 205, 207
    pure, 206
    symbolic attributes, 207
Libra, 12, 22, 26, 29, 32, 38, 39–41, 50,
    55, 58, 61, 64, 98, 133
Life line, 145, 173–74
Loops, 160, 161
The Lovers, 86–87
Luna mount, 160, 161, 168–69, 170,
    180, 186

The Magician, 76–78
Major Arcana, 74–117
    about: overview of, 68, 74
    astrology and. *See* Astrology, Tarot
        and
    Chariot, 88–90
    Death, 100–102
    Devil, 103–6
    Emperor, 81–83
    Empress, 80–81
    Fool, 75–76
    Hanged Man, 98–100, 139
    Hermit, 92–94
    Hierophant, 83–85
    High Priestess, 78–80
    Judgment, 114–16
    Justice, 97–98
    Lovers, 86–87

Magician, 76–78
Moon, 110–12
Star, 108–10
Strength, 90–92
Sun, 112–14
Temperance, 102–3
Tower, 106–8
Wheel of Fortune, 94–96
World, 116–17
Mars
    The Emperor and, 83
    energy quality, 10
    major influences of, 18, 19
    signs ruled by. *See* Aries; Scorpio
    symbol for, 12
Mars mount, 166–67
    balanced, 167
    Lower, 164, 166, 167, 170
    personality type, 167
    plain of, 167, 170
    Upper, 166, 170
Meditation
    benefits of, 185, 291
    intuition and, 129–30
    Librans and, 22
    numerology and, 198, 218
    Tarot and, 68, 70, 98, 128, 129–30
    yoga and, 291
Mercury
    energy quality, 10
    Magician and, 78
    major influence of, 78
    major influences of, 18, 19
    signs ruled by. *See* Gemini; Virgo
    symbol for, 12
Mercury (health) line, 145, 146, 178
Mercury finger, 178, 185, 187
Mercury mount, 172–73, 182, 187
Minor Arcana, 118–27
    about: overview of, 68, 118
    as backbone of Tarot, 118
    Cups, 118, 120–21, 133
    four suits, 118
    matching suits to life-area
        concerns, 119–22
    numerology and, 118, 122–27
    Pentacles, 118, 121–22, 133
    Swords, 118, 120, 133
    Wands, 118, 119–20, 133

Mixed hands, 155
Money questions
    astrological signs and, 57–59
    enneagrams for, 284–85
    numerology for, 236–37
    palmistry for, 184–85
    Tarot spreads for, 137–38
Moon. *See also* Luna mount
    energy quality, 10
    major influences of, 18, 19
    nodes of, 18–19
    symbol for, 12
    symbolism of, 71, 72, 79–80,
        110–12, 195
    Tarot card, 110–12

Neptune, 10, 12, 18, 19, 99–100. *See
    also* Pisces
Neptune mount, 169
North Node, 12, 18–19
Numerology. *See also* Flow lines;
    Numerology numbers
    about: overview and definition,
        189–90, 239
    alphabet and. *See* Letters
    basics, 190
    evolution of, 193–94
    geometric shapes (circles,
        semicircles, triangles) and, 195–96
    health questions and, 237
    intuition and, 196
    karma and, 230–32
    Kronos, Kairos, timing and, 227–30
    magi lineage and, 194–95
    mathematics vs., 191
    Minor Arcana and, 118, 122–27
    money questions and, 236–37
    personality masks and, 230
    relationship questions and, 234–36
    repetitions, rhythms of life and,
        232–33
    sex questions and, 236
    soul essence number, 215–27
    straight lines and, 195
    symbolic language of, 195–96
    unearthing power of you, 233–38
    work questions and, 237

Numerology numbers. *See also* Flow lines
    about: alphabet values/flow lines, 205–15; equality of, 204; flow lines of, 198–203; nature and, 191–93; nine pure numbers, 196–202; quality of, 196–97; soul essence number and, 215–27; as tools, 191–92
    Zero, 199
    One, 122, 196–97, 200, 218–19
    Two, 122–23, 196–97, 200, 219
    Three, 123, 196–97, 200, 220
    Four, 123–24, 196–97, 201, 220–21
    Five, 124, 196–97, 201, 221–22
    Six, 124–25, 196–97, 201, 222–23
    Seven, 125, 196–97, 202, 223–24
    Eight, 125–26, 196–97, 202, 224
    Nine, 126, 196–97, 202, 224–25
    Ten, 127, 197, 203
    Eleven, 203, 225–26
    Twenty two, 203, 226–27

Palmistry. *See also* Finger mounts; Fingers (palmistry and); *Hand references*; Palm lines; Palm marks and patterns; Palm mounts; Palm readings
    about: overview and definition, 143–44, 187–88
    basics, 145–47
    Divine Mind and, 147
    dominant hand and, 147–48
    right brain, left brain and, 148
    special markings, 147
    two-hand approach, 147–48
Palm lines
    Apollo (creativity) line, 145, 146
    basic varieties of (deep, clear, faint, broken), 156–57
    dermatoglyphics and, 158
    destiny line. *See* Saturn (fate/destiny) line
    head line, 145, 174
    heart line, 145, 175–76
    horizontal, 157
    inspecting, 156–57
    length of, 157
    life line, 145, 173–74

    meaning behind, 158
    Mercury (health) line, 145, 146, 178
    Saturn (fate/destiny) line, 145, 146, 176, 182, 183, 185, 186–87
    secondary, 177
    vertical, 157
    wrist lines (rascettes), 179–82
    wrist-to-finger lines, 181–82
Palm marks and patterns
    branches, 158, 159, 182, 187
    broken lines, 156, 158, 159, 183
    chains, 158, 159, 175, 181
    changing patterns, 159
    circles, 158, 159, 169
    crosses, 158, 159, 169, 170, 174
    crowd factor, 160
    dots, 158, 159
    forks, 159, 187
    grilles, 158, 159, 169
    islands, 158, 159, 175
    loops, 160, 161
    observing, 157–59
    ridges, 157
    secondary, 177
    shapes in patterns, 158–59
    shapes predicting creativity, 160–61
    squares, 158, 159, 169, 170
    stars, 159, 170, 181
    tassels, 147, 158, 159
    triangles, 158, 159, 169, 170, 181
    whorls, 160, 161
Palm mounts, 161–70. *See also* Finger mounts; Mars mount
    about: overview of, 161
    four-zone analysis, 164
    illustrated, 162
    Luna mount, 160, 161, 168–69, 170, 180, 186
    Neptune mount, 169
    reading clockwise, 169
    significance of, 163
    three-zone analysis, 163
    two-zone analysis (conscious and subconscious), 162
    Venus mount, 160, 161, 164–66, 168, 169, 174, 184, 185, 187

Palm readings. *See also* Finger mounts; Fingers (palmistry and); *Hand references*; Palm marks and patterns; Palm mounts
    avoiding charlatans, 148, 149
    communication pitfall precaution, 150
    finding good readers, 148–49
    hand shape and, 152–55
    health questions and, 185–86
    knuckles and angles, 156
    life length/quality questions, 174, 180–81
    money questions and, 184–85
    reading your own palm, 149–50
    relationship questions and, 174, 175–76, 183
    requirement for, 150
    sex questions and, 184
    unearthing power of you, 182–87
    work questions and, 176–77, 186–87
Pentacles, 118, 121–22, 133
Pisces, 12, 16–17, 23–24, 26, 34, 43, 45, 47, 50–52, 56–57, 59, 62, 65, 100, 111–12, 133
Planets, astrology and
    influences of each planet, 18
    nodes of moon, 18–19
    signs occupied, 19–24
    symbols of planets, 12
Pluto, 10, 12, 18, 19, 101, 115–16
Pointed (psychic) hands, 153
Power of you
    awakening energy centers, 291
    future vision, 290–91
    power of, 291–92
    sharing knowledge about, 290
    transforming your thinking and life, 290–91
    unearthing, 128–42, 182–87, 233–38, 279–88

Rascettes (wrist lines), 179–82
Relationships and love questions. *See also* Sex questions
    astrology for. *See* Astrology, relationships, love and
    enneagrams for, 280–82

numerology for, 234–36
palmistry for, 174, 175–76, 183
Tarot spreads for, 135–36

Sagittarius, 12, 22–23, 32, 36, 43, 44–45, 52, 55–56, 59, 62, 64, 103, 133
Saturn
    The Devil and, 105–6
    energy quality, 10
    major influences of, 18, 19
    sign ruled by. *See* Capricorn
    symbol for, 12
Saturn (fate/destiny) line, 145, 146, 176, 182, 183, 185, 186–87
Saturn finger, 171, 177, 178
Saturn mount, 171–72, 176, 182
Scorpio, 12, 22, 33, 34, 36, 38, 40, 41–44, 47, 52, 55, 58–59, 61, 64, 101–2, 133
Sex questions
    astrology for, 52–57
    enneagrams for, 282–84
    numerology for, 236
    palmistry for, 185–86
    Tarot spreads for, 136–37
South Node, 12, 18–19
Spatulate (action-oriented) hands, 154
Spreads. *See* Tarot spreads
Square (practical) hands, 154–55
The Star, 108–10
Strength (Tarot), 90–92
Sun
    energy quality, 10
    houses, cusps and, 16–18
    major influence of, 18
    Moon and, 111
    symbol for, 12
    symbolism of, 71, 92, 112–14
    Tarot, 79–80, 112–14
Sun signs, 20–24
Swords, 118, 120, 133

Tarot. *See also* Major Arcana; Minor Arcana
    about: overview and definition, 67–68, 142
    affirmations, 131–32
    astrology and. *See* Astrology, Tarot and

backbone of, 118
basics, 68–69
choosing deck, 69
doing readings, 127–28
handling cards, 69
health questions and, 138–41
journal, keeping, 131
learning to interpret, 70
meditation and, 68, 70, 98, 128, 129–30
money questions and, 137–38
opening to insight, 70
relationship questions and, 135–36
sex questions and, 136–37
shuffling cards, 69–70
Significators, 128, 132–34
spreads. *See* Tarot spreads
symbolism of. *See* Tarot symbolism
unearthing power of you, 128–42
work questions and, 142
Tarot spreads
    about: for health questions, 138–41; for money questions, 137–38; overview of, 134–42; for relationship questions, 135–36; for sex questions, 136–37; for work questions, 142
    four-card spread, 135–36
    general life-conditions spread, 137
    horoscope spread, 139–41
    immediate situation, 136
    quick spread for area of concern, 138
    single-card draw, 135
    thirteen-card spread, 142
    three-card, 136
    Tree of Life, 130
Tarot symbolism
    astrological indicators and imagery, 74
    changing interpretations of, 72
    color symbolism, 73
    personalizing symbols, 72
    symbols and their meanings, 71–72
    universal symbolism, 71–72
Taurus, 12, 16, 20, 27–29, 32, 34, 41, 43, 46, 52, 53, 57, 60, 63, 85, 133
Temperance, 102–3
Thumbs, 178–79

The Tower, 106–8
Tree of Life spread, 130

Universal law, 78
Uranus
    energy quality, 10
    The Fool and, 76
    major influences of, 18, 19
    sign ruled by. *See* Aquarius
    symbol for, 12
    The Tower and, 107–8

Venus
    Aries and, 26, 53
    The Empress and, 81
    energy quality, 10
    major influences of, 18, 19
    Neptune and, 99–100
    signs ruled by. *See* Libra; Taurus
    symbol for, 12
Venus, girdle of, 184
Venus mount, 160, 161, 164–66, 168, 169, 174, 184, 185, 187
Virgo, 12, 21–22, 34, 36–39, 46, 49–50, 54–55, 58, 61, 64, 93–94, 133

Wands, 118, 119–20, 133
Water hands, 153
Wheel of Fortune, 94–96
Whorls, 160, 161
Work questions
    astrological signs and, 62–65
    enneagrams for, 286–88
    numerology for, 237
    palmistry for, 176–77, 186–87
    Tarot spreads for, 142
The World (Tarot), 116–17
Wrist lines, 179–82

Zones, of hands, 161